IN PLAIN SIGHT

IN PLAIN SIGHT

EXPLORING THE NATURAL WONDERS
OF SOUTHERN ALBERTA

NEIL L. JENNINGS

RMB
Victoria Vancouver Calgary

Rocky Mountain Books
#108 – 17665 66A Avenue
Surrey, BC V3S 2A7
www.rmbooks.com

Rocky Mountain Books
PO Box 468
Custer, WA
98240-0468

Library and Archives Canada Cataloguing in Publication

Jennings, Neil L
   In plain sight : exploring the natural wonders of southern Alberta / Neil L. Jennings.

Includes index.
ISBN 978-1-897522-78-3

   1. National parks and reserves—Alberta—Guidebooks. 2. Natural history—Alberta—Guidebooks. 3. Alberta—Guidebooks. I. Title.

FC3663.J45 2010   917.123'4044   C2009-907199-1

Front cover photo: Dinosaur Provincial Park
Back cover photo: Writing-on-Stone Rock Art
Title page photo: Writing-on-Stone Provincial Park, NWMP Fort

Printed in Canada

Rocky Mountain Books acknowledges the financial support for its publishing program from the Government of Canada through the Book Publishing Industry Development Program (BPIDP), Canada Council for the Arts, and the province of British Columbia through the British Columbia Arts Council and the Book Publishing Tax Credit.

This book has been printed with FSC-certified, acid-free papers, processed chlorine free and printed with vegetable based inks.

Mixed Sources
Cert no. SW-COC-001271
© 1996 FSC
FSC

Disclaimer

The actions described in this book may be considered inherently dangerous activities. Individuals undertake these activities at their own risk. The information put forth in this guide has been collected from a variety of sources and is not guaranteed to be completely accurate or reliable. Many conditions and some information may change owing to weather and numerous other factors beyond the control of the authors and publishers. Individual climbers and/or hikers must determine the risks, use their own judgment and take full responsibility for their actions. Do not depend on any information found in this book for your own personal safety. Your safety depends on your own good judgment based on your skills, education and experience.

   It is up to the users of this guidebook to acquire the necessary skills for safe experiences and to exercise caution in potentially hazardous areas. The authors and publishers of this guide accept no responsibility for your actions or the results that occur from another's actions, choices, or judgments. If you have any doubt as to your safety or your ability to attempt anything described in this guidebook, do not attempt it.

Dedication

This book is dedicated to Linda – my wife, my best friend, my roommate, my hiking companion, my editor of first instance and one of the best flower spotters I know. I am mightily glad you're along.

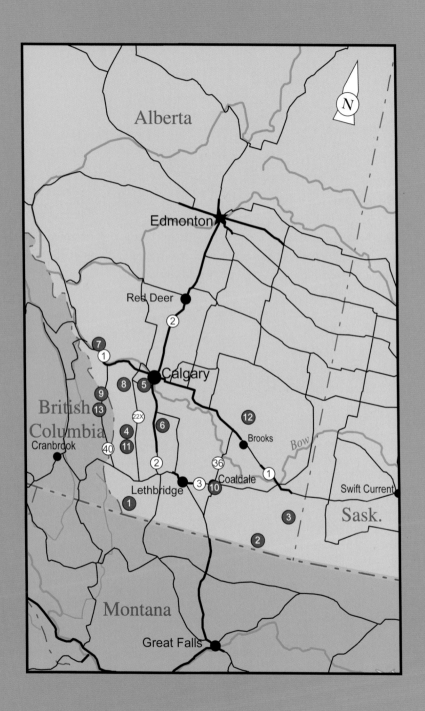

Contents

Western Anemone

Acknowledgements

The preparation of a book like this must, perforce, include the assistance of a variety of people who graciously give of their time, experience, expertise and other talents to complete the project. In that regard I would like to acknowledge and thank a number of people whose assistance along the way was invaluable. I include in that number Darian Kath, park interpreter at both Writing-on-Stone Provincial Park and Cypress Hills Interprovincial Park; Aaron Domes, visitor services coordinator at Writing-on-Stone Provincial Park; Duane Fizor, information services coordinator, Kananaskis Country; and Cyndi Smith, conservation biologist at Parks Canada, Waterton Lakes National Park. I also want to thank my friend Alan Youell for his advice and counsel on certain portions of the book, and my friends Brian Saunders and Susan Leacock for their efforts in reviewing drafts for portions of the work. I am particularly appreciative of the generosity of the photographers whose work graces these pages: Russ Webb; Russ Amy, and Carolyn Sandstrom, who collected, collated and delivered the images from Russ Amy; Chuck Murphy; Simon Jennings; Bev Lokseth; Jim McKean; Clay and Gill Ross; and Linda Jennings. I am, once again, in your debt.

Sky Pilot

Introduction

To many visitors, and indeed to many Albertans, no trip to southern Alberta would be complete without the obligatory drive to the splendour of the mountains of Banff and Lake Louise. The songs of those particular sirens have been sung and heard for several generations, and much of the world is acquainted with the wonders to be found in those places. With no wish to denigrate those two very special places and their appurtenances, this book is about some other special places in southern Alberta that are eminently worthwhile for the investment of some of your time. The places written about in this book have been chosen for their uniqueness. Some are easy to get to and easy to get around in; others require more time and energy. The common factor is that each place is worthy of your time and attention, and you will be stimulated, enlightened, enhanced, delighted, amazed, uplifted and broadened by the experience. Read on. I hope what you find here will prompt you to go see some of these marvellous things. They are awesome places, in the very real denotation of that adjective. All are in plain sight, though they are little visited. Some of the names may be familiar to you, some not.

For example, you have probably heard of Waterton Lakes National Park, Writing-on-Stone Provincial Park and Cypress Hills Interprovincial Park, but have you ever been there? They are all found in southern Alberta, each near the international boundary with the United States. You cannot see one from another but you are not far from that possibility. Each park is unique but all are connected in a number of ways. In the scheme of things, all three are rarely visited. For example, Waterton Lakes National Park experiences about 10 per cent of the traffic "enjoyed" by Banff National Park. All three are relatively out of the way. You do not "just happen to find yourself in the area" and drop in for a visit. You must set out to get to these places, because they are not really on the way to anyplace else. They have different geological histories, but their geological histories are interconnected nonetheless. Their human histories are also connected, with each place having seen some of the same people at relatively the same seasons for thousands of years, and with some of the same people having seen the same vistas at various times over the march of years.

Life today is complicated, and it appears that it will become more so sooner rather than later. For example, I recently made an application to become a volunteer for a local conservation organization. As part of the process, I was asked to deliver a letter to the local constabulary requesting that they do a security check on me and consenting to having the results delivered to the organization when completed. When I attended upon the local police district office to tender the letter of request, I was summarily and firmly denied service on the application because the letter from the conservation organization was not dated, my name in the body of the letter was printed in block letters by hand as opposed to being typed in, and the letter had been signed by the organization's representative using black, instead of blue, ink. My immediate reaction to the refusal was mirth, it being almost too preposterous to contemplate that life had become so complicated in the post-George W. Bush world that anarchy is assumed to be imminent when somebody takes the reckless step of using black ink to sign a letter. Perhaps there are some legitimate reasons for the police authorities to prefer typing to legible printing and blue to black ink, but those nuances are not intuitively obvious, at least not to me. On reflection, I suspect that in these days of constant scares about "security" it has become accepted wisdom that any failure to follow even patently cockamamie systems and procedures established by who knows whom for unfathomable reasons is the thin edge of the wedge that will lead us all down that slippery slope to who knows what awful end. The situation reminded me of the 1934 words of US social critic and contrarian H.L. Mencken: "The whole aim of practical politics is to keep the populace alarmed by menacing it with an endless series of hobgoblins, all of them imaginary." I suspect that he is, once again, right on the mark.

So what I am going to suggest is that you sit down and do some "mean considerin'" as to whether you really want to, metaphorically of course, "live life outside" by watching the Outdoor Life Network. I strongly recommend that you put down the remote, get off the couch and go outside to check on things. Kneel down and take a close look at the intricacies of a wildflower;

pick a safe location and watch a storm roll in; marvel at the grace of a red-tailed hawk as it wheels in the sky; watch a bee disappear inside a Yellow Columbine; get the liver frightened out of you by the flush of a covey of grey partridge as they bolt at your approach; climb a mountain trail to see the vista; and hear the booming of a blue grouse. There are lots of things out there that you really oughta see. That's what this book is about.

I should also say up front that it is a carefully considered opinion of mine that many hikers approach their outings like Julius Caesar approached the Battle of Zela: *Veni, vidi, vici,* "I came, I saw, I conquered." It seems as if the arrival at the intended destination, perhaps in a "personal best" time, is the ultimate point of the exercise. If you are that kind of hiker, seeking primarily to complete a mission, this book may not be for you. The approach here is quite different. I go hiking, and encourage others to go hiking, to discover a sense of wonder in things seen in the landscape. The "going" is the point of the whole thing, not just the "getting there."

As we commence, you should be aware of some matters of usage in the book. Native peoples figure greatly in the human history of southern Alberta. For purposes of clarity, the following explanation as to the names of the Native peoples might be beneficial.

Kootenay is the accepted Canadian spelling when referring to the Native peoples who inhabited the area that is present-day southeastern British Columbia, western Montana and Idaho. In the United States the spelling usually employed is "Kootenai." The Natives refer to themselves as "Ktunaxa" (pronounced "toon-AWK-ah," with the "K" being silent).

The Blackfoot Confederacy, defined in its broadest terms, is comprised of the following groups:

- the Blackfoot, also known as the Siksika;
- the Blood, also known as the Kainai; and
- the Peigan, also known as the Piikani (Pikuni). This group is often subdivided into the North Peigans, who reside in southern Alberta, and the South Peigans, who reside in Montana. Peigan is most often spelled "Piegan" in the United States, and the South Piegans are often referred to there as the "Blackfeet."

The Stoney, also known as the Nakota, is a tribe of the Sioux group that was pushed westward from its traditional lands near Lake of the Woods in the early 1700s by European expansion in eastern North America. White men called them "Stoney" because they employed a cooking technique that used fire-heated rocks. As the Stoney moved westward, they came into some conflict with the Blackfoot Confederacy, but over time they were eventually tolerated by the Blackfoot. As a rule, the Stoney moved into the western edge of the prairies. Where the Stoney came into contact with the Kootenay, fighting often resulted.

References to John George Brown will use the spelling of his nickname which he employed – "Kootenai." References to the Kootenay Lakes refer herein to the lakes today known as the Waterton Lakes – not the Kootenay Lake located on the western side of the Purcell Mountains in southeastern British Columbia.

"Buffalo" is the colloquial name applied to the American Bison (*Bison bison*). The name is quite arguably a misnomer, given that the relation between this animal and the "true" buffaloes of Africa and Asia is remote. However, the name "buffalo" as applied to the bison is so endemic in North American parlance and history – both oral and written – that the use of that name should not promote any serious misunderstanding on the part of the reader. Buffalo and bison are used herein synonymously.

On most of the hikes recommended in the book I have included Universal Transverse Mercator (UTM) coordinates for the convenience of readers. In my experience, such things are seldom seen in hiking books, and that is a mystery to me because the coordinates give a specificity and precision to location that cannot be equalled by even well-written directions. All pertinent maps are noted in the text. In each case where the coordinates appear, the eastings are shown first, the northings second. Though it is not a universally accepted practice, I have chosen to highlight the Grid References by using a larger font for those portions of the coordinates. By way of example used in the text, the trailhead for the Wishbone Trail in Waterton Lakes National Park has the coordinates 11U 0293728 5443354, meaning the GR is 937433. If you do not understand how coordinates work and how to read a map properly, read and absorb that information contained in the first chapter of this book. It is a skill easily acquired, and having it could save you a lot of grief. To those who might say it overly complicates the whole process of hiking, I say bosh. GPS receivers have become so ubiquitous in today's world that to eschew their use is folly, especially while advocating for hikers to carry a compass instead. While a compass is not as anachronistic as a slide rule, finding a competent user of either instrument carries with it a similar degree of difficulty. If you do not wish to use the included coordinates, that's fine, too. Their inclusion is not for purposes of setting up routes, but more for confirming locations in the field.

In closing, I must include the standard sort of disclaimer. There are inherent risks in hiking in mountainous and/or wilderness areas, and hikers should be cognizant of those risks, be ever aware of their surroundings and use their own judgment to avoid or reduce the risks to acceptable levels. Anyone using this book does so entirely at their own risk, and the author and the publisher disclaim any and all liability for any injuries or other damage that might be sustained by anyone hiking any of the trails described in this book.

Having said that, the final words are: go carefully and confidently, respecting the environment and other users, leaving things as much as possible as you found them. Enjoy.

Neil L. Jennings
Calgary, Alberta

PS The contents hereof are not a complete catalogue of amazing places in southern Alberta. If you have any suggestions as to other worthy places that are in plain sight, let me know. My curiosity quotient remains quite high. If you want to be a little bit rebellious, just send the word inscribed in black ink.

The author and his wife in the Cypress Hills in June, 2009

Some Preliminaries

My old dictionary says "preliminaries" are things coming before the main action, discussion, business or event *and* preparing for it. That definition sounds just right for a catalogue of items you should reflect, decide or act upon prior to going out there into the great wild.

DEGREE OF DIFFICULTY

Some of the places recommended in this book are very easy to get to and very easy to get around in. Virtually anybody can deal with those venues, irrespective of physical condition and level of experience. Just get up and go do it. However, some of the places discussed will require a more strenuous effort to get to and around in, and a relatively higher level of physical conditioning and woodcraft skills will be necessary to make the trip comfortably. You will have to make the decision as to which trips best fit your personal circumstances. Be realistic in your assessments of the difficulties involved and your skill set, all with a view to keeping your outings enjoyable. If you find the pace too fast, slow down to a manageable speed. If you find the going too tough, turn back, with good intentions of returning to the venue when you have improved your conditioning. This is supposed to be fun. It is not supposed to be all the fun you can stand.

WEATHER

The activities discussed herein take place outdoors, and weather is always a factor anywhere in outdoor Alberta. Around here it is always best to assume it will be warmer than they say it will be, colder than they say it will be, wetter than they say it will be and drier than they say it will be. It will also change for the better and change for the worse and do both more quickly than you can comprehend. If you read those last two sentences with a knowing nod, you are Albertan. Snow can fall during any month of the year and it is more probable at higher elevations. Steady rains are usually associated with June, but that is not to say that such rains are restricted to that month. Thunderstorms are most often associated with the

17

afternoon period on hot days during the height of summer, but that is not the only time they occur. If you are going outdoors, wherever you are going and whenever you are going, have clothing appropriate to all the weathers you may find out there. If you are inadequately clothed, it can, quite literally, kill you, so plan for all eventualities. If you are hiking at high elevations, monitor the weather continuously and be prepared to move off ridgelines if storms approach. If you are called upon to make a stream or river crossing during your hike, check the water conditions before committing to the hike. Spate conditions in the spring may make some rivers and streams impassable. If you multiply the depth of the water measured in feet by the speed of the water measured in miles per hour and the product of that multiplication is greater than 12, you *cannot* cross that stream safely. You should also bear in mind that stream levels during the spring of the year may be highest in the afternoon and lowest in the early morning. The reason for that is that air temperatures during the night may be falling below freezing, thus retarding the snowmelt from higher elevations in the early mornings. If you are going to a park, either provincial or national, you should be able to check trail and stream conditions by contacting the park. Making that call could save you a lot of grief.

TREKKING/HIKING POLES

I would recommend that you obtain and use a pair of trekking poles when you are hiking. They are not an affectation; they are a serious piece of equipment that will assist you in many ways. In fact, one long-time hiking friend told me she had gone to a shop to purchase new boots, but came away with poles instead after the helpful salesperson told her the poles would do her more good by far than new boots. The poles turn you into a four-legged animal and make you more stable, particularly in situations like stream crossings. Poles will help you avoid falls that could spell sprains, strains or even broken bones. They also relieve an astonishing amount of pressure from your lower back and knees, particularly on downhills. On a downhill grade, you reach the poles out in front of you and plant them on the way down, thereby allowing your upper body muscles to assist in slowing your forward momentum. That way, much of the strain on the

Trekking poles and carabiner

knees and lower back is removed, as would not be the case if you were walking without poles. If you use poles once, you will always use them in future and will wonder how you got by without them. If there is any problem with trekking poles, it has to be that hikers sometimes forget to pick them up after a break, and start off without them. After a while the forgetful hiker will suddenly remember the poles and will have to retrace his or her steps in hopes of recovering the mislaid property. That is, of course, a pain. To avoid that eventuality, obtain a non-weight-bearing carabiner from your outdoor retailer and attach it to your pack. Then make a habit of clipping the wrist straps of the poles into the carabiner whenever the pack comes off. That way you will never walk away from your poles again.

NAVIGATIONAL AIDS: GPS AND MAPS

If you are going to go traipsing in the "wildies," I recommend that you become proficient at reading a map. If this is a skill you do not have at present, learn it soonest and put it into practice when you go out. If you are sure you have this skill, feel free to skip this part. If you are not absolutely sure, please read on.

As a serious hiker, you should give more than just passing consideration to getting a GPS (Global Positioning System) receiver and learning how to use it. Together with the GPS, you should also get 1:50 000 NTS (National Topographic System) federal topo maps (or their commercial equivalent, such as Gem Trek Publishing maps) for your hiking venues and learn how to read them. Like the old guide says, the first priority is to bring 'em back alive, so it's best not to get plumb lost. GPS units for civilian use have now been around for years and the choices in the marketplace are extensive. The price of a receiver unit varies considerably with the features built in, but even a basic, no-frills model is well worth owning and using. You can program the device as to where you are starting from and where you are going, and it will remember such things and direct you to your destination and back. It will also keep track of how far you went, the route you took to get there and how long it took to get there. It will even calculate how long it will take to get back to the car by reversing the route. It will also record the locations of interesting things you discover on the way, so you can return to that exact spot at a later time for further investigation. I used a receiver years ago to mark the location of a particularly nice stand of Calypso orchids, and I have returned there in most years since to check on them. Another very legitimate reason to have a GPS is that it enables you to record the exact location of an injured hiker and then pass that accurate information on to the authorities when you seek assistance.

The workings of a GPS are not altogether intuitive, however, so you will have to apply yourself in learning how to use the device. Your efforts in that regard will be amply rewarded. In order to make the GPS function efficiently with your maps, set your receiver to display locations in UTM (Universal Transverse Mercator) format instead of latitude and longitude, and make sure the device is set to coincide with the proper map datum of the map you intend to use. A map datum is a mathematical model of the earth that is a reference point used to draw the map. Each map will have its datum noted on it. It may say, for example, NAD 83 (North American Datum 1983) or NAD 27 (North American Datum 1927) or WGS 84 (World Geodetic System 1984) or any one of many others.

As far as maps are concerned, I want to keep the explanation as simple as possible, while still remaining useful. Probably the most important thing to know when looking at a map is where *you* are. The easiest way to determine that is by reference to a coordinate grid. A coordinate grid is a pattern of intersecting lines drawn on the map which allows the user to uniquely describe every point on the map. That is to say, the grid lines, by their intersections, combine to identify all specific places on the map, and no two specific locations have the same coordinates.

One of the most commonly used, and useful, coordinate grids is the Universal Transverse Mercator (UTM) system.[1] It is incorporated in all of the NTS maps and their commercial equivalents. The grid appears as blue lines running east/west and north/south on the map. The distance on the

---

1 The UTM grid system splits the globe into 60 zones, each of which is 6° wide. Each zone is numbered. Zone 1 starts at west longitude 180°; zone 2 abuts zone 1 and starts at west longitude 174°; zone 3 abuts zone 2 and starts at west longitude 168°; and so on through zone 60, which abuts zone 1. By analogy, think of the globe as a huge orange. When the peel of the orange is removed, there are 60 segments underneath, all joined together to collectively make up the whole sphere. The province of Alberta is contained within UTM zones 11 and 12.

ground between any grid line and its next neighbouring parallel line on either side is 1 km, so the squares in the grid are all 1 km a side on the ground. Each grid line is assigned a two-digit number as a locator.

In the UTM grid, the numbers across the top and bottom edges of the map (or from the left side moving to the right side) are called eastings. They show your east/west positions on the map. If the easting number increases, you are moving east. If the easting number decreases, you are going west. The full easting coordinate has seven digits, with the first digit in an easting always being zero.

In the UTM grid the numbers on the left and right edges of the map (or the numbers going from the bottom of the map to the top) are called northings. They show your north/south positions on the map. If the northing number increases, you are going north. If the northing number decreases, you are going south. The full northing coordinate has seven digits, and the northing numbers are the distance, measured in metres, from the equator.

GPS with UTM

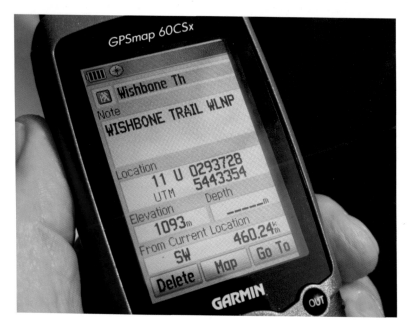

The coordinate for a particular location on the map consists of an easting and a northing. Where the two intersect is the particular spot.

When your GPS receiver is set to deliver locations in UTM format, the device will generate two lines of numbers. The top line is the easting, the bottom line the northing. The easting will be displayed as a seven-digit number starting with zero. (If your device displays the easting as only a six-digit number, you should insert a zero as the starting number.) The northing will also be displayed as a seven-digit number. For purposes of finding your exact position on a map, you need only address the middle three numbers in the easting and the middle three numbers in the northing.

The first two of the middle three numbers in an easting coincide with the UTM easting numbers shown on the map. The first two of the middle three numbers in a northing coincide with the UTM northing numbers shown on the map. Where those two lines intersect on the map you have found the southwest corner of the square kilometre where you are. The third numbers in the easting and northing tell you more precisely where you are inside that square kilometre. In each case, the third number tells you how far you are east and north of the southwest corner of the square, measured in tenths of a kilometre, that is, units of 100 m.

By way of example, let's look at photograph A below. The photograph shows a very small section of the Gem Trek map "Waterton Lakes National Park." Notice that there is a blue-lined grid on the map segment shown. In the lower middle portion of the photo the vertical blue lines are numbered, starting at the left "92," then moving right to "93," then moving farther right to "94," then moving farther right to "95." Those numbers are the eastings. As the numbers increase, you are moving farther to the east. Likewise, in the right-hand third of the photo you will see that the horizontal blue lines are numbered, moving from bottom to top, reading "41," then "42," then "43," then "44." These are the northings, and as the numbers increase you are moving farther to the north.

Hike No. 34 on the Gem Trek map (shown as a red dot with a white "34" inside) is the trailhead for the Wishbone Trail. If I turn on my GPS

Above: Photograph A
Below: Photograph B

while standing at the trailhead for the Wishbone Trail, the readout shows two lines as follows:

11u 0293728
5443354

In the top line, 11u refers to the zone in the UTM system – in this case zone 11 – and the u indicates it is in the northern hemisphere (the whole of Alberta is contained in zones 11 and 12). Of the set of numbers 0293728, we take the middle three – 937 – as the easting. In the lower set of numbers – 5443354 – we also take the middle three – 433 – as the northing. The Grid Reference for the trailhead is 937433.

Now look at photograph B. If you follow the vertical blue line "93" up to its intersection with the horizontal blue line "43," you will see that the intersection occurs at the tip of the pen in the photo. Where those two lines meet is at the southwest corner of a 1-km square that contains the trailhead. The last number in the easting – 7 – indicates that the precise location inside that square is 7/10 of the way across the square from west to east – that is 700 m east of the southwest corner of the square. The last number in the northing – 3 – means that the precise location inside that square is 3/10 of the way up the square from south to north, or 300 m north of the southwest corner of the square. If you then project 7/10 of the width of the square east and 3/10 of the height of the square north, you will be looking at the dark dot on the map that represents the trailhead. That dot is at Grid Reference 937433.

The coordinate might also be written 11u 0293728 5443354.

As an exercise, calculate the Grid Reference for the park gate on the east side of the Waterton River in the photos. It is in the square kilometre where the southwest corner is the intersection of easting 93 and northing 43. The gate is about 2/10 of the distance across the grid square (200 m), so the easting is 922. The gate is about 5/10 of the distance up the square from the south side (500 m), so the northing is 435. The Grid Reference for the gate is therefore 922435.

Once you understand how these eastings and northings work, you can take any Grid Reference and quickly find that exact spot on the map. In the alternative, you can take any spot on the map and quickly work out the Grid Reference for that point. A very useful hint from my friend Alan Youell is to get a clear plastic ruler that is calibrated in metric. You can see through the ruler to the map underneath, and the metric calibration can greatly assist with pinpointing places inside the squares on the grid.

If I am planning a hiking trip to any place I am unfamiliar with, I first gather as much information about the hike as I can, including, if possible, speaking to somebody who has done the hike before. I also check the available guidebooks and do a search on the Internet, all in an effort to acquaint myself as much as possible with what might be expected on the hike. I also obtain the relevant map for the area and make a copy of the pertinent portions for carrying with me on the hike. On the copy I plot the course for the hike and include such information as how to get to the trailhead and any known geographic features on the trail that I want to further investigate or avoid, such as a swamp or a cliff. With the route plotted on the map, I have a game plan for the hike. I know where I am starting and what waypoints I will encounter along the route. I know which turns to make when I get to an intersection in the trail, and I know how far ahead I should expect to find the junctions. I can also key all that information into my GPS if I wish. If I don't choose to do that, I can turn on the GPS unit from time to time during the hike, get a current position from the device and compare that position to my map to confirm exactly where I am at any point. If you think I am making too much of all this, that's okay with me. You deal with it as you deem appropriate. But I can tell you this, without any fear of contradiction by those who know only too well – getting and/or being lost on a hike SUCKS. In fact, once you have been lost (assuming you were found and rescued), you will most likely revisit the wisdom of your earlier convictions about not having a GPS device and map. I do not recommend taking a hike in unfamiliar country without first attending to the necessities of navigation, any more than I would recommend taking a hike without attending to the necessities of sufficient water, food and clothing to get you home safely even if the worst happens.

One final word on this subject. A Grid Reference, if properly recorded, can get you to within 100 m of any point on the map. If you require more precision than that, you can get it from your easting and northing. Look once again at the coordinates for the trailhead for the Wishbone Trail:

11u 0293728

5443354

By using the last three digits of the easting and northing, the trailhead is precisely 728 m east and 354 m north of the southwest corner of the square kilometre where grid lines 93 easting and 43 northing intersect.

And what of your old, trusty compass? Most authorities will tell you to carry it in the field as a backup navigation system in case your GPS goes down for any of a variety of reasons. They point out that a GPS can fail as a result of battery exhaustion, canopy cover that blocks reception from satellites, having the unit get dropped and broken, fall in a lake, fall over a cliff, get gnawed by a bruin, etc. Yes, any of that can happen, but none of it likely will if you take the simple expedient of carrying extra batteries and treat the instrument with a modicum of the care it deserves. After all, compasses can get misplaced and damaged too. So, in the final analysis, carry your compass as a backup, but make sure that you know how to properly use it as such in the unlikely event that your GPS goes down.

DRINKING WATER

Be advised that there are no surface waters in the province of Alberta that are safe to drink. This is particularly so on the eastern slopes of the Rockies, where water is often contaminated with *Giardia lamblia*, a protozoan parasite that can lead to a condition called giardiasis – commonly known as "beaver fever." The condition causes severe gastrointestinal distress, including bloating, gas, excessive flatulence, abdominal cramps and pain, diarrhea, loss of appetite, weakness and a general lassitude. Anybody who has ever suffered with the condition would never choose to repeat the experience. Cryptosporidium is another group of protozoan pathogens that are present in many surface waters in Alberta. They also will cause acute infections of the intestines and will present symptoms similar to giardiasis. So, bring your water from home and bring sufficient quantities to keep yourself properly hydrated during your outings. Experienced hikers do not share their water bottles, because of a justifiable fear of contamination. In the same vein, hikers should never answer "nature's call" within 50 m of any body of water, whether the water is moving or still. If you cannot carry all of the potable water you may require for an outing, make certain you have effective filtration devices and purification chemicals with you and use them as necessary to safeguard your water supply.

LEAVE WORD WHERE YOU ARE GOING AND WHEN YOU WILL BE BACK

Before you go on an outing, make certain you advise a responsible person of where you are going and when you expect to return. You might also include in your plan a time certain for the contact person to notify the appropriate authorities should you not report in before that time. If your plans change after first delivering the notice, make certain the change of plans is communicated to the contact person before setting out on the different course. There is an ongoing debate as to whether one should carry a cell phone while hiking. Some people are adamant that carrying one is an affront to the whole rationale of getting into the wild to "re-create" yourself. Others are of the opinion that having a cell phone is a reasonable safety measure in the event of accident, breakdown or delay. Sometimes this debate is quite moot, given that cell service may be severely restricted in mountainous terrain. One thing is certain, however. The cell phone has now become so ubiquitous that the likelihood is good that somebody will have one, even in a small party of hikers. My wife and I often hike with a wonderful group from High River, and many of us are now over 60. The founder/leader of the group, recognizing that things can go wrong with older people, dedicates a portion of the club dues each year to leasing a satellite phone, which he carries on all hikes as a precaution. He also makes a habit of making sure that all members of the group are acquainted with its operation. I applaud his resourcefulness.

HIKE WITH COMPANY

And speaking of parties of hikers, it is usually preferable to go out in the company of others, rather than alone. It is generally true that there is more safety in numbers. Hikers in a group can assist one another, particularly when an accident occurs. If a member of the group becomes incapacitated for any reason, there is sufficient manpower to render aid and comfort to the ill or injured while still having some members who can hike out and raise the alarm with rescue personnel. Should this eventuality occur, make certain that the members going for help have a GPS fix on the injured companion. Groups of hikers are also much less likely to get cross-threaded with aggressive wild animals than might a solo hiker. When hiking in a group, remember that the group must stay together at all times, and consequently the pace of the group is dictated by the pace of the slowest member. If the slowest member begins to lag behind, the rest of the group should stop and wait for the slowest member to catch up – and also give the late arriver a chance to catch a short rest before heading on again. When the hike is restarted, reduce the pace to accommodate the slowest member.

KEEP THE GROUP TOGETHER

Splitting a group with the idea of the laggers "catching up later" is a very bad procedure. That error may come back to haunt you at the very next junction in the trail, where you don't know if the advance party went to the left or to the right. I was once on a hike where two teenaged girls were quietly given permission by their mothers to head out in advance of the rest of the party, provided they stop and wait at the next bridged stream crossing. Before that plan was announced to the group, the girls had taken their leave. When the main party arrived at the bridge, there was no sign of the girls, and that presented quite a quandary. Did the girls fail to reach the bridge, in which event they went astray before getting there and therefore were still somewhere back up the trail? Or did they fail to stop at the bridge, in which event they were still ahead of the main party? The situation was made even more stressful because the girls had set out without extra clothing and water – and they were now moving as a party of two in tremendous bear habitat. In the end, the girls were found safe at the vehicles at the trailhead, but the whole experience taught all of us that it is a really bad idea to split a party unless the circumstances are dire. Even if the circumstances are dire and you have a legitimate reason to split a group, make sure you firmly establish the ground rules as to what is now to happen, and confirm that everybody understands them implicitly.

TRAIL ETIQUETTE

Acceptable conduct on the trail means being courteous to and respectful of your companions, other users and the environment. Where the trail is sufficiently wide, proceed as you would if you were on a public sidewalk. Walk single file and provide room for others to pass in either direction without having to step off the trail. If you are being overtaken by a faster hiker, give way and let the person by. If you are overtaking a slower hiker, be courteous and request permission to pass. If someone steps off the trail to allow you to pass, acknowledge their courtesy with a "thank you." Stay on the trails as much as possible and never cut switchbacks. If you are stopping to take a break, step off the trail so as not to impede other hikers. Acknowledge others when you meet them, but do not assume they want to engage in conversation with you. If you have some news that might be useful to the stranger – like you saw a bear 300 m back – mention it in passing. If the trails are used by hikers and bicycles, you might as well assume that the bikers have the right of way, because in my experience they assume that is the case. Keep your head up and your ears open for their approach and let them know you are going to step out of their way. If I encounter horses on the trail, I treat them the same way as bikes, but with more justification.

WILDLIFE

If you are hiking in Alberta and are not in the desert, you could well encounter a bear, either black or grizzly, or a cougar. The odds are somewhat long for bear encounters and even longer for cougar, but such things do happen. Before it happens to you, make sure you have studied

Grizzly print

and understand how you should behave in the situation. The more you know about how to act when confronted by one of these animals, the greater the likelihood you will get through the meeting without damage. Literature about bear and cougar encounters can be obtained from park visitor centres, hiking/backpacking manuals and online sources. It is recommended that all hikers carry bear spray, but make no mistake about it, having bear spray does not obviate your knowing what to do. The best thing would be to avoid any encounter in the first place. The best defence against an encounter is to move in groups of five or more and make a lot of noise to alert the animal that you are in the area. If you give the animal that advance warning of your approach, it will almost always make an exit rather than risk a confrontation. In areas where you are near running water or where thick vegetation might absorb sound, make sure you increase your volume accordingly. Make the assumption that bears and cougars do not like surprises, and try your best not to give them any.

Quite apart from bears and cougars, you should never approach any wildlife. Elk, deer and moose can be very dangerous, particularly when they have young of the year or during the rut in the autumn. Interestingly enough, between 1978 and 1992 in Yellowstone National Park, four times as many people were killed or injured by bison as by bears. The score was bison 56, bears 12. Feeding any wildlife is absolutely prohibited and completely ill advised. Even small animals can bite, and sometimes they carry diseases that are communicable to humans.

OTHER CRITTERS

Two species of wildlife you are liable to encounter wherever you hike are mosquitoes and ticks. Mosquitoes seem to be everywhere, regardless of elevation. Indeed, I have encountered swarms of the pesky things well above treeline and have often wondered how they make a living up there on top of the world. Though we don't seem to hear as much these days about the West Nile virus as we once did, taking prophylactic measures against disease caused by mosquito bites cannot be a bad thing.

Ticks occur in many locations in Alberta and are most active during the months of April through June. Ticks pose a risk of a variety of diseases, including Lyme disease, Rocky Mountain spotted fever and tick paralysis. Most of these diseases are communicated by agents contained in the saliva of ticks, it being the mouthparts of the tick that attach to your skin when it feeds. Even if ticks did not carry diseases, the very thought of something burrowing into your skin is sobering enough. Yuck. So your best defence is to get them before they get you. Ticks get on us from vegetation we pass through or sit down in, and once aboard they crawl upward looking

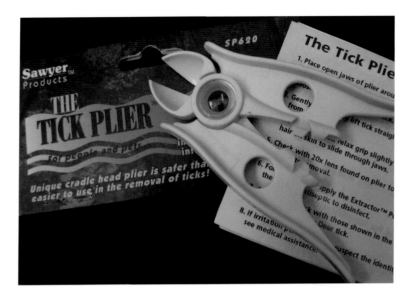

The Tick Plier

for a place to feed. Generally they are slow movers and usually take quite a while to settle in. During that time you might be able to see the tick and destroy it before it starts to feed. Ticks, being dark, show up better on light coloured clothing, so that is what is recommended. During your hike, use the buddy system to check yourself and your companions from time to time to see if any ticks have slipped aboard. Make another check before getting into your vehicle at the conclusion of the hike. Pay particular attention to your hair, your crotch, your armpits and any places where clothing fits tightly. If a tick does get through your defences and gets its mouth parts inserted into your skin, do not remove it by ripping it off of your skin. That process will probably leave the mouth parts buried in your skin, exposing you to disease and setting up a potential infection. If you pull slowly and gently on the tick, it will gradually withdraw from your skin. Outdoor equipment shops sell a simple device for tick removal called the Tick Plier. It is good planning to have such a device at hand when needed.

HIKING WITH A DOG?

One other matter you should consider is whether to take your dog on a hike. In Alberta provincial and national parks, dogs must be on leash at all times, and that can be a nuisance for the owner, particularly when traversing technically difficult terrain. In national parks in the US, dogs are banned from the trails. When the dog relieves itself, the owner should, as a matter of course, clean up after the dog as a courtesy to other people using the trail. In all areas dogs must be "under control" at all times. Under Alberta law, any dog found coursing game animals can be shot on sight and the shooter is statutorily shielded from any liability to the dog owner. I understand that everybody likes their dog, but I also understand that not everybody will like *your* dog. If you are going hiking with companions, check with them first to see if they will welcome your dog on the hike. Do not assume your companions will want your dog along. If they say "no," be prepared to leave Fido at home or give up going yourself. Many hiking clubs have a "no dogs allowed" policy. The crux of the problem is how well trained your dog is and how good your control over the pet is when in the field. In my experience, the vast majority of dogs will not measure up as being under control in the field. I like dogs and have lived with a number of them over the years, but I can honestly say I have only ever hiked with a mere handful of dogs that were really under control and pleasant to have as trail companions. Most of the dogs I see on hikes are out of control and qualify only as abject nuisances. When I used to bird hunt regularly, I had a wonderful German shorthair pointer that I followed around for years. He was a joy to be with most of the time, but he did have a couple of bad habits I could not make him break. He would often pick up skunks and shake them to see if they were empty, and any time he encountered a porcupine, he would try to get even for every other time he had encountered one. Would I take Luke hiking? Not on your life. One final thing to ponder on this issue: it has happened more than once that a dog on a hike will get tangled up with a bear, and when the dog decides it is time to break off the harassment and run back to the master, it will, unfortunately, have a very angry bruin in hot pursuit. Oops.

SOME ESSENTIALS

There are a few essential items that you should have with you every time you go hiking for the day. I recommend that you make a checklist of these items and revisit the checklist regularly with a critical eye to confirm that it is an adequate reflection of what you really want and need. You want to keep the weight to a minimum of course, but you also want to be ready for problems if they arise. My suspicion is that most experienced hikers will have very similar checklists. Mine would contain the following:

hat to shield you from rain and sun

fleece jacket or sweater

rain jacket and pants

bandana

sunglasses

butane lighter in zip-lock bag to keep it dry

sunscreen

insect repellent

headlamp

pocket knife

toilet paper in zip-lock bag

GPS and map

spare batteries for GPS

whistle

large, brightly coloured plastic garbage bag

assorted sizes of zip-lock bags

first-aid kit with all basic items included

notebook and pen

water bottles

water purification kit

food as required

camera and spare batteries

tripod

CAMERAS

If you are going out there, you will see some amazing things and you might want to make a record of some of them. Carrying a camera is always better than wishing you were carrying a camera. If you do carry one, and assuming it is digital, here is a potpourri of things you might want to consider.

Spend some time to adequately acquaint yourself with the camera's workings and capabilities. Read the operator's manual and become familiar with the camera's functions. If there is something you do not understand, seek advice from your camera dealer before you go into the field.

You do not have to make a huge financial investment to obtain the results you are seeking. A point-and-shoot camera is quite adequate for what most people want. Such cameras are significantly lighter in weight and much lower in cost than digital SLR cameras. Your results will not be better simply by investing in a more expensive camera. Unless you are going to make huge enlargements, a five-megapixel or larger processor is quite sufficient. Happily, in today's market that is about any new camera you see for sale. A more robust processor will capture an image that is larger, but not necessarily better.

The larger the LCD screen on the camera, the easier it is to see the image. An adjustable-angle screen is preferable to a fixed screen because you can adjust the angle to defeat glare. Bear in mind that when you use a point-and-shoot camera in macro mode, the photo must be framed in the LCD screen, not in the viewfinder, so it is critical that you be able to see the LCD, even in bright sunshine.

From the outset, adjust the camera to the highest resolution available and leave it there. Likewise, set the compression to the highest quality setting and leave it there. These settings will use up more memory, but memory is cheap and the better results from such settings are worth it.

Do not use the Auto ISO feature on the camera. Set the ISO to one of the lowest values available and leave it there. Make a change to a higher ISO only if low light forces you to that eventuality.

Do not use the Auto White Balance (AWB) setting on the camera. Set the white balance to match the light in which you are shooting. In most

Camera in Pelican case

cases outdoors, that will mean setting it to "Sun" or "Cloudy" or "Shade." Do not assume that the AWB setting will give you the best result in all circumstances. It won't.

Turn off the flash and leave it off. The flash will remove shadows in your photos, making the subjects look "flat."

On macro subjects like wildflowers, you generally want the flower to be in focus and the background to be somewhat blurred. You get this effect by setting the camera to the aperture priority mode and using a more open (larger) aperture. Do not use the Auto mode on the camera. It robs you of this effect. If the wind is really blowing, you might try using the shutter speed priority mode to get the subjects to stop shaking. Aperture priority or shutter speed priority modes will give you better results overall.

When taking close-up photos, camera shake is the biggest villain. To reduce camera shake, use a tripod. The sturdier the tripod the better, because you must demand a stable shooting platform.

Rechargeable batteries are the most cost effective for cameras. Generic "no-name" rechargeable batteries are usually just as good as those sporting the camera maker's name and logo, and they are considerably less expensive. Check with your dealer on this issue if it concerns you to buy generic. If the dealer is honest with you, you will come away with the no-name and will be adequately served. Get spare batteries, keep them charged and always carry them with you in the field. Rotate your batteries so all of them experience relatively the same amount of use. They will last longer if you treat them this way. If it is cold outside, keep the spare batteries in a pocket next to your body so the batteries stay a little warmer. They will hold their charge longer when treated that way.

If you are going to use your camera outdoors, you eventually will get caught in a rain squall. To protect the camera, consider getting a Pelican brand case from your camera dealer or outdoor equipment seller. Pelican cases are made in an enormous variety of sizes, so you will find one that fits your camera. These cases are waterproof, dustproof and virtually indestructible. In fact, they are guaranteed against all hazards other than shark attack, bear attack and children under five. Happily, they are not terribly expensive in sizes that fit point-and-shoot cameras. The one shown on the previous page has been adapted to hold an extra battery and several extra memory cards by the use of some Velcro and five-minute epoxy. That keeps those things in a waterproof condition, too.

Learn the basic manipulations in the photographic software you are going to use. That software is the digital darkroom and can be quite a fascinating and rewarding undertaking in itself. Deal with your photos promptly after returning home. Do not let them pile up unsorted for long or you will soon be overwhelmed by their sheer volume. Discard poor images immediately. In this regard, be absolutely ruthless. Bad photos will not get better with age!

Shoot, shoot, shoot. One of the best things about digital photography is that you do not have to pay for film and processing, so you can keep shooting. Review your images in the camera in the field. If you find you did not get what your really wanted, try again until you get it right.

BE CAREFUL OF THE BOTANY

When you are moving around in the backcountry, go carefully on the botany. As much as possible, stay on established trails so you can avoid damaging the wild plants. **Do not pick the flowers.** Leave them for others to enjoy. Bear in mind that in national, state and provincial parks **it is illegal to pick any flowers.** In my considered view, picking wildflowers is reprehensible, irresponsible and socially unacceptable behaviour. The most usual results are clearly demonstrated in the photograph below. Shameful.

Carthew Lakes

Waterton Lakes National Park

NATURAL HISTORY

The "Shining Mountains" was the name used by Native peoples to refer to what we today call the Canadian Rocky Mountains. Officially those mountains are bounded on the east by the Interior Plains, on the west by the Rocky Mountain Trench, on the north by the Liard River in northern British Columbia and on the south by the international boundary with the United States. Geologically, topographically and biologically, however, the "Canadian" Rocky Mountains actually extend farther south than the international boundary. That boundary was arbitrarily drawn along a line of latitude that does not accurately reflect the extent of the similarities of geological origin and natural environment that exist on both sides of the line. The southern end of this part of the Rocky Mountains actually extends some 40 km south of the border, to a place near to the southern edge of Glacier National Park in Montana. Indeed, many scientists in the United States refer to this portion of the Rocky Mountains – starting at or near Marias Pass and extending northward and westward into northern British Columbia as the "Northern Rocky Mountains." These mountains are principally made of sedimentary rock up to 1.5 billion years old that was once at the bottom of an ancient sea that covered this part of North America. Starting about 140 million years ago, and extending for an estimated 95 million years, that rock has been pushed, bent, broken, piled up and eroded to become what we see today.

In order to comprehend how the Rocky Mountains came to be, we can use an area rug on the living room floor as an appropriate analogy to explain in general terms how the mountains were built. If the rug is lying flat on the floor and you push one edge of the rug with your foot, the rug will start to slide and then buckle or wrinkle up. This is the same sort of mechanism that built the Rockies. Before the mountains were created, the area now occupied by them was part of a continental shelf that was covered by ocean. Sediment had been arriving in that ocean for hundreds of millions of years, and during that time, much of it turned to sedimentary rock. Beginning

41

an estimated 140 million years ago, Earth's crustal plates collided on the west coast and began to push the sedimentary rock inland in a roughly northeasterly direction, not unlike a grader pushing gravel on a roadway. As the continental plates continued to collide, the sedimentary layers overlying the plates were compressed and began to fold. Some broke, creating cracks or faults. When the faults formed, sections of the rock began to thrust upward as thrust sheets, climbing up and over other sections, creating a thrust fault. There was a general shifting, breaking, tilting and upward movement in the rock, resulting in the creation of the mountains – just like the wrinkle in the rug analogy. For most of the Rocky Mountains north of the Crowsnest Pass, this routine was repeated a number of times, creating foothills, mountain fronts and main mountain ranges aligned roughly southeast to northwest, extending about 150 km from eastern edge to western edge. However, south of the Crowsnest the mountains were created in a slightly different fashion, and that is apparent as soon as one sees the mountains of Waterton Lakes National Park.

In Waterton-Glacier International Peace Park the mountains were created by one principal movement, wherein a single, flat-lying massive thrust wedge originated about 100 km to the southwest and slid, more or less as a single horizontal unit, in a northeasterly direction. In the process the wedge – 9 km deep and over 100 km long – overlapped much younger rock. There was little folding in the thrust sheet, and it lies more or less flat. Geologists call this event the Lewis Overthrust or Lewis Thrust Sheet. There were no major faults in the thrust sheet, ergo nothing to divide the mountains here into separate ranges as seen farther north. All of the mountains at Waterton-Glacier are in the front range. They are also more colourful, many showing red rocks (argillite with oxidized iron) and green rocks (argillite with unoxidized iron). The mountains here also look like peaks, castles and spires when compared to the mountains farther north. The lateral distance from eastern edge to western edge is also quite abbreviated here, as little as 40 km. And, perhaps most noticeable to the visitor familiar with the Rockies farther north, foothills are virtually non-existent. The Lewis Thrust Sheet ground over smaller, younger rock and stopped on the prairies. What might have become foothills were ground away, leaving a relatively flat, treeless grassland margin that runs right up to the base of the mountains. This truly is the place where the mountains meet the prairies. On the eastern approach to the mountains of Waterton, the elevation soars over 1000 m only 1 km from the plains.

But in the scheme of mountain building, the foregoing is only part of the story. As soon as the mountains appeared, they were subjected to the erosive forces of wind and water, which shaped the mountains significantly. And perhaps most important, they were shaped by ice – in many cases vast rivers of ice.

During the most recent three million years, North America has been locked in several major glacial events. During those events snow fell and accumulated faster than it dissipated. As the snow deepened, it compressed and compacted the lower layers of snow into hard snow and ice. The ice recrystallized under the pressure, and in the right circumstances, given sufficient mass and slope, it would begin to move. The landscape was significantly altered by the passage of the ice. Deep u-shaped valleys, deep lakes, hanging valleys, cirques, arêtes, eskers, kames, kettles, moraines and glacial erratics are all evidence of glacial activity. As each glacier moved it picked up and transported rocks and boulders, sand and silt, all of which acted as rasps upon the landscape. Debris was carried by the ice and deposited elsewhere. During those periods there were advances in ice during the colder times and retreats during warmer periods between the ice events. At each advance and retreat, the ice was shaping and reshaping the environment. The last of these ice events ended between 10,000 and 12,000 years ago.

In addition to glacial activity, erosion from wind and water was significant. Those elements would also sculpt the landscape. As the glaciers began to recede, vast quantities of water were released and that water also shaped the landmass. Indeed, the mountains began to decompose almost as soon as they were formed, with natural forces breaking down the sedimentary rock into its component sediments, going back to be deposited once again in water bodies. Rates of erosion varied with elevation, climate, plant cover, soil composition and precipitation, but the weathering process was unrelenting and remains so today.

43

CLIMATE AND WEATHER

The climate of any place is its long-term averages of elements such as temperature, amount of precipitation, amount of sunlight, humidity, wind speed and direction and other factors. The weather is the status of these things at any particular given time.

Waterton's climate is strongly influenced by prevailing Pacific maritime systems. Typically, warm, moist air moves over the coastal mountains and the Columbia plateau before spilling across this narrowest point in the Rocky Mountains. The moist air from the Pacific meets colder, drier air masses and the warmer air is forced upward, creating precipitation in the form of rain or snow. As a result of its location and topography Waterton receives more annual precipitation than any other place in Alberta: 1072 mm. Most of this precipitation falls as snow. There is also a decided difference in the moisture levels from west to east in the park. Cameron Lake receives considerably more precipitation than does the Waterton townsite, and the townsite receives more than does the park gate, only a few kilometres away.

In Waterton, the weather can be variable at any time of the year, typical of the mountain environment. Summers tend to be short and can be interrupted by cool spells, some of which can bring snow. Winters are snowy but tend to be mild as a result of frequent chinook winds.

"Chinook" in Blackfoot parlance means "snow eater," a name given because these warm winds can make snow disappear virtually before your eyes. Typically, chinooks occur when the eastern slopes of the mountains are overlain by an arctic high-pressure cell, giving very cold temperatures. At the same time, a low-pressure system builds in the Gulf of Alaska and that sends winds eastward over the mountains. If conditions are right, the Pacific flow strengthens and produces an enormous standing wave downwind of the Rockies. In the trough of this standing wave, air rushes quickly downward, compressing and heating as it descends. It is estimated that for every 100-m drop, the temperature in the air mass rises 1° Celsius. It is not uncommon for chinook winds to raise temperatures from −20°c to 10°c overnight. In fact, the greatest swing of temperature ever recorded during a chinook was a 57°c rise recorded in Chouteau County, Montana, in 1972. As the air flows down, it creates a band of stationary stratus clouds parallel to the mountains. The cloud band appears to arch as it follows the curvature of the earth, and consequently is referred to as a "chinook arch." The warm air from the chinook pushes the cold air eastward across the prairies. Chinook events may last a few hours or several days. Typical wind speeds during a chinook are 30–50 km/h, but can reach 100 km/h. In a typical winter, Waterton can receive chinook winds for 30 of 120 days. Spells of extreme cold can occur, but they tend to be short-lived.

Quite apart from the chinook events, the most important climatic factor in the Waterton area is the wind. Waterton is the windiest place in Alberta, with the exception of the Crowsnest Pass. The prevailing winds blow from the west and southwest and average 30 km/h. Winds up to 120 km/h are not uncommon. The highest wind velocities are usually experienced in January and November, when gusts of over 150 km/h have been recorded. As the prevailing winds strike the western slopes of the Rockies, they tend to compress and slow down, creating an increase in pressure on that slope. They then expand and speed up on the lee side of the mountains, creating a decrease in pressure on the eastern slope. Winds move from high-pressure zones toward low-pressure zones. Added to this phenomenon is the fact that the Continental Divide in Waterton is generally lower in elevation than it is both to the south and to the north of Waterton. This creates a gap in the mountains, and the wind moves to that gap. Unlike the valleys in the Rockies farther north, which tend to run parallel to the ridges, the valleys in Waterton tend to be perpendicular to the Divide and this causes the wind to funnel, an effect that can increase the velocity of the winds.

The wind at Waterton also redistributes the snow. Windward slopes often lose their snow, while leeward slopes accumulate drifts. This phenomenon often provides forage areas and travel corridors for wildlife in the winter months. The accumulation of snow in drifts on the leeward slopes usually means slower melting in the spring and consequent steady inputs to streams and rivers later in the summer months.

PLANT LIFE IN WATERTON

All of the climatic factors mentioned above influence the variety and distribution of the flora (and fauna) in the park. However, there are other important factors also at play, such as the angle of the sun, elevation or altitude, alignment or orientation, and soil properties. For example, southerly and westerly facing slopes will be warmer, drier and have more sunlight than will northerly and easterly facing slopes; leeward slopes will accumulate more snow than windward slopes will, and as a consequence they will also be generally wetter and cooler during the spring; higher altitudes will generally be colder than lower altitudes; etc.

There are several ecoregions within the park, each with its own defining plant community. The foothills parkland and montane ecoregions are particularly rich areas with very productive streams, valleys, wetlands and woodlands. The subalpine and alpine ecoregions are perhaps less productive, but they feature species that are mainly limited to those areas. In its totality, Waterton Lakes National Park is an astonishing place for the abundance and diversity of its vegetation. There are said to be almost 1,000 plants in the park, including trees, wildflowers, grasses, sedges, lichens and others. Indeed, one-half of all of the plant species found in the whole of the province of Alberta are found in Waterton. Among the plants in the park, there are an estimated 170 species that are provincially rare and 50 that are nationally rare. Counted among the plants in the park there are nearly three dozen that occur nowhere else in the province. Suffice it to say, Waterton is an extraordinary place for wildflower viewing.

HUMAN HISTORY

Archaeological sites in the Waterton area have produced evidence that some nomadic peoples probably arrived in the area shortly after the last glacial retreat, approximately 10,000 years ago. The record is unclear as to exactly which peoples these were, but the best speculation seems to be that they probably represented the ancestors of two of the cultures who would come later: a mountain/interior-plateau culture like the Kootenay, and a prairie culture like the Blackfoot.

It is posited by some that prior to the introduction of the horse into this area of North America in the early 1700s, the Kootenay and the Blackfoot co-existed in relative harmony east of the Rocky Mountains. This is reinforced by the oral history of the Kootenay, which traces their ancestry to present-day southern Alberta, but little physical evidence of that exists. If it were once so, that occupation almost certainly ended before Europeans appeared in the area. After the introduction of the horse, the Natives' relationship with the land and each other changed. The horse allowed for hunting while mounted and also allowed for a dramatic expansion of territory. This expansion undoubtedly led to conflicts between neighbours. It is speculated that while the Kootenay were the first to acquire horses, the Blackfoot were first to acquire both horses and firearms. The balance of power shifted in favour of the Blackfoot, and the Kootenay were pushed off the plains and into and beyond the mountains to the west. There is also some speculation that any Kootenay that continued to live east of the mountains were wiped out, or virtually so, by the arrival of smallpox. The first smallpox epidemic arrived on the prairies in the 1730s and was followed by resurgent epidemics in 1781, 1835 and 1869. In each case all of the Native tribes suffered woefully. Each epidemic carried off large portions of the Native population.

There seems to be little doubt that by the time of arrival of Europeans, the Kootenay inhabited the headwaters of the Columbia River drainage and the Kootenay River drainage, including the Flathead River and the Tobacco Plains, a north/south-oriented valley west of the Continental Divide that straddles the British Columbia/Montana border near present-day Roosville, Montana. The bison herds of the great plains did not extend into that country, so the Kootenay regularly travelled through the mountains to get access to the bounty of the bison on the prairies. The route they used most often was through the mountains leading to the valleys of the Waterton area. The Kootenay often hunted and traded around Chief Mountain, then took their harvest back over the mountains at the end of the hunt. Indeed, the Kootenay were such regular visitors to the area that the lakes we know today as Waterton, were for many years referred to as the Kootenay (Kootenai) Lakes. The trail through the mountains was known to the Kootenay as the Buffalo Trail. White men called it the South Kootenay Pass.

Prior to the introduction of the horse, the members of the Blackfoot Confederacy were highly nomadic and followed the bison herds on foot, using only dogs as beasts of burden. Because they were pedestrian hunters, they developed some ingenious ways to obtain bison. By luring, baiting and driving the herds – over cliffs, into pounds and into marshes as traps – the Blackfoot were able to obtain bison, and their culture was centred on the animals and their movements. The animals were certainly a food source, but they were much more than that, too. The meat was cooked by roasting on a spit or boiling in a skin bag. Meat was also cut into thin slices and dried to produce jerky or rendered into pemmican. Pemmican was a high-protein food made by pounding dried meat into a powder and then mixing it with melted bison fat and berries. That was packed in skin bags and would remain edible for years. Apart from meat, bison bones were fashioned into tools, horns were used as containers and vessels, sinew was used as thread and other cordage, hair was braided into halters, hooves were made into rattles or rendered for glue, hides were made into clothing or stitched together for tipi covers. In addition, the bison was inculcated into the spiritual and cultural mosaic of the Native peoples.

With the advent of horses and guns, the Blackfoot were able to significantly expand their territory, and they would eventually dominate the lands between the North Saskatchewan River and the Missouri, and between the Rocky Mountains and the present-day boundary between Alberta and Saskatchewan – virtually all of the territory in present-day southern Alberta and much of Montana. The Confederacy presented a formidable impediment to European expansion in western British North America. There certainly were Europeans on the scene by the early 1700s, but it is important to bear in mind that the fur-trading companies that first pushed into the western portions of North America were not there for any purpose apart from commercial exploitation of the fur resource. They were not interested in annexing territory; they were interested only in *profit à prendre*. The traders were not nation builders and were not in any way interested in advancing settlement or European expansion in the area. Indeed, such expansion would not have been good for business, because it could easily have led to increased competition for the region's bounty. Likewise, the fur traders would have been loathe to share any knowledge of the area with potential rivals, because giving away that information would also interfere with their commercial advantage. Any local knowledge of the area, including rudimentary maps, were treated as proprietary information by the companies, not to be shared unless a commercial advantage could be obtained in return. The traders were there for lucre, not for science and not for political expansion. However, an irresistible movement was already under way. The Lewis and Clark Expedition of 1804–1806 resulted in significantly increased interest in what would become the western United States, together with a steady rise in the numbers of white adventurers and fortune seekers entering those environs. Expansion was underway in the United States, and soon western British North America, its Native inhabitants and the bison would not escape similar attentions.

In that context, the timing was right to make an exploration of the territories that would become western Canada. Enter John Palliser.

The Palliser Expedition, 1857–1860

John Palliser was born in Ireland in 1817, a son of the landed gentry. He attended Trinity College, Dublin, but was never awarded any degree. He served some intermittent time in the Waterford militia, rising to the rank of captain, but his military pursuits ended there. His keenest interests ran to being a sportsman, adventurer and explorer. In all such pursuits he was certainly a star. Indeed, his five brothers were all adventurers who were often engaged in explorations around the world. His youngest brother, Walter, was lost with Sir John Franklin on his final polar expedition.

In 1847 Palliser travelled up the Mississippi River from New Orleans to the site of present-day Kansas City. In September of that year, in company with a party of traders for the American Fur Company, he made his way up the Missouri River into the western wilderness that had been explored by Lewis and Clark at the start of that century. He spent the winter of 1847–48 in the upper Missouri country, exploring, hunting elk, grizzly bear, antelope and buffalo in the Yellowstone country, and becoming acquainted with some of the Native tribes. He departed this sojourn with great regret in July 1848 to return to Ireland. His adventures in North America were recounted in his book *Solitary Rambles and Adventures of a Hunter in the Prairies*. The book was published in 1853, and it became an immediate popular success.

After his return to Ireland, Palliser retained a fierce desire to revisit the western wilderness. In 1856, after his election as a fellow of the Royal Geographical Society, Palliser made an application for the Society to fund an expedition through the prairies of British North America and on to the Rocky Mountains. The application was referred to the Expedition Committee of the Society, which looked favourably on the project but recommended that the plan be expanded to include trained scientists who could use the best available instruments to make sophisticated records along the way.

After some considerable discussion, the Society made a formal request to the Colonial Office for a contribution to finance the expedition. Palliser was to be the leader, supported by scientists and technical men. The Colonial Office reviewed the request and, after some dithering, approved a plan to put the expedition into the field as the British North America Exploring Expedition. The venture was to be funded for two seasons of exploration (later expanded to three), with the express proviso that the Colonial Office, not the Royal Geographic Society, took full responsibility for the expedition.

The mandate of the expedition was very broad indeed, and could quite accurately have been referred to as daunting. The expedition was to assess and report on the state of the prairies, including the location of the border with the United States; determine the feasibility of transportation routes, including possible rail routes through the mountains; assess the potential for sustainable agricultural settlement in the region; collect and catalogue minerals and other resources, flora and fauna along the way; and keep meteorological and magnetic records. The area of interest for exploration, study and mapping was the plains between the North Saskatchewan River and the US border, as well as any mountain passes in the Rocky Mountains that led to the Pacific coast. As mentioned above, at the time the Palliser expedition set out, the prairie region of British North America was titularly under the jurisdiction of the Hudson's Bay Company and would remain so until the Deed of Surrender was signed in 1869, transferring ownership in Rupert's Land to the new country of Canada. Realistically, however, the country was under the jurisdiction of the Blackfoot Confederacy, and every move the expedition made would be inside their territory. The geographic scope of the area is immense. Quite apart from the sheer volume of country, the expedition would be approaching the plains and the Rocky Mountains without any reliable maps, and virtually none of the geographic features were named. Compounding the problem even further, the Convention of Commerce signed at London in 1818 had settled the border between the United States and British North America from Lake of the Woods to the Rocky Mountains as the 49th parallel of latitude. That sounds simple enough, but in truth nobody knew exactly where that parallel lay. It did not run along a river, lake, mountain range or any other obvious topographical feature. It was just an invisible, virtually imaginary line that formed a frontier. None of it had been properly mapped, surveyed or marked in any meaningful way. Viewed from the perspective of the present century, the plan of exploration was well past audacious. Fortunately for history, Palliser did not view his mission in that light. He looked upon the whole plan as an answered prayer and could hardly wait to set forth.

Once the plan of exploration was outlined and approved, Palliser and his advisers began to recruit the men who would join the expedition. In addition to Palliser as leader, the expedition would have four members.

Eugène Bourgeau, a native of the French Alps, was chosen as botanist and plant collector. Sir William Hooker, the first director of the Royal Botanical Gardens at Kew, had received many specimens from Bourgeau over the years and referred to him as a "prince of botanical collectors." Hooker recommended Bourgeau to the expedition organizers. Parenthetically, Bourgeau collected specimens from over 800 species of plants during his two years with the expedition. Many of them are still preserved at Kew. Bourgeau left the expedition after two years because he had commitments elsewhere that could not be set aside. There is a mountain west of Banff that bears Bourgeau's name. It was named by James Hector in 1860 in honour of the botanist.

Thomas Wright Blakiston, a lieutenant in the Royal Artillery, was chosen to be the magnetic observer. He was recommended by his erstwhile commanding officer, General Sir John Henry Lefroy, an astronomer who had travelled extensively in British North America several years earlier making magnetic and meteorological observations. Lefroy would later become head of the Toronto Observatory. Mount Lefroy, which can be seen from Chateau Lake Louise, was named in his honour. After receiving the recommendation, Blakiston volunteered for duty with the expedition. Several natural features in southern Alberta bear Blakiston's name, but more on that shortly.

Dr. James Hector from Edinburgh University was chosen as geologist, medical doctor and naturalist for the expedition. As it turned out, Hector probably contributed more to the expedition than any other member. He was indefatigable in his explorations, and his talents in medicine proved very worthwhile in dealings with Native peoples. Following the expedition, Hector moved to New Zealand, where he would remain for most of the balance of his life, eventually becoming the founder and head of the Geological Survey of New Zealand.

John W. Sullivan, a mathematician and instructor at the Naval College at Greenwich, was chosen as sextant observer and put in charge of astronomical observations for the expedition. He was also named recording secretary of the expedition.

With all of the members of the expedition chosen, they soon set out. Blakiston travelled alone, sailing from England to York Factory, a Hudson's Bay Company fort on Hudson Bay, and on to the prairies by York boat. He was to join the rest of the party at Fort Carlton on the North Saskatchewan River. This means of proceeding was deemed best given that Blakiston was carrying a number of delicate scientific instruments, and it was believed they would have a better chance of arriving intact by using that route rather than risk the jolting overland journey across the prairies to the south.

Palliser, Bourgeau, Hector and Sullivan left from London in May 1857, bound for Liverpool and then on to North America. They docked in New York, then travelled by train to Detroit, where they caught a lake steamer to Sault Ste. Marie and Isle Royale. From there they travelled by canoe to Thunder Bay and on to Fort William, a Hudson's Bay Company fort. The members of the expedition entered winter quarters at Fort Carlton after gruelling travel to get there.

Owing in part to the vastness of the area under study, Palliser regularly split the expedition in hopes of better canvassing the country. As one example, in the summer of 1858 he split the expedition into three parts. Palliser himself travelled west over the Rockies by going up to the headwaters of the Kananaskis River, over a pass, then down the newly named Palliser River to the Kootenay, where he travelled farther south. He returned eastbound through the Rockies by way of the North Kootenay Pass.

At the same time, Hector rode up the Bow Valley, over Vermilion and Kicking Horse passes and explored the North Saskatchewan valley, Howse Pass and the Athabasca River. It was on this exploration that Hector, while exploring a mountain pass near the Continental Divide of the Rockies, lost a pack horse in a river. As he worked to recover the horse, Hector's horse bolted and, in the process, kicked Hector in the chest so hard it rendered him unconscious. His companions, believing him to be dead, prepared a grave for him and were about to put him into it when Hector regained consciousness and stopped his own premature funeral. The pass and the nearby river were immediately dubbed "Kicking Horse," and are known by that name to this day. While Palliser and Hector were so engaged, Blakiston was to go south to explore the Crowsnest and Kootenay Pass country. It is these travels of Blakiston that particularly relate to the Waterton country.

Virtually from the outset of the expedition, Palliser found that personality clashes between Blakiston and the other members of the expedition, particularly Sullivan, were an ongoing problem. Blakiston's views were undoubtedly coloured by his military background, where an institutional regimentation was constantly at work, with every member of the troop being told how and what to do on a consistent and continuous basis. Palliser did not run the expedition even remotely with military precision, and that almost surely grated on Blakiston's sense of military propriety. Blakiston regularly opposed many of Palliser's decisions as to the conduct of the expedition, and he was at no pains to conceal his opinions about how Palliser conducted himself as the leader of the expedition. Blakiston opined openly that "this expedition is no more than a party of pleasurers out on a hunting excursion." This attitude, while perhaps understandable, is surprising given that Blakiston, as a military man, would understand, presumably better than the others, the dangers of the breakdown in discipline among the troops.

At one point, the dispute became so raw that Blakiston demanded that Palliser choose a second in command who would take over the expedition during times of Palliser's absence. Blakiston surely was expecting Palliser to choose him as second in command, but instead Palliser chose Dr. Hector. Blakiston undoubted took this as a personal affront, and his relationship with Palliser never recovered from the perceived slight.

On August 3, 1858, while Palliser was absent on his Kananaskis valley exploration, Blakiston penned a letter to Palliser and left it with Hector and Sullivan, to be delivered to Palliser upon his return. In the letter Blakiston, in his words, "threw off Palliser's command" and went about exploring on his own to the south. He left Hector and Sullivan near Peigan Post (Old Bow Fort), a fort that had been built by the Hudson's Bay Company in 1832 in an unsuccessful attempt to lure the Peigan and Blackfoot away from American traders in the Missouri River country.

After Blakiston split from Hector and Sullivan, he headed down the eastern edge of the Rockies along a route similar to the present-day Hwy 22 from Turner Valley to the Crowsnest Pass. On the trek south Blakiston noted

John Palliser

an eastern range, of very regular form, extending … for a distance of five and twenty miles without a break. The crest of the range was of so regular a form that no point could be selected as a peak, I therefore gave the whole the name Livingstone's Range, it is a very marked feature when seen from the plains outside.

The reference is to Dr. David Livingstone, a British explorer, geographer and missionary who for over 30 years travelled through Africa. Livingstone is the same one whom Henry Morton Stanley was said to have asked on meeting: "Dr. Livingstone, I presume?" Later explorers revered Livingstone, and this undoubtedly led to the honour bestowed by Blakiston. It seems somehow strange to have a portion of the Rocky Mountains named for an African explorer who never came within thousands of miles of setting foot in the very mountains that bear his name to this date. However, this was a practice of many of the explorers who left the British Isles to take the measure of the world.

Near the Oldman River, Blakiston noticed a gap in the mountains in which appeared a "very decided dome-shaped mountain." This he named Gould's Dome after a distinguished British naturalist, John Gould (1804–1881). Gould's Dome is now known as Tornado Mountain, with its southern outlier still being referred to as Gould's Dome. John Gould was a British naturalist who illustrated over forty volumes on birds, leaving over 3,000 coloured plates by the time of his death. He learned taxidermy at Windsor Castle, where his father was foreman of gardeners. In 1827 Gould became the taxidermist to the Zoological Society of London. He produced a five-volume set on the birds of Europe and he also worked in Australia on birds and mammals. He was elected to the Royal Society in 1843. So far as I can discover, Gould, like Livingstone and others for whom Blakiston named things, never set foot in North America, much less in Alberta.

On the trek south, Blakiston also named a mountain Castle Mountain – which name was later changed to Windsor Mountain to avoid confusion with the mountain in present-day Banff National Park that James Hector coincidentally named Castle Mountain at about the same time.

Blakiston crossed the Crowsnest River on August 20, 1858, and gained the entrance to Kootenay Pass. The Kootenay Trail followed up today's Carbondale River, which in turn flows into the Castle River. Blakiston called the present-day Castle River the Railway River. From the Crowsnest Pass he travelled across North Kootenay Pass into present-day southeastern British Columbia, the first recorded crossing by a white man. Shortly after the crossing he encountered the Flathead River, then continued west to the Wigwam River. He followed the Wigwam down to its confluence with the Elk River – in the process naming the Galton Range after a distinguished British scientist Francis Galton. Sir Francis Galton (1822–1911) was an English explorer, scientist and anthropologist who was a cousin to Charles Darwin. Galton is credited with coining the word "eugenics." He was also a pioneer in the use of fingerprints for personal identification, the correlation of calculus in applied statistics, the study of twins, blood transfusions, criminality and meteorology.

Blakiston then turned south into United States territory, most probably near the present-day border crossing at Roosville, Montana. It was after that crossing that Blakiston met some Kootenay Indians and heard of another pass through the mountains farther to the south of the one he had travelled. With the assistance of the Kootenays he headed back north and east and, moving into present-day US Glacier National Park, entered the South Kootenay Pass. He then followed Kishinena Creek north of the 49th parallel. Blakiston referred to this southern route as "Boundary Pass." He noted in his journal:

> After two hours travelling on level ground along Red-stone creek [present-day Red Rock Creek] we emerged on the Saskatchewan plains, just six geographical miles north of the 49th parallel and camped at the lakes ... The scenery here is grand and picturesque ... game is abundant, including, Grizzly bears ... and we obtained both fresh meat and fish.

Blakiston named the lakes Waterton, after Charles Waterton, a British scientist, ornithologist and naturalist. Waterton made four journeys to

British Guiana (now Guyana) and wrote extensively about his travels. In later life he retired to his ancestral home in Yorkshire, Walton Hall, and established his estate as a protected environment for wildlife – perhaps the first such reserve in the world. At the time Blakiston named the lakes, they were known as the Kootenay (Kootenai) Lakes, a name taken from the Kootenay Indian tribe. That name persisted for some years, in spite of Blakiston's honouring Charles Waterton.

While in the area, Blakiston named Mount Blakiston – the highest peak in Waterton Lakes National Park, at 2910 m – and Blakiston Creek after himself.

From Waterton, Blakiston turned north, returning to Fort Edmonton, there to reunite with the other members of the expedition. He returned to England alone in 1859. Though Blakiston repudiated Palliser's command, he did not quit exploring. Indeed, he used assets and hired personnel of the expedition to complete his explorations in western Canada, and later refused to share his findings, observations or notes with other members of the expedition. When the final report was written on the expedition, Blakiston delivered his report separately. All in all, this behaviour by a military officer is most peculiar. If he handled himself similarly in a setting where military discipline were the rule, he undoubtedly would have been cashiered for mutiny.

In his report on the expedition, Blakiston recommended the North Kootenay Pass as a route west for the railway. That suggestion was never taken up, owing to the later "discovery" of the Crowsnest Pass route. Blakiston was aware of the existence of the Crowsnest Pass route, and indeed "Crows Nest Pass" is written on the map he made during his journey. However, he thought that route was not easily passable based upon what he was told by Indians in the area. They told him it was a "bad route and seldom used." In retrospect, the Indians were most likely referring to the Crowsnest Pass as a bad route owing to extensive numbers of blowdowns and deadfalls, which would indeed make it a bad route for horses and men on foot but nothing that would be problematic for a railway. Blakiston did not venture along the Crowsnest Pass and it would not be travelled by white men for another 15 years. When it was explored, it was deemed to be a perfect pass for a railway because it had "no mountains to go over."

After completing his report on the Palliser Expedition, Blakiston was detailed to China to protect British interests during a civil war. While there he organized an expedition up the Yangtze River, and he explored almost 1200 km more of that river than any westerner had ever done before. Blakiston later published important works on ornithology, spending many years in the Far East. He retired to the United States, where he died in 1891 at the age of 58.

Without question, the Palliser Expedition was a pivotal point in the history of western British North America. The expedition produced the first maps of the Rocky Mountains, named many of the prominent topographical features, and revealed a number of heretofore unrecorded passes through the mountains and on to the Pacific coast. Hundreds of specimens of heretofore unknown flora and fauna were delivered to men of science for study. The expedition concluded that the Palliser Triangle – a triangularly shaped area of present-day southern Alberta and Saskatchewan – was too arid for agriculture, but that finding was ultimately overlooked and over-ruled by government officials. In the scheme of things, however, the expedition opened up the western territories of British North America and beckoned in more exploration and settlement. In the two decades following Blakiston's arrival at Waterton the landscape and culture would alter quickly and permanently. The culture of the Blackfoot Confederacy would dramatically decline, the bison herds would disappear, law and order would be brought to the west, and Kootenai Brown and others would successfully lobby to preserve the lands that would become Waterton Lakes National Park.

Decline of the Native culture

In the panorama of history, the Blackfoot Confederacy's domination of the prairies was extraordinarily short-lived. In about two generations, European diseases, the whisky trade and the disappearance of the bison herds took a quick and collective toll to destroy the dominance of the culture.

As referred to earlier, diseases brought to North America by Europeans repeatedly devastated Native peoples. The Native people had no immunities to the diseases, and smallpox, measles and any number of other communicable diseases regularly wiped out large segments of the indigenous societies. As bad as it was, disease was not the only issue.

A US law passed in 1832 made it illegal to sell liquor to Indians, but that law was seldom, if ever, enforced in the Montana Territory. When the Territorial Government was formed in 1864, that began to change. As the law was enforced, it put constraints on the American businessmen operating in Montana, so they moved to British North America, where there was no law enforcement. One of the first to take advantage of the opening was John ("Johnny") Jerome Healy, then of Fort Benton, Montana. Healy was an Irish immigrant who at various times during his colourful life was a soldier, prospector, Indian fighter, scout, merchant, lawman, whisky trader and con man. As a matter of interest, John Healy was to later hear of and promote a copper discovery in present-day Banff National Park, whereby he became the namesake for Healy Creek and Healy Pass. Healy touted the discovery as also containing silver, and he is credited with creating a shanty town called Silver City, where he intended to get rich by dealing with prospectors who were lured into the area by his touts. After that, Healy moved north to the goldfields of the Klondike. It was there that he prospered financially by trading, proving once again that it is easier to make money from miners than from mining.

In 1869 Johnny Healy, in company with Alfred Baker Hamilton, crossed the border into present-day southern Alberta with a permit granted by General Alfred Sully, the Indian Commissioner for Montana, for "a scientific expedition of exploration." Once in British North America, the two established Fort Hamilton at the confluence of the Oldman (formerly the Belly River) and the St. Mary's rivers, near present-day Lethbridge. Such an action was quite in keeping with the audacity of Healy and Hamilton. The location was chosen because it was a traditional winter camping place for the Blood and the Peigan. The primary purpose was to gain a quick profit from an illicit trade – whisky and firearms in exchange for buffalo robes from the Native people of the unpoliced prairies north of

Montana. Trade was immensely profitable, with "whisky" going for a price of $30–$40 per gallon. The term "whisky" is used loosely in this context. Pure alcohol was shipped to Fort Hamilton in five-gallon tins. At the Fort the alcohol was diluted with a variety of other ingredients, including but not limited to water, chewing tobacco, molasses, ink, ginger, red pepper and various patent medicines, to give it colour and taste. The exact amount of alcohol in the final product varied enormously, depending on the recipe used. Without doubt, however, the various concoctions marketed could be referred to, literally and figuratively, as "rotgut."

Business was brisk. Six months after Healy and Hamilton started Fort Hamilton, they were reported to have returned to Fort Benton with $50,000 worth of buffalo robes. The original fort burned down at the end of its first year (some say at the hands of the Blackfoot), but it was replaced quickly by an even larger facility. Though initially called Fort Hamilton, the place quickly became known by a more appropriate and infamous name – Fort Whoop-up – and it became arguably the most formidable and notorious of the several American-owned and -run whisky forts located in the area. Indeed, the whole region soon became known as "Whoop-up Country" and the trail leading to the fort as the "Whoop-up Trail." The name Whoop-up, most likely, is a shortened form of "whoop it up," meaning to celebrate boisterously.

In a short time, the fort's dealing in contraband spawned so much violence and disorder that lawlessness became the norm in the region. This general state of affairs hastened the formation of the North-West Mounted Police (NWMP) in 1873, a force established to maintain law and order in western Canada. Their marching orders were clear, though perhaps a little grandiose given the number of men and the breadth of country to be patrolled. They were delegated to end the illegal whisky trade, patrol the border, end smuggling, gain the confidence of the Native peoples, prepare the west for the coming railway and maintain law and order. What they were to do in their spare time is unclear.

After its establishment, the force was headquartered in Lower Fort Garry, an old Hudson's Bay Company supply fort on the Red River a few miles north of Winnipeg. When the force was started, it comprised 150 men, organized along the lines of a cavalry regiment and equipped with sidearms, rifles and small artillery. The force was increased by an additional 150 men within a few months of its creation, and it grew regularly over the years as new contingencies arose. Interestingly, of the original force assembled at Lower Fort Garry, there were only two members who had any previous experience as peace officers, and the very large majority of the recruits knew nothing of horses or how to ride them.

On July 8, 1874, nearly 300 "mounties" of the NWMP accompanied by 114 ox-drawn carts, 73 supply wagons and a number of Métis freighters left Dufferin, Manitoba, and headed west, bound for the southern plains of the North-West Territories. When they left Manitoba they were facing a journey of over a thousand kilometres through country unknown to them, without the assistance of competent guides, with green men unused to such travels and having no practical knowledge of what pitfalls or pestilence might be encountered. In the words of Sir Cecil E. Denny, then one of the young officers in the march west: "I doubt if any expedition ever undertook a journey with such complete faith and such utter ignorance."

As might be expected, the column moved much slower than first expected. Progress was hampered significantly by terrible weather, including thunderstorms, torrential rains, even a tornado; sick and dying livestock; desertions; grasshopper plagues that denuded the countryside of fodder for the livestock; lack of game or other food in many parts; scarce water; and buffalo herds that ate off forage and fouled water sources for "leagues on end." Two months after departure, commissioner George A. French and second in command James F. Macleod left the main contingent in camp near the Sweetgrass Hills and, with a small escort, made their way to Fort Benton.

In the 1830s Fort Benton was the principal trading post on the upper Missouri River of the American Fur Company, John J. Astor's competitor to the Hudson's Bay Company. By the time French and Macleod arrived in 1874, Benton was no longer a "fort" but a wide open town in one of the wildest, least civilized parts of the US frontier. All manner of business took place there, some legal but much not. There was not much law and very little order. The town was served by steamboats operating on the Missouri, and was the supply house for the whole of the area, including territory both above and below the 49th parallel.

In Fort Benton, arrangements were made to resupply the column, and commissioner French received orders to return to Manitoba with part of the troop. Jerry Potts, a Métis with a Scottish father and a Blood Indian mother, was hired as guide, and Potts led the Macleod contingent back to the main troop to continue north.

On October 9, Potts, Macleod and three troops of police arrived at Fort Whoop-up, where a rudimentary copy of a US flag was fluttering above the palisade. The police expected trouble but the scene was one of stillness and silence. To their surprise, they met no resistance and were welcomed by the manager, David Akers, who was accompanied by two Native women. Otherwise, the fort was unoccupied. According to Potts, buffalo hunters had warned the whisky traders of the approaching "red coats" and they had fled to the south. Macleod had the fort searched, but no liquor was discovered. Macleod then left the premises and established a permanent post farther west on the Oldman River, which place was named after him – Fort Macleod. One year later Macleod divided his force, sending Inspector E.A. Brisebois north to the confluence of the Bow and Elbow rivers to establish Fort Calgary, and sending Inspector James Walsh east to the Cypress Hills to establish Fort Walsh. Mounted patrols were sent out from the forts to police the region, and within a short period of time the illicit trade in whisky was brought under control.

Ironically, in 1875 the police entered an agreement with John Healy to rent a building at Fort Whoop-up, which building was used as a barrack to house a contingent of police – two during the winter and six to eight during other times of the year. The whisky trade was essentially at an end. The effects of the whisky trade on the Natives cannot be overestimated or overstated. Whisky caused fights and accidents, many resulting in fatalities. Death by freezing became rampant and commonplace, with imbibers dying after lying down outdoors in a drunken state. Many Natives traded everything for whisky. When their buffalo robes were traded away, they

James Macleod

could not keep themselves warm in winter. When their horses were traded away, they could not pursue buffalo and other game. As a direct and indirect consequence of all this, the Indians were leaving themselves even more susceptible to diseases for which they had no natural immunity. And perhaps the cruelest irony is that while the Indians were hampered or prevented from pursuing their previous nomadic lifestyle following the bison herds, the white men were systematically and rapidly wiping out the very foundation of prairie Native life and culture – the bison.

Prior to European contact, North America was the home to an estimated 60 million bison. There were two principal herds, the southern and the northern, each with its own migration route. The northern herd travelled in a somewhat circular loop that ran south in present-day Saskatchewan to the Cypress Hills, then meandered west into present-day Montana, then north along the eastern slope of the Rockies up to the North Saskatchewan River drainage, then wending back east into Saskatchewan, there to repeat the pattern of migration. Many Native groups based their entire existence on the movements of the bison herds and the availability of the animals for sustenance. Starting in about 1820, a market began to develop for buffalo hides, and white traders began to trade with Natives to obtain hides. White hunters also started to hunt the animals independently, and their weapons were superior to those of the Natives. By the mid-1800s a good hide was worth $3 on the frontier but might fetch more than ten times that amount in the markets of eastern North America and Europe. In addition, the hide market was tremendously augmented by the rising demand for leather for use in the manufacture of industrial belting. By the 1860s the slaughter was at its height, and hundreds of commercial buffalo hunters were harvesting bison skins. It has been estimated that by that time only about four out of every 100 animals killed were actually consumed as food. The carcasses were left in the field to rot and feed a growing number of scavengers. By the early 1870s the end of the bison herds was obvious to all who saw the carnage. In one episode known as the Great White Hunt, 5,000 white hunters and skinners went into the field between 1870 and 1873 and took over three million animals.

By the mid-1870s the market for hides was glutted, prices fell precipitously and the hunt was over. By that time the largest natural mammal herds ever seen and recorded by man were decimated. Bison were essentially extirpated in what is now Alberta by 1880. By 1887 it was estimated that only about 1,100 bison were left alive in all of North America.

As the herds began to wane precariously, some voices were raised in favour of protection for the remaining animals, but those voices were drowned out by those who called for a governmental policy of annihilation of the bison as a method of bringing fractious plains Indians to heel. Deprive them of their livelihood and they will surrender became government policy in the United States.

In September 1877, Treaty Seven was signed by members of the Blackfoot Confederacy, the Tsuu T'ina and the Stoney at Crowfoot Crossing on the Bow River downstream from Calgary. In that treaty the Native peoples gave up their claims to most of the land they had occupied, in exchange for sustenance and reservations. The Blackfoot were settled on the Bow downstream from Calgary; the Blood are near Cardston; the Peigan are in two groups, with the North Peigan near Pincher Creek, Alberta, and the South Peigan in northern Montana; the Tsuu T'ina are near Calgary; and the Stoney are upstream on the Bow near Morley, Alberta. The extinguishment of the Native peoples' claims opened up huge tracts of land for white settlement.

In the same year, Johnny Healy sold out his interest in Fort Whoop-up and moved back to Fort Benton, where he became sheriff of Chouteau County. In the spring of that year, one of his deputies, William Rowe, was called upon to track and arrest one John George Brown on a charge that he had murdered a rather notorious Montana wolfer known as Louis Ell (sometimes spelled "El"). Rowe caught Brown and delivered him into the custody of Healy, who held Brown in jail in Fort Benton until the fall of the year. In November, Healy delivered Brown to a grand jury that was meeting in the territorial capital, Helena. The grand jury failed to return a bill of indictment against Brown, and he was set free. He immediately gathered up his family and moved north, settling in the vicinity of Waterton Lakes for the rest of his life. Mr. Brown was more familiarly known as Kootenai Brown, and he was to play a pivotal role in the establishment of Waterton Lakes National Park.

John George "Kootenai" Brown

Kootenai Brown had a reputation for embellishment, and many aspects of his life and times have been inflated to the point of unreality. Indeed, many apocryphal tales of his life are circulated and believed to be true. What we do know to be true is as follows:

John George Brown was born in County Clare, Ireland, on October 10, 1839. As a young man he was given a commission in the British Army and was stationed briefly in India shortly after the Indian Mutiny of 1857. By 1860 his unit was transferred back to England. Within two years Brown had sold his commission and embarked on an adventure to the Pacific Northwest goldfields in company with another Irishman, an army veteran named Arthur Vowell. Their destination was the Cariboo country of British Columbia. They took a ship to Panama, crossed the isthmus by train and caught a ship up the west coast to Victoria. From Victoria they made their way to the Cariboo goldfields but found the rewards meagre and soon left. Vowell returned to Victoria and entered the civil service, eventually rising to be the gold commissioner for the Kootenay Region and later superintendent of Indian affairs for British Columbia.

Brown went from the Cariboo to the East Kootenay area, where there was a gold rush in progress at Wild Horse Creek, near present-day Fort Steele. Brown worked briefly there as a policeman, then as a miner/prospector. That boom was soon ended, however, and Brown moved on, departing in the company of several other men for rumoured gold strikes near Edmonton. They travelled east from the Kootenays, across the Tobacco Plains, into the Flathead Valley and up the South Kootenay Pass into present-day Waterton.

Brown first arrived at Kootenay Lakes (Waterton) in 1865. Upon seeing the lakes and their surroundings, Brown was said to have remarked, "For this is what I have seen in my dreams, this is the country for me," and vowed to return to settle there at some point in future. From Waterton, Brown drifted north and east, living in different places on the prairie frontier. He worked at various times as a buffalo hunter, packer, trader, scout, wolfer, whisky trader, pony express rider and a number of other vocations. He married a Métis woman, Olivia (Olive) Lyonnais (D'Lonais), and fathered two children. He was involved in the "whisky troubles" and was familiar with the Whoop-up Trail and Fort Benton and undoubtedly many of the characters associated with the trail and infamous fort. By 1877 Brown's wanderings found him in the Fort Benton area, where he was accused of murder and arrested, as referred to above. Following his release from custody, Brown made good on his vow of 12 years earlier and settled in Waterton, where he would remain until his death. There he made a living as a trader, packer, commercial fisherman and guide. During his years in Waterton he witnessed the waning throes of the frontier, with the final slaughter of the bison, the confinement of the Native peoples on reservations and the arrival of the cattle ranchers and settlers who would occupy the country.

The source of Brown's nickname, Kootenai, is not altogether clear. Some say it arose because of his long association with the Kootenay tribe, while others say it was a result of his long residence near the Kootenay Lakes. It is also quite conceivable that Brown himself adopted the nickname rather than had it foisted upon him. The spelling would indicate an association with the Indians in the United States. It is interesting to note, however, that *The Record*, the local Fort Benton newspaper that reported on Brown's arrest – in the finest traditions of yellow journalism under the headline "A Bloody Deed" – makes no mention whatsoever of Brown's nickname, and that would have been the kind of fodder that such a newspaper would thrive on. However the nickname arose, Brown was known by it from his arrival in Waterton up to the present.

In 1885 Brown's wife, Olivia, grew ill from complications of giving birth to their third child and she succumbed. After her death, Brown placed the children with people he considered more capable of caring for them than he was, and returned to Waterton to live alone. In 1886 he became seriously ill himself. Through good fortune, W.F. Cochrane, a neighbouring rancher, happened to look in on Brown during the spring roundup and found him gravely ill. Cochrane arranged for medical assistance and Brown was relocated to the North-West Mounted Police Hospital in Fort Macleod. There he recovered and returned to his cabin in Waterton, but with this forceful reminder of the dangers of living alone on

"Kootenai" Brown

the frontier, he soon took a Cree woman as his second wife – Isabella or "Chee-pay-tha-qua-ka-soon," or "the blue flash of lightning." It is unclear where Brown met Isabella or whether the relationship was solemnized by a civil or church service or was a common-law relationship, which was usual at the time. In any event, they stayed together for the balance of Brown's life. Isabella survived Brown, living until 1935. During their lives together, Isabella was an admirable companion and Brown became increasingly dependent upon her as the years went by. It was during this latter part of his life that he became a consistent and outspoken proponent for the area, and was instrumental in the effort to preserve the country around the Kootenay Lakes. Brown lobbied hard for protection for the area, and one of his early and influential allies in the fight was Fredrick William Godsal.

Godsal was an English immigrant who started a large ranch in the Cowley area of southern Alberta. In 1883 he wrote to his friend William Pearce, the superintendent of mines for Canada, saying:

> I believe that some years ago in an official report you recommended that the Crows Nest Pass, Kootenay or Waterton Lakes, etc., should be reserved as National Parks. I wish now in the strongest manner to urge upon the Government the adoption of this suggestion without delay.

Pearce sent the letter along to the Department of the Interior with his strong and enthusiastic recommendation for action.

On May 30, 1895, the Governor General, by order-in-council, created the Kootenay Lakes Forest Reserve pursuant to the Dominion Lands Act. The reserve was a township and a half in size – six miles by nine miles – and included lands extending from a point just north of the lower lake to the international boundary. However, the reservation did not provide any special supervision or protection for the lands in the reserve. Forestry and other resource extractive pursuits were still allowed if permits were obtained. Making the area a forest reserve was a good first step, perhaps, but it did not afford protection to the area that might be expected from the name.

Indeed, as peculiar as it may sound, the Kootenay Lakes Forest Reserve was the site of a brief oil boom and the location of the first oil well ever drilled in western Canada.

In 1879 a Dominion Land Surveyor by the name of Allan Poyntz Patrick, known as "A.P." to friends and acquaintances, was shown a seep of petroleum substances on Cameron Brook, a small tributary to the Kootenai River, as the Waterton River was then known. This seepage was almost surely the same one that Kootenai Brown had been shown by the Stoney Indians a few years earlier. The Natives called it "stinking waters." Patrick took a sample of the substance and had it analyzed, but the results were not terribly exciting, and Patrick simply filed the information away in his memory.

Ten years later, Patrick filed two mining claims on Cameron Brook. Patrick did not have the financial resources to commence an exploration on his claims, but he was fortunate to soon meet John Lineham, a successful sawmill owner/operator in Okotoks and former member of the Territorial Legislature. Patrick "pitched" his claims and prospects, and on February 12, 1901, Lineham, Patrick and Calgary businessman George K. Leeson incorporated Rocky Mountain Development Company, Limited. They soon opened an office in nearby Pincher Creek and invited public subscription for shares in the company, offered at $1 per share. The company then paid $700 for a cable tool drilling rig in Petrolia, Ontario, then the only oil-producing area in Canada, and had the rig shipped to Fort Macleod by rail. After arrival, the equipment was taken by horse-drawn wagons to a drilling location prepared at Cameron Brook. There, an experienced driller by the name of Alex Calvert erected the three-pole derrick and commenced drilling in November 1901. Amidst continual breakdowns and other tribulations, drilling continued until September 21, 1902, at which point the driller encountered light, sweet crude oil at a depth of 310 m. An estimated flow of approximately 300 barrels per day was encountered, but shortly thereafter disaster befell the operation. The surface casing of the well apparently failed, and surface gravel poured into the well bore. In an effort to clear the hole, the boiler on location was over-pressured and exploded, and all operations ceased for that year. But a "find" had been made, and the owners of the Rocky Mountain Development Company jubilantly named the well "Discovery No. 1" and began to make grandiose plans for the future. Two additional rigs were purchased and a new prospectus was issued for the purpose of distributing more stock. Expectations ran wild and even included rumours of a pipeline to be constructed and railroad spurs arriving at the oil field. Speculation was rampant, claim staking was brisk, prices spiked in the area and plans were afoot for a new town to be called Oil City. A boom was on.

However, like most booms, this one turned to bust almost as quickly as it arose. The following year a pump was installed on the discovery well and eventually a total of about 8,000 barrels of oil was produced. However, the early enthusiasm proved unjustified. Production from that well declined quickly and significantly, and by the close of 1904 the well was dry. The Rocky Mountain Development Company drilled two more wells in the area in the following couple of years, but neither discovered oil in commercial quantities and the company withdrew from the area.

Another outfit, the Western Coal & Oil Company, also drilled three wells in the area. One of those was located on Seepage Creek, a small tributary to Cameron Brook. That well blew out and ran wild for two days, pouring oil into Cameron Brook. The water carried the oil downstream to the Kootenay Lakes, killing untold numbers of waterfowl and fish. The oil sheen was eventually seen all the way to Lethbridge. After the blowout, the well quickly ran dry. Of the other two wells drilled, one was dry and the other found production of only one barrel per day. By 1908 the boom was ended. However, the very fact of a brief oil boom that might have forever changed the landscape in the Reserve led Brown and his supporters to press even harder for protection for the area.

As of April 1, 1910, Kootenai Brown was appointed as forest ranger in the Kootenay Lakes Forest Reserve. At the end of March 1911 he submitted his first annual report to Howard Douglas, at that time the commissioner of national parks, resident in Banff. Included in his report was a strong recommendation by Brown to increase the size of the park dramatically to better afford protection to the large mammals that lived there. The recommendation was strongly supported by Douglas when he forwarded Brown's report to his superiors in Ottawa. Douglas was very much in favour of an expanded park "to have a preserve and breeding ground in conjunction with the United States Glacier Park." (Glacier Park had been established May 11, 1910.)

A few months later the Department of the Interior moved "to make provision for the proper administration of the reserve." As part of that "proper administration," the distinct identity of a national park as a "set aside" reserve came into being with the passage of the Dominion Forest Reserves & Parks Act of 1911. In that legislation "forest reserve" and "park" were defined. A "forest reserve" was withdrawn from settlement but certain controlled resource usages and extractions were allowed under permit. "Parks" were to be used as "public pleasuring grounds," and Kootenay Lakes Forest Reserve was officially made a national park. While the status of the reserve was changed to national park, inexplicitly but simultaneously the powers that be completely ignored the call by Brown and others to increase the size of the reserve. In fact, they chose to *reduce* its size considerably, to a mere 35 km². Indeed, under the reduced dimensions, the reserve no longer contained any portion of the very lakes referred to in the reserve's name! Brown was promoted to superintendent of the park, which sounds more glorious that it really was. In fact, Brown was the only person employed in the park in 1911.

Brown and his superiors kept pressing for an extension of the park boundaries to match up with Glacier Park in the United States. Brown was a vocal advocate for the park and he was constantly engaged in schemes to bring more people to marvel at the wonders it contained. In his words: "The scenery is simply magnificent – many have said it is far superior to Banff or any of the other parks." As time went by, more and more visitors came to the new park.

In June 1914, with virtually the same suddenness and surprise as the park had originally been declared, its boundaries were expanded to encompass roughly 1095 km² – extending the park to become, with adjacent Glacier Park, one of the great game preserves in the world, in one of the most beautiful landscapes in the world. As part of that declaration, the department chose to revert to the name "Waterton" for the lakes. Henceforth the park would be known as Waterton Lakes National Park.

In a final irony, concurrent with the expansion of the park so long advocated by Brown, the then commissioner of parks, James Bernard Harkin, called for the appointment of a new superintendent of Waterton Lakes National Park, saying: "Ranger Brown cannot exercise proper supervision over extended area owing to extreme age." Brown's term as superintendent ended on September 1, 1914.

Over the next several years the boundaries of the park were adjusted between Waterton and local forest reserves, eventually leaving Waterton Lakes National Park at a size of approximately 500 km^2.

Brown did continue as a ranger in the park until his death in July 1916. He died quietly at home with his wife Isabella and was buried on the western shore of Lower Waterton Lake, near the site of his first homestead. Brown specified in his will that he "did not desire the attendance of any clergyman of any denomination at his funeral in an official capacity." That express wish was, sadly, ignored.

By 1930 the National Parks Act passed, under the watchful eye of Commissioner Harkin. A clear mission directive for the parks was proclaimed: "National Parks are hereby dedicated to the people of Canada for their benefit, education and enjoyment, and such parks shall be maintained and made use of so as to leave them unimpaired for the use of future generations." In 1932, Waterton Lakes National Park was joined with Glacier National Park in Montana to form Waterton-Glacier International Peace Park. In 1979 the International Peace Park was declared a Biosphere Reserve by UNESCO, an international conservation designation. There are at present more than 500 such reserves in over 100 countries. In 1995 UNESCO declared the park to be a World Heritage Site, a designation that catalogues, names and conserves sites of outstanding cultural or natural importance to the common heritage of mankind.

ACTIVITIES IN WATERTON

When you visit Waterton, there are a number of activities recommended. Almost without question, your chances of seeing wildlife along the roadways are greater here than in any other Rocky Mountain national park. Bear sightings – both grizzly and black – are far more common in Waterton than elsewhere. You may also see large ungulates – deer, moose, elk and Rocky Mountain sheep – and there are bison in a fenced paddock in the park. Mule deer are extraordinarily common in the townsite, where they wander up and down the streets. In the early summer, you might witness the birth of fawns, and you certainly will see the young deer clumsily galloping around, following their mothers. Mountain goats are a relatively common sight on some of the backcountry trails. Birdwatching is particularly good here, with the great diversity of habitat available in a relatively small geographical area.

With its great plant diversity, Waterton is a tremendous place for flower-watching and photography. Every year in the middle of June the Waterton Wildflower Festival runs for ten days. The festival features guided walks and hikes, lectures on wildflower topics, seminars on flower identification and photography, and other related activities. Many of the events are available by preregistration only and payment of a registration fee, so check out the program at www.watertonwildflowers.com in advance of your arrival. Early bookings for accommodations are also recommended.

Hiking possibilities are limited only by the enthusiasm of the visitor. There are short interpretive walks available, as well as relatively easy strolls, easy to moderately challenging day hikes, and strenuous treks that might involve an overnight camping component. Trail maps and advice are available at the Visitors Centre and local businesses, and arrangements can be made with qualified local guides. As on all backcountry excursions, be prepared and equipped properly for your own safety and comfort. Wear good-quality hiking shoes or boots, take plenty of drinking water, have proper clothing for the conditions (which can change quickly) and carry sunscreen, insect repellent and a hat. Plan your trip carefully and be realistic in your expectations. Failing to plan adequately is a recipe for failure and potential disaster. Trail condition reports are available at the Visitors Centre or go to www.pc.gc.ca/pn-np/ab/Waterton and in the left-hand sidebar, under Public Safety, click Trail Conditions Report.

PHOTOGRAPH: JIM McKEAN

PHOTOGRAPH: RUSS WEBB

Above left: Mule deer buck
Above right: Bear
Below: Bison and Waterton

PHOTOGRAPH: CLAY ROSS

If you are so inclined, a moderately strenuous, day-long hike called the Carthew-Alderson Traverse is highly recommended. It is, in the opinion of many experienced Waterton "hands," the best hike in the park for showcasing the marvels of the area. The hike starts at Cameron Lake and finishes 18.4 km later at Cameron Falls in the Waterton townsite. The elevation gain from Cameron Lake to Carthew Pass is about 650 m; the elevation loss from the pass to the townsite is just over 1000 m and the hike takes 6–8 hours to complete. It should not be attempted if rain or thunderstorms are forecast, because much of the way is through terrain that is near or above treeline. Bear in mind that weather in the area can change dramatically and quickly, so carry rain gear and extra clothing. It is always best to assume the worst will happen in the weather department, so be prepared for all eventualities. Pertinent maps for the hike are NTS maps o82G01 (Sage Creek) and o82H04 (Waterton Lake) or the Gem Trek map "Waterton Lakes National Park."

The trailhead for the Carthew-Alderson Traverse is the bridge over Cameron Creek, the outflow from the lake, which is on the east side of Cameron Lake at coordinates 11U 0716120 5433849. You can leave a vehicle at the parking lot for Cameron Lake or can arrange for a shuttle to the trailhead from the Waterton townsite by checking with Tamarack Outdoor Outfitters in Waterton. From the bridge, the trail steadily climbs a series of switchbacks that ascend the forest slopes some 275 m in the first 3 km. The trail then levels off somewhat and reaches Summit Lake at 4 km and an elevation of 1906 m. On a clear day, the vistas from Summit Lake are wonderful, and the floral community in the meadows around the lake is diverse. If you have the time, some investigation in the area is worthwhile.

At Summit Lake there is a junction in the trail at coordinates 11U 0717548 5432609. The right fork leads to Glacier National Park in Montana, so you turn left to climb to Carthew Pass. From this point up to the pass at 7.6 km from trailhead, the trail is a steep traverse up the slope to a bare, windswept ridge at 2311 m elevation – a climb of 375 m in 3.6 km. As you ascend, the trees become more stunted and eventually give way to steep meadows and scree slopes. Openings are dominated by Beargrass (*Xerophyllum tenax*), a large, torch-shaped white lily that is emblematic of the high country in Waterton Lakes National Park, one of the only places in Alberta where it is found. Some authorities attribute the common name Beargrass to the fact that

PHOTOGRAPH: LINDA JENNINGS

Above: Cameron Lake
Below: Mount Carthew and pass

PHOTOGRAPH: CHUCK MURPHY

Above: Trail to Alderson Lake
Below: South from Carthew Pass
Opposite: Red Rock Canyon

bears have been reported to eat the leaves of the plant in the spring. My research, however, has led me to believe that this notion of the etymology of the name is incorrect. The plant was first collected for science by Meriwether Lewis in 1806 in present-day Idaho. At the time of the collection, Lewis believed the plant to be a kind of Yucca, a plant that was known to Lewis by one of its common names, Bear Grass. While the two plants do have some like characteristics, Yucca is more of a desert plant and it only grows in more arid environments at lower elevations. Even though Lewis was mistaken about this plant being a type of Yucca, the name Beargrass stuck. Various animals may indeed eat various parts of the plant, but none of that has anything to do with the common name. Another locally common name for the plant is Indian Basket Grass, the reference being that some Native peoples once used the long leaves of Beargrass to weave intricate and exquisite baskets, capes and hats.

As you break out of the trees, there is a long traverse over scree, leading to a series of switchbacks that will deliver you to the summit at coordinates 11u 0719205 5434187. The floral community on the scree slopes is quite beautiful, with colourful wildflowers appearing in patches and strips wherever they can get any purchase. Bright yellow Alpine Buttercups and Snow Cinquefoil are here, as are white patches of Spotted Saxifrage, large numbers of purple Silky Phacelia (Scorpionweed) and bunches of blue Sky Pilot. The latter plant is also known as Skunkweed and Stinky Jacob's Ladder, and the redolence of skunk emanating from the plant is clearly apparent as you climb the switchbacks. On a clear day the vistas from the summit are spectacular in all directions. The bare summit of Mount Carthew is to the left. It was named for William M. Carthew, a surveyor who worked on the boundary survey between Alberta and British Columbia in 1913 – a mere three years before he was killed in action at Ypres, Belgium. Mount Alderson is on the right. It was named for Lt. Gen. E.A.H. Alderson, the commander of the Canadian Expeditionary Force in France during part of the First World War.

From the ridge, the remainder of the hike is all downhill (literally, not figuratively). Upper Carthew Lake is visible to the northeast and the trail descends toward the lake on steep scree slopes that are marked with knee-high trail markers. The trail winds around Upper Carthew Lake at about 8.5 km from trailhead and then descends a couple of switchbacks to Lower Carthew Lake. As you descend, the waterfalls connecting the lakes are quite beautiful and you will find a large diversity of wildflowers along the trail, including Yellow Columbine, rare Pygmy Poppy, Roseroot, Mountain Gentian and many others.

Look also for *kruppelholz*, the scrubby, shrub-like, misshapen evergreens that have been stunted in this extreme environment. As explained in Ben Gadd's watershed volume *Handbook of the Canadian Rockies*, *kruppelholz* means "crippled wood" in German. Gadd points out that the word *"krummholz"* (sometimes spelled *"krumholtz"*) is often incorrectly applied to these trees. Citing treeline ecologist Kevin Timoney, Gadd draws a distinction between the two terms by explaining that *krummholz* means "crooked wood" in German, and it refers to trees that grow stunted and bent for genetic reasons, not because of their environment.

Shortly after passing Lower Carthew Lake, the trail drops out of the lake basin into an alpine valley, steepens and drops sharply over the next several kilometres to reach Lake Alderson, some 12.2 km from the trailhead. Lake Alderson lies at the base of a massive 700-m cliff on Mount Alderson. At the trail junction that leads to the campground at the lake, stay left and continue down the trail through the forested valley between Buchanan Ridge and Bertha Peak to Cameron Falls at coordinates 12U 0286890 5437332, and the Waterton townsite just beyond.

HOW TO GET THERE

Waterton Lakes National Park is located 270 km south of Calgary. From Calgary go south on Hwy 2 to its junction with Hwy 3 (near Fort Macleod), then proceed west on Hwy 3 to Pincher Creek, then south on Hwy 6 to Waterton. Alternatively, from Calgary go south on Hwy 22 to its junction with Hwy 3 (near Lundbreck Falls), then proceed east on Hwy 3 to Pincher Creek, then south on Hwy 6 to Waterton.

From Lethbridge, go south on Hwy 5 to Cardston, then continue west on Hwy 5 to Waterton.

Underfit river

Writing-on-Stone Provincial Park: Áísínaí pi – "Where The Drawings Are"

On May 8, 1805, as he was ascending the Missouri River on his way west, Capt. Meriwether Lewis made a journal entry as follows:

> "we nooned it just above the entrance of a large river ... the water of this river possesses a peculiar whiteness, being about the colour of a cup of tea with the admixture of a tablespoonful of milk. from the color of the water we called it the Milk river..."

Thus did the Milk River receive its name. The river originates in Glacier County in northwestern Montana. Two streams, the South Fork and the Middle Fork, rise in the Blackfeet Indian Reservation just east of Glacier National Park, and their confluence marks the beginning of the Milk. From there the river flows east-northeast into Canada, then turns east and tracks across southern Alberta, passing through Writing-on-Stone Provincial Park, just north of the Sweetgrass Hills. It then turns southeast and flows back into Montana, just northwest of Havre. The river continues past Glasgow, Montana, and soon thereafter joins the Missouri River on its way to the Mississippi and the Gulf of Mexico. The Milk is the only river in Alberta that contributes water to the Missouri drainage. The relatively constant turbidity seen in the river is the result of fine-grained glacial till and silt in the upstream reaches being washed into the river.

At the time Lewis and Clark found the Milk River, they would have wondered, first and foremost, how far north the Milk extended. The implications of the answer to that question were significant. Napoleon sold the Louisiana Territory to the United States in 1803. However, the extent of the lands covered in the sale were unclear to everybody. The northern parts of the Louisiana Territory were *terra incognita*. The purchase gave the United States all of the lands of the western half of the Mississippi drainage. That is to say, they extended from the Gulf of

Mexico northward to the northernmost tributary of the Missouri River, and west from the Mississippi to the Continental Divide. If the Milk originated to the north and drained portions of present-day Alberta and Saskatchewan, the United States could, with some legitimacy, lay claim to those lands. Indeed, obtaining the answer to that very question was one of the principal objectives of the Expedition of Discovery. As it turned out, however, the hopes of Lewis and Clark to extend US territory northward were dashed.

The Blackfoot believed the valley was sacred and the home of spirits. It does not require an abundance of imagination to understand how they arrived at that conclusion. As you drive east and then south from the town of Milk River, Alberta, the prairie is mostly flat country, interrupted occasionally by a rise, a depression or a coulee. Looking east and south, the prairie appears to stretch on, all the way to the horizon. Approaching Writing-on-Stone Provincial Park, the panorama looking south is more of the same. The optical illusion takes the eye all the way to the Sweetgrass Hills rising in the distance, hardly admitting that the Milk River valley is cutting the flat prairie somewhere just in front. However, when you crest the top of the breaks above the river and quickly cast a glance down into the valley, if you possess even the tiniest flickering of curiosity, imagination or wonder in your being, the first word to escape your lips will be "Wow." The wide valley is filled with spectacular sandstone formations – strangely shaped hoodoos and monstrous abstract forms – scattered haphazardly around on the rolling grassy verges and sandstone cliffs overlooking the meandering, milky river. You will have the feeling of stepping into a mysterious and alien world, fascinating and somehow hugely appealing.

The Milk has been described as an "underfit" river system, meaning that the river itself is considerably smaller than the valley in which it flows. This phenomenon is the result of the river's canyon being carved during a geologic time when virtually all of the runoff from melting glaciers in present-day southern Alberta was directed into the Milk River drainage by an enormous ice dam to the northeast near the Cypress Hills. Prior to the recession of the Laurentide glacier, meltwater could not get around the ice dam, and thus it was diverted south. As the glacier receded, the meltwater eventually found a route around the Cypress Hills and began to drain into the South Saskatchewan River, ending up eventually in Hudson Bay. By the time that happened, the canyon of the Milk was "oversized" to the river's volume, hence the river is said to be underfit.

About 85 million years ago, a large section of what is now North America was covered by an enormous inland sea. Over millions of years, layers of sand were deposited by rivers into and adjacent to this sea. Over time those layers were compressed and compacted into sandstone rock. Sandstone is a rock that is comprised of sand-sized particles that are cemented together by calcite, silica and iron oxide. The sandstone varied in hardness – some of it was fairly soft, some relatively hard. Over millions of years, the sandstones were covered and overlain by other sediments, which also turned to various kinds of rock. In the most recent glacial period, commencing about 110,000 years ago, ice sheets formed over much of North America, sometimes resulting in ice as much as three kilometres thick.

As alluded to above, approximately 15,000 years ago the ice sheets of the last glacial period began to melt, sending enormous volumes of meltwater rushing south and eastward. In the process, the moving water eroded the younger rock overbearing the sandstone formations and the Milk River canyon was formed. The sandstone exposed in the process is known as the Milk River Formation. That formation, once exposed, was further eroded by water, wind and a continuous cycle of freezing and thawing. Water would enter cracks in the stone, then freeze. As it froze, the ice would expand, putting enormous pressure on the rock to crack further. Over time, the cleaving of the rock by repeated freezing and thawing would be accomplished. Water from rain or the river would wash away particulate matter from the sandstone. Wind would entrain sand particles and pelt the rock with them, in the process knocking loose other particles. Over thousands of years the canyon of the Milk River was altered by such forces, leaving a landscape dominated by hoodoos and sandstone cliffs. Indeed, the process of erosion still continues inexorably, changing the landscape further with each day. The process is too slow to see it happen, but rest assured that it continues.

A hoodoo is a sandstone rock formation, many of which bear a striking resemblance to a mushroom. The odd-shaped formations are the result of erosive forces working on stones that contain materials with different resistances to erosion. That is, some parts of the stone are harder than others, and those parts do not erode as quickly as the softer parts. On the typical hoodoo formation the top is called the "caprock." It is usually made up of many small, thin, compact layers that are very hard and do not erode easily. The caprock often protects soft sandstone underneath it, keeping it from eroding. The softer areas of the formation that are unprotected by

Hoodoo and caprock

the caprock are subject to faster erosion, thus lending the formation the mushroom stem and cap appearance.

There seems to be some dispute among authorities as to where the word "hoodoo" originates, but the predominant school of thought holds that the term comes from the African language Hausa. It is believed that kidnapped and enslaved African natives brought the term to North America, and it meant "a cause of bad luck or a jinx" or "a person or thing whose presence brings bad luck." Thus the term denotes an aura of malignant and evil forces at work. The fur trappers were the first to apply the term to the strange rock formations in the badlands, and the name stuck. The Blackfoot and the Cree believed that the hoodoos were giants that were turned to stone by the Great Spirit in retribution for evil deeds. It was said that if one disrespected the hoodoos, they could awaken at night and cast down stones upon passersby.

Hoodoos with holes in them are not uncommon. This phenomenon is usually the result of an ironstone concretion that was locked in the sandstone millions of years ago. When the sand was being laid down at the time of the ancient sea, organic material from living organisms would often become trapped in the sand. That material would slowly attract iron molecules, which would cover it (collectively called the concretion), and, over millions of years, produce a very hard stone – an ironstone. When the sandstone holding a trapped ironstone is exposed to erosive forces, the ironstone, being extraordinarily hard, will not erode much but the sandstone holding it *in situ* will. Eventually the sand holding the ironstone in place will erode away, and the ironstone will simply fall to the ground, thus leaving a hole – or a depression – in the hoodoo where the ironstone once resided. Further erosion will then enlarge that hole over time. These holes are referred to as tafoni (the singular is "tafone"), and the small cave-like structures often provide nesting places for small mammals and birds.

Writing-on-Stone Provincial Park was dedicated as a park in January 1957. It has one of the largest concentrations of rock art on the North American plains. The area is hot during the summer, with daytime maximums near 40°c, and cold in the winter, with minimum temperatures near -40°c. Chinooks are quite common in the winter months. Annual precipitation is only 330 mm, qualifying the area as quite arid. June is the rainiest month, followed by May and July. The park comprises 1780 ha of the dry, mixed-grass subregion of Alberta's Grassland Natural Region.

Visible to the south are the Sweetgrass Hills (spelled "Sweet Grass" in the US) of north central Montana, a few kilometres south of the international boundary. The Blackfoot called them the "Sweet Pine Hills," a reference to the Balsam Fir that grows there, but the perversion of the name to "Sweetgrass" apparently arose over an inaccurate translation made long ago and never corrected. The hills were formed approximately 45 million years ago when molten rock (magma) was pushed up a volcanic neck from the bottom, causing the surface ground layers to bulge upward. The molten rock then cooled and hardened as a dome, holding the bulged layers above it. Over time, through weathering, the surface layers were eroded away, leaving the igneous rock exposed. When the glaciers next swept through the area, the lands surrounding the tops of the hills were further eroded but the tops of the hills were not. They were nunataks, standing above the ice sheet. The Cypress Hills to the northeast were also nunataks. Today, the Sweetgrass Hills stand almost a full kilometre above the surrounding prairie. Because the hills escaped the glaciation of the last ice age, there are plants and animals found there that are not found on the prairies that surround them. The Sweetgrass Hills extend for almost 80 km east to west and almost 15 from north to south. There are three major buttes in the hills. The West Butte stands 2128 m tall, the East Butte, 2114 m. Gold Butte, in the middle, measures 1969 m. The high ground of the hills was used by Native peoples for centuries to sight bison herds moving on the plains below.

The Blackfoot believed that Writing-on-Stone and the Sweetgrass Hills possess abundant spiritual powers. Many young Blackfoot went on their vision quests in these places. The vision quest was a rite of passage in the Blackfoot culture whereby the young man went off alone to some lonely place and engaged in fasting and prayer until he had an encounter with a supernatural spirit, usually in the form of a dream or vision. That encounter was believed to be an indication of the youth's intended spiritual and life direction. It is speculated that at least some of the rock art at Writing-on-Stone was created as a result of vision quests. Archaeological evidence at Writing-on-Stone indicates that Native peoples camped there as long as 3,000–3,500 years ago. Anecdotal and oral evidence indicates that the occupation of the area by the Native peoples persisted well into the early 20th century. The valley and the coulees joining it provided shelter, wood and water. Over that time, the Native peoples created petroglyphs (rock carvings) and pictographs (rock paintings) on the sandstone cliffs around the valley. There is no technique available to precisely date the rock art, though approximate dates can be surmised by examining the style of the art and its contents. For example, human figures bearing large body shields can be assumed to have been done before the advent of horses among the Native peoples, circa 1730. After the arrival of the horse, such large body shields fell from use and fashion. Guns depicted in the art must have been done later rather than sooner, because the firearm did not appear on the plains until roughly the same time as the horse. Many of the older petroglyphs were incised or scratched into the cliffs using bone implements or antlers. More recent art might have been created using metal tools, following the arrival of metals with the Europeans in western North America.

The pictographs were drawn with charcoal or painted with red ochre. Ochre was sourced in various sites known to the Native peoples. It was collected, cleaned and kneaded into small balls, then flattened and baked to render a red powder of iron oxide. The red powder was then mixed with fish oil or animal grease and the resulting concoction was used to paint things – tipis, bodies, clothing or rock art. In 1858 Dr. James Hector of the Palliser Expedition found large ochre beds near the Vermilion River in present-day Kootenay National Park. In his journal he noted:

"... Kootenaie Indians come to the plain sometimes to ... convert the ochre into the red oxide which they take away to the Indians of the low country and also to the Blackfoot."

The rock art in the valley is assumed to have been done for biographical or ceremonial purposes. The biographical art commemorates events that actually happened, like hunts, battles etc. Ceremonial art most probably depicts images from dreams, visions, prayers or other rituals. Subject matter

Hoodoo, cliffs and the Milk

of the art includes animal figures like horses, bison, dogs, deer, bears, elk and mountain sheep. Also depicted are shields, bows, guns, spears, hatchets, tipis, travois and other objects. Some of the subjects remain mysteries. It is assumed that most (or the majority) of the art was created by Blackfoot people, though there is evidence that at various times the area was frequented by other groups, including the Cree, Gros Ventre, Assiniboine, Crow, Kootenay and Shoshone, any or all of whom could have contributed to the art.

One particularly spectacular and complex petroglyph is known as the Battle Scene. It depicts a force of warriors closing in to attack an encampment of tipis. The encampment is defended by a line of guns. Most of the apparent attackers are on foot, but there are also horses depicted. There is some oral evidence that the scene commemorates an actual battle. According to an account related in 1924 by Bird Rattle, an elder of the Aamsskáápipikáni (South Piegan or Blackfeet tribe, as they are known in the US), the petroglyph was of a battle called "Retreat up the Hill," which took place in the late 1800s. According to Bird Rattle, during that battle the Aamsskáápipikáni earned a decisive victory over a combined war party of Gros Ventre, Crow and Plains Cree warriors, killing over 300 of them.

Many Native peoples believe the rock art was the work of spirits, perhaps trying to communicate with those still living. Whatever the significance, the rock art at Writing-on-Stone represents hundreds of years of Native culture, and it is an irreplaceable treasure. Over the years graffiti and vandalism have destroyed or marred many of the items of rock art. The Archaeological Preserve was set aside in 1977 to restrict access to many of the rock art locations in the park and thereby offer them more effective protection from wanton human destruction. Heavy fines and jail terms can result from damaging the rock art. It is illegal to remove anything from the park. If you discover any artifacts or archaeological remains, leave them in place and report the find to park personnel. Such things are more valuable to archaeologists if they are left undisturbed.

As in much of the rest of southern Alberta, the North-West Mounted Police (NWMP) have had a long association with the Milk River area and Writing-on-Stone in particular. As alluded to elsewhere in this book, the NWMP was formed in 1873 in Fort Garry, Manitoba, principally to interdict the illicit whisky trade in the North-West Territories of Canada – present-day Alberta and Saskatchewan – that was having a disastrous impact on the Native peoples. The following year, a force of some 300 "Mounties" set off en route to southern Alberta. After two months of hardship on the trail, the force arrived at Writing-on-Stone in early September and camped there for four days of rest and recuperation before continuing west. They would eventually build Fort Macleod in October and extend other forts into other parts of the territories in the coming years.

The arrival of the NWMP in the territory effectively put a stop to the cross-border traffic in liquor, with most of the American whisky traders removing themselves back into Montana. In 1887, as part of a border patrol system established by the NWMP, a tent camp was set up at Writing-on-Stone, located at the mouth of a coulee across river from the present Archaeological Preserve. That was replaced two years later with a two-room log building, but it turned out that little policing was required in the area, and boredom was more the standard lot of the men stationed there. Indeed, desertion rates were high. By 1897 there were never more than three men posted to Writing-on-Stone. As the new century was set to open, homesteaders began to arrive in the area in numbers, and the duties of the force shifted from fighting crime to assisting settlers. By 1918 the post was deemed dispensable, the men were reposted and the fort closed down. A short time after the closure, the building burned to the ground.

In 1973, as part of a centennial project for the NWMP, which became the Royal Canadian Mounted Police (RCMP), an archaeological assessment was done on the site of the fort. Two years later the barracks, barn and tack room were rebuilt on the site to replicate the original fort. Visitors may be able to tour the site on special guided hikes that are scheduled from time to time.

Inside the park, the Archaeological Preserve is a restricted area and can only be accessed by the public if accompanied by park personnel acting as a guide. Hikes in that area are regularly scheduled and tickets must be obtained to attend. In addition, there is a backcountry hiking zone across the river from the campground, that is, on the right bank of the Milk River as one looks downstream. This area is a primitive hiking area that has no established trails, employing game tracks instead. There are two coulees to explore on that side of the river – Davis Coulee and Humphrey Coulee. The grasslands on that side are more extensive and generally in better condition than those on the campground side. Access to the backcountry hiking zone is achieved by fording the river on foot. Before crossing the river to the backcountry hiking zone, check in with park personnel at the Visitor Information Centre and file a "flight plan." Do not attempt the crossing in times of high water. The river is usually less than 1 m deep, approximately 15 m wide, and the bottom is a mix of smooth cobbles and sand.

The most popular hike in the park is the Hoodoo Interpretive Trail. This trail commences at the campground and runs upriver to the boundary with the restricted area. Trail length is 4.4 km return. Along the trail you will pass through samples of all three of the vegetative zones found in the park: hoodoo habitat, riparian habitat and prairie/grassland habitat. Along the way there are numbered posts which correspond to the descriptions contained in a self-guiding brochure that is available from the Visitor Information Centre. The descriptions contained in the brochure will significantly add to your enjoyment and education on the hike. To protect the fragile environment, stay on the trails. For your comfort and safety, take a hat, wear good quality hiking shoes or boots on the trail, and take plenty of drinking water and sunscreen. In rainy conditions the clay content in the hoodoos habitat can become very slick, so be careful if things are wet. Smoking is not allowed in the park owing to the significant danger of grass fires.

There is a very rich and diverse plant and animal community occupying the valley, the coulees leading to the river, and the surrounding grasslands. Animals seen in the area, either occasionally or commonly, include pronghorn antelope, coyote, yellow-bellied marmot, rabbit, hare, bats, bushy-tailed wood rat (pack rat), beaver, mink, badger, skunk, long-tailed weasel, mule deer and bobcat. There is a huge diversity of bird life on the river, including raptors such as golden eagle, northern harrier, prairie falcon, sharp-shinned hawk, Swainson's hawk, American kestrel, red-tailed hawk and ferruginous hawk. Before you go, take the time to review the information below about a fellow denizen of the park, the prairie rattlesnake.

THE PRAIRIE RATTLESNAKE

Anyone visiting Writing-on-Stone should be aware (and well briefed) on one of the animals found there – the prairie rattlesnake (*Crotalus viridis viridis*). The genus name, *Crotalus*, is derived from the Greek *krotalon*, which means "a rattle, clapper or castanet," referring, of course, to the rattle that is characteristic of many members of the genus. The species name, *viridis*, means "green," most probably a reference to the colour of the animal. Though these animals live in the park and surrounding countryside, it should be pointed out that the overwhelming majority of visitors will never set eyes on a prairie rattlesnake. They are very timid animals and will go to virtually any length not to get involved with humans. And make no mistake about it, the right-of-way here belongs to the rattler. It is illegal to harass, injure or kill a rattlesnake in the park.

Some facts about the prairie rattlesnake

Prairie rattlesnakes are venomous but their bite is seldom fatal to humans, particularly if medical assistance is sought in a timely fashion after being bitten. Unless provoked or cornered, rattlesnakes will almost never strike at large moving objects. Leave snakes alone and they will return the favour.

The snakes display a wide variation in colour, from green to dark brown, but they always have dark blotches along the back. The head is decidedly triangular in shape. They usually have rattles at the end of their tails, though that is not always the case. An adult snake may be 1–1.5 m long, the rattle about 5 cm long.

Rattlesnakes live in prairie grassland and rocky outcrops, and the park is ideal habitat for them. They are cold-blooded animals, taking their body temperature from the environment, and in cool weather they are lethargic. In cold weather they retreat underground into hibernacula, where they stay until warm weather returns.

Rattlesnakes are live bearing, with the young being born in the fall. Young rattlesnakes are born with fangs and venom but no rattles. Instead, they have only a small "button" on the end of the tail, which in actuality is a scale covering the tip end of the tail. With each molt, a new scale is added with the shedding of the skin, and the addition of these new scales creates the rattle, which is an appendage that consists of a series of loosely interlocking, hollow scale segments that make an audible noise when vibrated by the snake. Therefore, young snakes will not have rattles until after their second shedding. Young snakes may shed as many as five times during their first year of life. Mature snakes usually shed only once, and no more than twice, a year. Consequently, the number of rattles is not a reliable indicator of age. Rattles may also be damaged or lost, so not all rattlesnakes can in fact rattle.

Rattlesnakes usually lie in wait for prey to approach, then strike with astonishing speed, injecting venom into the victim through hypodermic fangs. Their diet consists of small rodents, rabbits, birds, reptiles and amphibians, all of which they ingest whole after the prey is immobilized by toxin. Rattlesnakes have a keen sense of smell and have heat-sensing organs between their eyes and nostrils.

Some precautions to take while in the park

Stay on the trails. Avoid climbing on rock piles and walking through bushes. Stay out of tall grass where visibility at the ground level is obscured. Keep dogs on leash at all times. If you are with small children, be very vigilant and keep them close to you at all times.

Do not put your hands into cracks or holes in rocks. Do not put your hands under vegetation.

Do not climb on ledges or reach above you if you cannot see where you are putting your hands.

Prairie rattlesnake

PHOTOGRAPH: RUSS AMY

Rattlesnakes like to bask on ledges, so visually inspect such places before moving onto ledges.

Do not touch or handle snakes. As peculiar as it might sound to many people, the decided majority of snakebite victims receive their bites while they are attempting to handle or capture snakes. I was told by one physician who is intimately familiar with treating snakebites that bites that are the result of unintentional, accidental contact with snakes are a very tiny percentage of the overall number of bites he treats.

Do not assume that the snake will always rattle prior to striking. They usually give this warning, but it is by no means a sure thing. Bear in mind that a juvenile snake cannot rattle anyway.

If you hear the distinctive buzz of a rattling snake, stop immediately, stand still, and survey the area until you determine the exact location of the snake. Having done that, back away slowly. Do not throw things at the snake to get it to move. It has the right-of-way. Snakes will almost never strike unless harassed, pestered, cornered or stepped on.

In the unlikely event that you do get bitten in spite of these precautions, stay calm and send a companion to get assistance. Your life is not in danger, but rapid movement, running and panic will certainly not assist your situation. If you must move to find assistance, do so slowly and, if possible, immobilize the bitten area below heart level. Locate park personnel for help or go immediately to the hospital in the town of Milk River. Do not try to capture or kill the snake that bit you. Do not apply a tourniquet to the bitten area. Do not incise the bite wound and attempt to suck out the venom.

PLANTS IN THE PARK

The plant life in the park is quite diverse, with over 250 flowering species reported to be found within the park's boundaries. Flowering times vary from species to species and from year to year depending on seasonal weather and other factors. As indicated earlier, there are three main habitats in the park: upland prairie grassland, hoodoo and riparian, or riverside. Some plants may be found in only one habitat, while others might overlap several habitats. While moving through the park, try to keep your feet off the botany. Remember that it is illegal to remove or damage any plant life within the park. A checklist follows for some of the more common flowering plants. The checklist is sorted to give the common name(s) of the plants, their scientific names, approximate time of blooming, the preferred habitat, the usual flower colour and the relative abundance in the park. Legends are at the top of the checklist.

Flower colour legend – BP is blue or purple; Y is yellow; ROP is red, orange or pink; W is white, brown or green

Preferred habitat – P is prairie; R is riparian, riverside; H is hoodoo, dry slopes

* Locally common but provincially rare

**Rare species

EARLY SPRING

Common name(s)	Scientific name	Colour	Preferred habitat	Occurrence
Low Larkspur	Delphinium bicolor	BP	R	Common
Moss Phlox	Phlox hoodii	BP, W	H, P	Common
Shooting Star	Dodecatheon pulchellum	BP	P, R	Common
Smooth Blue Beardtongue	Penstemon nitidus	BP	H, P	Common
Butter-and-Eggs, Toadflax	Linaria vulgaris	Y	R	Common
Common Groundsel, Prairie Groundsel, Woolly Groundsel	Senecio canus	Y	H	Common
Dandelion	Taraxacum officinale	Y	H, P, R	Common
Early Yellow Locoweed	Oxytropis sericea	Y	H	Common
Golden Bean, Buffalo Bean	Thermopsis rhombifolia	Y	H, P	Common
Leafy Musineon	Musineon divaricatum	Y	H	Common
Lemonweed, Puccoon	Lithospermum ruderale	Y	H	Common
Narrow-leaved Puccoon, Yellow Stoneseed	Lithospermum incisum	Y	H	Common
Skunkbush	Rhus trilobata	Y	H	Common
Thorny Buffaloberry	Shepherdia argentea	Y	R	Common
Yellow Prairie Violet	Viola nuttallii	Y	P, R	Occasional
Yellowbell	Fritillaria pudica	Y	H, R	Common
Bearberry, Kinnikinnick	Arctostaphylos uva-ursi	ROP	P, R	Common

Three-flowered Avens, Prairie Smoke, Old Man's Whiskers	*Geum triflorum*	ROP	P	Common
Veiny Meadow Rue	*Thalictrum venulosum*	ROP	R	Common
Western Meadow Rue	*Thalictrum occidentalis*	ROP	R	Common
Cushion Milk-vetch	*Astragalus gilviflorus*	W	H	Common
Low Townsendia	*Townsendia exscapa*	W	H	Common *
Pale Comandra, Bastard Toadflax	*Comandra umbellata*	W	H	Common
Star-flowered Solomon's Seal	*Maianthemum stellatum*	W	R	Common
Wild Strawberry	*Fragaria virginiana*	W	R	Common

LATE SPRING

Common Name(s)	Scientific Name	Colour	Pref. Habitat	Occurrence
Ascending Purple Milk-vetch	*Astragalus adsurgens*	BP	H, P	Common
Blue Flax	*Linum perenne ssp. lewisii*	BP	H	Common
Missouri Milk-vetch	*Astragalus missouriensis*	BP	H	Common
Silvery Lupine	*Lupinus argenteus*	BP	P	Common
Smooth Fleabane	*Erigeron glabellus*	BP	H	Common
Tufted Vetch, Bird Vetch	*Vicia cracca*	BP	R	Common
Two-groove Milk-vetch	*Astragalus bisulcatus*	BP	P	Common
Brown-eyed Susan, Gaillardia, Blanketflower	*Gaillardia aristata*	Y	H,P	Common
Butte Marigold, Stemless Rubber Weed	*Hymenoxys acaulis*	Y	H	Common
Colorado Rubber Plant	*Hymenoxys richardsonii*	Y	H	Common
Goat's-beard, Yellow Salsify	*Tragopogon dubius*	Y	H, P	Common
Golden Currant	*Ribes aureum*	Y	R	Common
Low Whitlow-wort	*Paronychia sessiflora*	Y	H	Occasional
Poison Ivy	*Toxicodendron radicans*	Y	H, R	Common
Prickly-pear Cactus	*Opuntia polyacantha*	Y	H	Common
Sand Bladderpod	*Lesquerella arenosa*	Y	H	Common
Silverweed	*Potentilla anserina*	Y	P, R	Common
Small-flowered Rocket	*Erysimum inconspicuum*	Y	H	Common
Spatulate Bladderpod	*Lesquerella alpina*	Y	H	Common

Wolf Willow, Silverberry	Elaeagnus commutata	Y	H	Common
Yellow Flax	Linum rigidum	Y	H, P	Common
Yellow Umbrella Plant, Yellow Buckwheat	Eriogonum flavum	Y	H, P	Common
Cushion Cactus, Ball Cactus	Coryphantha vivipara	ROP	H	Common
Northern Hedysarum	Hedysarum boreale	ROP	H, P	Common
Prickly Rose	Rosa acicularis	ROP	P, R	Common
Scarlet Butterflyweed, Scarlet Gaura	Gaura coccinea	ROP	P, R	Common
Scarlet Mallow	Sphaeralcea coccinea	ROP	P, R	Common
Wavy-leaved Thistle	Cirsium undulatum	ROP	H	Common
Wood Rose	Rosa woodii	ROP	R	Common
Chokecherry	Prunus virginiana	W	R	Common
Clustered Oreocarya	Cryptantha nubigena	W	H	Common
Cut-leaved Anemone, Windflower	Anemone multifida	W, ROP	P, R	Common
Canadian Milk-vetch	Astragalus canadensis	W	P	Common
Creamy Peavine	Lathyrus ochroleucus	W	R	Common
Drummond's Milk-vetch	Astragalus drummondii	W	P	Occasional
Ground Plum	Astragalus crassicarpus	W	P	Common
Gumbo Evening Primrose, Butte Primrose, Rock Rose	Oenothera caespitosa	W	H	Common
Macoun's Cryptanthe	Cryptantha macounii	W	H	Common
Mouse-eared Chickweed	Cerastium arvense	W	H	Common
Narrow-leaved Milk-vetch	Astragalus pectinatus	W	H, P	Common
Nodding Umbrella-plant	Eriogonum cernuum	W	H	Rare**
Northern Gooseberry	Ribes oxyacanthoides	W	P, R	Common
Pearly Everlasting	Anaphalis margaritacea	W	H· P	Common
Prairie Onion	Allium textile	W	P, R	Common
Prickly Milk-vetch	Astragalus kentrophyta	W	H, P	Common*
Red-osier Dogwood	Cornus stolonifera	W	R	Common
Saskatoon, Serviceberry	Amelanchier alnifolia	W	R	Common
Tufted Fleabane	Erigeron caespitosa	W	H	Common
Western Canada Violet	Viola canadensis	W	R	Common
White Beardtongue	Penstemon albidus	W	H, P	Common
Wild Licorice	Glycyrrhiza lepidota	W	H, P	Common
Yarrow	Achillea millefolium	W	H, P	Common

EARLY AND MIDSUMMER

Common Name(s)	Scientific Name	Colour	Pref. Habitat	Occurrence
Blue-eyed Grass	Sisyrinchium angustifolium	BP	R	Common
Harebell	Campanula rotundiflora	BP	H, P	Common
Stickseed	Hackelia floribunda	BP	R	Common
Common Annual Sunflower	Helianthus annuus	Y	H, P	Common
Hairy Golden Aster	Heterotheca villosa	Y	H	Common
Owl Clover	Orthocarpus luteus	Y	P	Common
Prairie Coneflower	Ratibida columnifera	Y	H, P	Common
Shrubby Cinquefoil	Potentilla fruticosa	Y	P, R	Common
Yellow Evening Primrose	Oenothera biennis	Y	R	Common
Yellow Sweet Clover	Melilotus officinalis	Y	P, R	Common
Water Smartweed	Polygonum amphibium	ROP	R	Common
Western Snowberry, Wolfberry	Symphoricarpos occidentalis	ROP	R	Common
Common Nettle	Urtica dioica	W	R	Common
Cow Parsnip	Heracleum lanatum	W	R	Common
Creeping White Prairie Aster	Aster falcatus	W	H, P	Common
Evening Star, Sand Lily	Mentzelia decapetala	W	H	Common
Northern Bedstraw	Galium boreale	W	R	Common
Western Clematis	Clematis ligusticifolia	W	R	Common
White Clover	Trifolium repens	W	R, P	Common
White Evening Primrose	Oenothera nuttallii	W	R	Common
White Sweet Clover	Melilotus albus	W	P, R	Common

LATE SUMMER

Common Name(s)	Scientific Name	Colour	Pref. Habitat	Occurrence
Common Burdock	Arctium minus	BP	P, R	Common
Dotted Blazingstar, Dotted Gayfeather	Liatris punctata	BP	H	Common
Purple Prairie Clover	Petalostemon purpureum	BP	P, R	Common
Smooth Blue Aster	Aster laevis	BP	H, R	Common
Wild Bergamot	Monarda fistulosa	BP	R	Common

Black-eyed Susan	*Rudbeckia hirta*	Y	H, P	Common
Broomweed, Snakeweed	*Gutierrezia sarothrea*	Y	P	Common
Canada Goldenrod	*Solidago canadensis*	Y	P	Common
Common Tall Sunflower	*Helianthus nuttallii*	Y	P, R	Common
Gumweed, Resinweed, Gum Plant, Tarweed	*Grindelia squarrosa*	Y	H, P	Common
Late Goldenrod	*Solidago gigantea*	Y	R	Common
Low Goldenrod	*Solidago missouriensis*	Y	R	Common
Pasture Sagewort, Pasture Sage, Fringed Sage	*Artemisia frigida*	Y	H, P	Common
Perennial Sow Thistle	*Conchus arvensis*	Y	H, P, R	Common
Sagebrush, Winter-fat, Winter Sage, White Sage	*Eurotia lanata*	Y	H, P	Common
Silver Sagebrush	*Artemisia cana*	Y	H, P	Common
Bee Plant, Spider-flower, Stinking Clover	*Cleome serrulata*	ROP	P	Occasional
Bull Thistle	*Cirsium vulgare*	ROP	H, P	Common
Canada Thistle, Field Thistle	*Cirsium arvense*	ROP	H, P	Common
Nodding Onion	*Allium cernuum*	ROP	H, P	Common
Skeletonweed, Prairie Pink	*Lygodesmia juncea*	ROP	H	Common
Showy Milkweed	*Asclepias speciosa*	ROP	H, R	Common
Green Milkweed	*Asclepias viridiflora*	W	H	Common*
Prairie Sagewort, Prairie Sage, Cudweed, Mugweed	*Artemisia ludoviciana*	W	H, P	Common
Wild Mint	*Mentha arvense*	W	R	Common

A number of the plants in the park are provincially rare and/or restricted to the habitats that exist there. A more detailed description and photographs of some of the more unusual plants follows.

Yellowbell
Fritillaria pudica
LILY FAMILY

This diminutive flower is a harbinger of spring, blooming often just after snowmelt in dry grasslands and coulees in the southern portion of the province. The early appearance of the flower is most probably the source of another common name, Yellow Snowdrop. It can easily be overlooked because of its small size, usually standing only about 15 cm tall. The yellow, drooping, bell-shaped flowers are very distinctive. The flowers turn orange to brick-red as they age. The leaves (usually two or three) are linear to lance-shaped and appear more or less

opposite each other about halfway up the stem. The Yellowbell sometimes appears with two flowers on a stem, but single blooms are more common.

The genus name, *Fritillaria*, is derived from the Latin *fritillus*, which means "a dice box," most probably a reference to the fruit, which appears as an erect, cylindrical capsule atop the flowering stem. The species name *pudica* means "bashful" and is probably a reference to the nodding attitude of the flower on the stem. Native peoples gathered the bulbs and used them as food, eating them both raw and cooked.

Low Townsendia (Easter Daisy, Stemless Townsendia)
Townsendia exscapa
COMPOSITE FAMILY

This early-blooming plant grows from a taproot and appears on dry hillsides and prairies. The leaves are basal and crowded, linear to narrowly spatulate, 3 cm long and 2 mm wide, and covered in soft hairs which lend the foliage a greyish-green colour. The flowerheads are about 3 cm in diameter and appear overly large for the size of the plant. They are virtually stemless and the flowers appear to be sitting on the ground. The 20- to 40-ray florets are bright white (sometimes tinged with pink) surrounding bright yellow disc florets. The ray florets curl under at night.

The genus name, *Townsendia*, honours David Townsend, a 19th-century American amateur botanist. The species name, *exscapa*, is botanical Latin meaning "without a stem," referring to the plant's low growth habit. That also gives rise to the alternative common name, Stemless Townsendia. The other alternative common name, Easter Daisy, arises because of the plant's early blooming time. The plant was first collected for science by Sir John

Richardson, a Scottish biologist who was attached to Sir John Franklin's expedition to the Arctic in search of the Northwest Passage. A similar, related plant, Parry's Townsendia (*T. parryi*), also appears in the region at various elevations, but its ray flowers are violet to purple.

Golden Currant (Yellow Currant)
Ribes aureum (also *Ribes odoratum*)
CURRANT FAMILY

This early-blooming plant is an upright shrub that grows to 3 m tall along riverbanks and in desert grasslands. The leaves are alternate, deeply palmately lobed like maple leaves, wedge-shaped at the base, and blunt-tipped. The leaves turn to lovely red and maroon colours in the fall. The bright yellow flowers are numerous, occurring in clusters of 5–15 tubular blossoms with five spreading lobes. The flowers exude a clove-like fragrance. The fruits are round berries, first golden, then turning orange, then red. They are also, as testified to by Meriwether Lewis, "agreeably flavored."

The origin of the genus name, *Ribes*, is a matter of some dispute. Some authorities say it is from the Danish *ribs*, a name for red currants. Others say the name arises from the Arabic name for a similar plant. All of the currants and gooseberries are in this genus.

The species name, *aureum*, is Latin for "golden," most likely a reference to the flower colour. The species was first collected for science by Meriwether Lewis in 1806, and was first described for science by Frederick Pursh in 1814 in his book *Flora Americae Septentrionalis*. The plant is also known by the locally common names Buffalo Currant, Missouri Currant and Clove Currant. It was used as food by Native peoples, either eaten raw or dried for future use. Hummingbirds are drawn to the flowers.

Poison Ivy
Rhus radicans (also *Toxicodendron radicans*)
SUMAC FAMILY

This plant is a sprawling to erect deciduous, somewhat hairy shrub that grows in a variety of habitats including rocky areas, disturbed places, in woods and along streams. It often grows like a vine, forming low-growing, dense colonies. The leaves are distinctive, being compound with three leaflets. Each leaflet is more or less of equal size (3–12 cm long), almond-shaped, pointed, shiny green, prominently veined, and smooth or shallowly toothed on the margin. The leaves are green during the spring and summer, turning bright red in the fall. The flowers are inconspicuous, white to yellowish, and occur in clusters on erect stems at the leaf bases. The flowers give way to berry-like drupes that are greyish-white and waxy.

The genus name, *Rhus*, is derived from the Greek *rhous*, which is an ancient name for Sumac. The species name, *radicans*, means "with rooting stems," a reference to the fact that this plant spreads both vegetatively by rhizomes and sexually by the distribution of seeds. Seeds are usually spread by birds eating the fruits. The seeds must pass through the digestive tract of a bird in order to be viable. The alternate genus name, *Toxicodendron*, is derived from the Greek *toxikos*, meaning "poisonous," and *dendron*, meaning "tree," thus "poison tree." DO NOT TOUCH THIS PLANT. The plant produces a volatile oil called urushiol, which can cause serious contact dermatitis in many people. The reaction to contact is usually a severe itching on the skin that turns to a reddish inflammation, then blistering. It is said that the same reaction can happen if

one breathes in smoke from the burning plant. Several mnemonics have been coined to remind people not to come into contact with this plant: "leaves of three, let it be – hairy vine, no friend of mine – berries white, run in fright."

Cushion Milk-vetch (Plains Milk-vetch)
Astragalus gilviflorus (also *Astragalus triphyllus*)
PEA FAMILY

This low-growing plant occurs on dry hilltops and buttes in the prairie habitat. It forms dense mats of leaves and flower stems on the ground, and blooms early in the season. The leaves are palmately compound, with three elliptic leaflets. The leaves and stems are densely covered with soft, silvery hairs, giving the plant a greyish-green hue. The flowers are creamy to yellowish-white, typical of the pea family in construction, have a purplish tint on the keel, and occur in short-stemmed clusters that are somewhat buried in the leaves. In fact, the flower stems are so short that the flowers appear to arise directly from the foliage. The distinguishing feature of this species that sets it apart from other members of the genus is its three-parted leaves. All of the other members of the genus have pinnately compound leaves with numerous leaflets.

The origin of the genus name, *Astragalus*, is explained in the note on Ground-Plum (*A. crassicarpus*), shown below. The species name, *gilviflorus*, means "yellow flowered" in botanical Latin. This plant was first described for science by 20th-century American botanist Edmund Perry Sheldon, an authority on *Astragalus*. Plants in the genus *Astragalus* are said to be accumulators of selenium, often concentrating the element in their tissues to toxic levels. In trace amounts, selenium is necessary for cellular function in most animals, but if ingested in large amounts it can inhibit locomotor functions, giving the affected animal symptoms like the blind staggers.

Ground-Plum (Buffalo Bean)
Astragalus crassicarpus
PEA FAMILY

This hardy perennial grows in open prairie and on grassy hillsides, and sprawls over the ground, sometimes forming dense mats up to 1 m in diameter. The stems are decumbent – lying on the ground, with tips ascending – and the inflorescence appears in a loose raceme of 8–10 pea-like flowers at the tip of the stems. The flowers are pale yellow to whitish, with the keel fringed in purple. The fruits are nearly round pods, up to 12 mm in diameter, which are reddish and lie on the ground like small red plums. The pods give the plant its common name.

The origin of the genus name, *Astragalus*, is a matter of some dispute. Some authorities say it is derived from the Greek *astragalos*, which means "ankle bone," a reference to the pod shape of some members of the genus. Indeed, the talus bone in the human ankle is sometimes referred to as the astragalus. At least one authority takes the etymological connection of "ankle bone" slightly further,

pointing out that Greeks once used rattling bones as dice, and the sound made by them when shaken is reminiscent to that made by the ripe seeds inside a pod from an *Astragalus* plant. Others say the name is derived from the Greek *astron*, which means "star," and *gala*, which means "milk," it once being believed that milk production would increase in cows grazing on members of the genus. The young pods were eaten, raw or boiled, by some Native peoples. The roots were boiled and used as a toothpaste and for treatment for insect bites. The dried, powdered roots were used as a coagulant to stop bleeding. The plant was first described for science by renowned 19th-century English botanist Thomas Nuttall, when he visited the Mandan tribe in the Dakotas in 1810. The plant is occasionally referred to as Buffalo Bean, but should not be confused with Golden Bean (*Thermopsis rhombifolia*), another member of the Pea Family that blooms in the area and also goes by the name Buffalo Bean. It has upright stems and bright yellow flowers that are decidedly larger than those of Ground-Plum.

Butte Primrose (Gumbo Evening Primrose)
Oenothera caespitosa

EVENING PRIMROSE FAMILY

This low-growing, tufted perennial grows from a woody root, and is found in the park most often on dry clay slopes and eroded prairie. The leaves are basal, entire, spoon- to lance-shaped, wavy-margined, prominently mid-veined and irregularly toothed. They occur in a rosette on the ground and may have a reddish tinge. The sweet-scented flowers are showy and white, with four large, shallowly lobed petals and four sepals that are often reflexed and pale pink. The flowers are short-lived and become pinker as they age and wilt.

The genus name, *Oenothera*, is derived from the Greek *oinos* meaning "wine," and *thera* meaning "to imbibe." The name is said to arise because an allied European plant was thought to induce a taste for wine. The specific epithet, *caespitosa*, is Latin for "tufted," a reference to the growth habit of the plant. The flower usually opens late in the day and remains open at night, using moths as pollinators. This plant goes by a number of common names, including Tufted Evening Primrose, Rock Rose, Gumbo Evening Primrose, Stemless Evening Primrose and Gumbo Lily, though it is not a member of the Lily Family. The plant was first collected for science by Meriwether Lewis in 1806 near the Great Falls on the Missouri River in present-day Montana. Lewis wrote that he collected the plant from "... a light-coloured soil intermixed with a considerable proportion of coarse gravel without sand, when dry it cracks and appears thursty and is very hard, in its wet state, it is as soft and slipry as so much soft soap." That is a good description of the wet, clayey soils known to hikers as gumbo.

Butte Marigold (Stemless Rubber Weed)
Hymenoxys acaulis
COMPOSITE FAMILY

This creeping, tufted, hairy perennial grows up to 30 cm tall from a woody rootstock and often forms small colonies on dry, rocky or sandy exposed slopes in grasslands and in badlands habitat. The leaves are all basal, entire, narrowly lance-shaped to spoon-shaped and softly hairy. The flowers are bright yellow, solitary heads that are borne on a leafless flower stalk arising from the ground – an organ called a scape. The ray flowers are yellow, three-lobed at the tip, and reflexed with age. The disc flowers are yellow or orange-yellow.

Top: Butte Marigold, Bottom: Colorado Rubber Plant

The involucral bracts are white, hairy, linear and not united at the base.

The genus name, *Hymenoxys*, is derived from the Greek *hymen*, meaning "membrane," and *oxys*, meaning "sharp," a reference to the scales on the pappus of the fruit of the plant. The species name, *acaulis*, means "without a stem," a reference to the scape that supports the flower. The roots of plants in this genus exude a white sap when cut or crushed, and that is most likely the origin of the common name Rubber Weed. Colorado Rubber Plant (*H. richardsonnii*), also shown, is a related species that occurs in the same habitat. The chief difference between the two plants is the leaves. In the Colorado Rubber Plant the leaves are divided into narrow, rubbery, smooth segments.

Smooth Blue Beardtongue
Penstemon nitidus
FIGWORT FAMILY

This erect, often branched perennial usually has several stems that grow to 30 cm tall, and it often occurs in clumps, on dry grassy slopes, eroded areas and sandy soils. The stems are hairless. The oval to lance-shaped leaves are opposite, thick and fleshy, pale green and covered with a greyish bloom, similar to the skin on a grape. The blue flowers are numerous and occur in dense clusters from the leaf axils at the top of the plant. The flowers are tube-shaped and up to 2 cm long and have purple pencilling inside the lower floral lip. There are two lips, the lower being three-lobed, with soft, smooth hairs, and the upper being two-lobed.

The common name, Beardtongue, describes the hairy, tongue-like staminode (sterile stamen) in the throat of the flower. The genus name, *Penstemon*, originates from the Greek *pente*, meaning "five," and *stemon*, meaning "stamen," five being the total number of stamens in the flower. The species name, *nitidus*, is derived

from Latin and means "shining," or "lustrous," most probably a reference to the bright flowers. This Beardtongue is an early bloomer on the prairie, and its bright blue flowers on a smooth stem are quite striking. White Beardtongue (*P. albidus*), also shown, is a related species that also blooms early in prairie habitat in the region. As the scientific name might suggest, it has white flowers.

Prickly-pear Cactus
Opuntia polyacantha
CACTUS FAMILY

This easily recognized plant is prostrate and can form mats on dry, exposed slopes in eroded areas and badlands, often growing on sandy or rocky soil.

The stems are flattened and covered with modified leaves that are clusters of hard, sharp spines that have tufts of sharp bristles at the base. The flowers are large and showy, with numerous yellow petals that are waxy, and up to 5 cm long. There is a conspicuous large green stigma and numerous yellow or orange stamens inside the flower. The fruits are reddish, soft, spiny berries, which are edible and are often browsed by antelope.

The genus name, *Opuntia*, is derived from the Greek name of a spiny plant that grew in Greece. The species name, *polyacantha*, is derived from the Greek *poly*, which means "many," and *acantha*, which means "thorns." Native peoples roasted and ate the plant stems, after removing the spines and outer skin. The juices inside the stem were often used as an emergency water supply. The plant contains calcium, phosphorus and vitamin C, and is said to taste of cucumber. The spines on the plants are very sharp, and will easily pierce thin footwear. Indeed, these plants were a continuing bane to early explorers in western North America.

In addition to Prickly-pear Cactus, you will also find Cushion Cactus (*Coryphantha vivipara*), also known as Ball Cactus, in the park. It is a low-growing, squat perennial that grows singly or in clumps, often on south-facing slopes. Its pincushion stem rises only a few inches above the ground. The whole surface of the rounded stem is covered with evenly spaced, spine-tipped projections. The beautiful purplish to pink flowers have numerous lance-shaped petals and occur between the spines. Each flower also has a shower of yellow

stamens in the centre. The flowers are short-lived and grow into round, soft, edible berries which are consumed by antelope. The berries are said to taste like gooseberries and can be made into a jam.

Evening Star (Sand Lily)
Mentzelia decapetala

BLAZING STAR FAMILY

This stout, leafy, branched biennial grows up to 90 cm tall and appears on exposed clay hillsides and eroded badlands in the hoodoo habitat of the park. The leaves are alternate, prominently veined, sharply toothed, up to 15 cm long and roughened with thick, whitish, spine-like hairs. The upper leaves are stalkless. The large white flowers appear at the terminal ends of the branches. They are showy and have five sepals and ten lance- to spatula-shaped, pointed petals, five of which are modified sterile stamens (staminodes). There are numerous yellow stamens. The petals are surrounded by hairy, triangular, pale-orange bracts that are joined at the base. The flowers open in the evening and bloom during the night, thus the common name Evening Star. By morning the flowers will have closed. The nighttime blooming may be explained by the plant's use of moths as pollinators. As the flowers bloom, they emit a wonderful fragrance.

The genus name, *Mentzelia*, honours Christian Mentzel, a 17th-century German botanist. The species name, *decapetala*, means "ten petals." The plant was first collected for science by Meriwether Lewis in 1804, most probably near the mouth of the James River in present-day South Dakota. It has a variety of locally common names, including Ten Petal Blazing Star, Ten Petal Mentzelia, and Sand Lily, though the plant is not a member of the Lily Family. Another member of the genus, Blazing Star (*M. laevicaulis*), occurs in similar dry habitats in southern British Columbia. It has very large, showy, yellow flowers.

If you want to witness the blooming, plan to be in the hoodoos just before sundown on a mid- to late-summer evening, say between the last two weeks of July and first ten days of August. By that time the buds will be showing on the plants during the daytime. I would recommend a reconnoitre of the hoodoo habitat in the late afternoon in order to locate some plants that are in bud. Return to the plants about 8:00 p.m. The buds on the plant will start to open as the direct sunlight ceases to hit the ground. The whole blooming process may take up to an hour. Make sure you have a flashlight for the walk back to the campground. While we were watching the bloom, we were joined by a small butterfly called a Gray Hairstreak. It seemed almost as interested in the process as we were.

Western Clematis (White Virgin's Bower)
Clematis ligusticifolia
BUTTERCUP FAMILY

This plant is a climbing or trailing woody vine that commonly occurs in coulees, along roadsides and in riparian habitat in the park. It clings to and climbs over other plants by a twist or kink in its leaf stalks. The leaves are opposite and compound, with five to seven long-stalked leaflets. The flowers are white and borne in dense clusters. The flowers are unisexual. The male flowers have many stamens but no pistils, while the female flowers have both pistils and sterile stamens. The fruits are masses of hairy achenes, each with a long, feathery style. The genus and common name, *Clematis*, is derived from the Greek word *klema*, meaning "vine branch or tendril." The whole plant is toxic if ingested. Some Native peoples mashed the leaves and branches and used the juices as a headwash. Some Native peoples also boiled the leaves and applied the decoction to boils and sores. Clematis often goes by the locally common names of Virgin's Bower and Traveller's Joy, both names arising because the plant makes bowers along trellises and fences, creating shelters and shady areas. Two related species occur in the region. Blue Clematis (*C. occidentalis*) is common in shaded woods in western and central parts of the province, while Yellow Clematis (*C. tanguitica*) is a naturalized species. The flowers of those species are quite different in appearance from Western Clematis. They occur as solitary on the stem and have four to five sepals that resemble crepe paper.

Prairie Coneflower
Ratibida columnifera
COMPOSITE FAMILY

This is a plant of dry grasslands, coulees and disturbed areas and can reach heights of up to 60 cm. The leaves are alternate, greyish-green in colour and deeply divided into oblong lobes. The distinctive flower appears atop a tall, slender stem and consists of dark-purple disc florets formed into a cylinder up to 4 cm long, the base of which is surrounded by bright yellow petals. An associate of mine once declared: "This flower looks like it is sporting a tutu." Indeed it does.

The origin of the genus name, *Ratibida*, is unknown. The species name, *columnifera*, is a reference to the column or cone-shaped flower. Some Native peoples dried the flowers for food, while others made a tea from the disc florets and leaves. The roots of the plant yield a yellow dye. The plant is relatively common in the southern third of the province. One of the naturalists at Writing-on-Stone recently showed me a photograph taken in the park of a very distinctive specimen of the plant that had reddish-brown ray florets instead of the usual yellow.

114

Green Milkweed
Asclepias viridiflora
MILKWEED FAMILY

This rare perennial plant occurs only in the far south-central part of the province. It grows up to 60 cm tall on dry hillsides, usually in sandy soils. It occurs along the roadway that leads down to the campground in the park. The leathery leaves are opposite, up to 8 cm long, egg-shaped to oblong lance-shaped, short-stalked, prominently veined, and wavy on the margins. The flowers are pale green, sometimes with a purplish tinge, and they occur in dense, rounded, umbrella-shaped clusters

at the tops of the stems and in the leaf axils. Each flower is up to 1 cm long, and the corolla is five-parted, with the petals arranged around a projecting tube of fused stamens.

The genus name, *Asclepias*, honours Asklepios, the Greek god of medicine, perhaps a reference to the plant's medicinal properties. The species name, *viridiflora*, is Latin for "green flower." The common name, Milkweed, arises because plants in the genus exude a milky latex when the plant is damaged or cut. The plant contains alkaloids and resins in its stems and leaves which may cause it to be poisonous to livestock. Showy Milkweed (*A. speciosa*) is also native to the park. It has pink flowers that occur in large clusters.

HOW TO GET THERE

To get to Writing-on-Stone Provincial Park, travel south from Lethbridge on Hwy 4 to the town of Milk River. At Milk River turn east and proceed 32 km east on Hwy 501. At the junction with Hwy 500, turn south and proceed 10 km to the park entrance. The route is well signed and paved throughout.

View of Elkwater Lake

Cypress Hills Interprovincial Park

If you have never been to the Cypress Hills, you should know that when you arrive you will not see any cypress trees. There are none there. The name "Cypress Hills" came about because of some misunderstandings and misinterpretations that were not corrected before it was too late. The Métis are the descendants of marriages between Native peoples of present-day Canada and Europeans who came to explore North America and capture its bounty. The history of mixed-race marriages and their offspring dates back to the mid-1600s in eastern Canada. As the fur trade commenced in earnest in the 1700s, the Métis emerged as a distinct culture, particularly along the Red River in present-day Manitoba. They mixed Native and French traditions and language, and many of them became a semi-nomadic community that followed the bison herds. As such, the Métis were early visitors to the Cypress Hills country, and they apparently mistook the Lodgepole Pine (*Pinus contorta*) that grows there for another pine that was familiar to them from further east – the Jack Pine (*Pinus banksiana*). In the Métis tongue the Jack Pine was referred to as "cyprès," so they incorrectly applied that name to the Lodgepole Pine, and they accordingly referred to the area as "Les montagnes des cyprès." That name translated to the Europeans as the "cypress mountains," and they did not appreciate the distinction between "cyprès" and "cypress." Thus the die was cast. Henceforth these were the Cypress Hills, though there are no cypress anywhere to be found.

The hills themselves are more properly termed a high erosional plateau rising above the plains that surround it. The plateau generally runs east/west, straddling the Alberta/Saskatchewan boundary about 75 km north of the border with the United States. The hills are approximately 150 km from east to west and 40 km from north to south. When you arrive, you may well think something very peculiar is afoot. Approaching from the west or northwest, you have left the foothills and mountains behind you and have been driving across relatively flat, treeless prairie for several hours. Suddenly – or at least it seems sudden – you see an island of tree-covered, rolling highland coming into view, rising above the plains to the east or southeast. The plateau rises sharply from the north, then drops gradually to the south, there rejoining the prairies. In fact, the Cypress Hills are the highest point in Canada between the Rocky Mountains and Labrador. How can this be, you may well wonder. What trick of nature or conjuring has made this place? Welcome to the Cypress Hills, a magical place with a fascinating natural and human history, even if it does not have any cypress.

Prior to the arrival of the white man and the Métis, the Blackfoot Confederacy were the dominant Native peoples and culture in the geographic area that includes the Cypress Hills. The Blackfoot called the hills *l-kim-e-kooy*, which translated as "striped earth," a reference to the ground's appearance in places where glacial erosion has exposed ancient strata in the hills. The Cree were frequent visitors to the area, and they knew the place as "mun-a-tub-qow," which meant "beautiful upland." Neither of those names would prevail once the Europeans began to arrive, but both were quite appropriate.

HOW THE HILLS WERE BUILT

Looking at the Cypress Hills, one might assume they were built by forces similar to those that created the Rocky Mountains: rock that has been pushed upward, then bent, folded, broken, piled up and eroded. Though that is perhaps a logical assumption, these hills were not built in quite that way. In fact, these hills might be said to have been built in rather an opposite way. The Cypress Hills – the plateau – is better described as a work of bas relief, where the surrounding area has been ground away, leaving the plateau intact, standing above the now lowered plains. The hills are truly an intriguing geological anomaly.

More than 70 million years ago most of present-day southern Alberta, including the Cypress Hills area, was covered by a shallow sea. Rivers carried clay and silt to the sea and those sediments settled to the bottom. Extending over millions of years, the sediments were buried by later sediments in a continual cycle. In time, the basement sediments were compressed into dark-grey shale. As time went by, the sea became shallower on its western edge and began to retreat to the east. As it did so, over long periods of time, sand and mud were deposited at the margins of the sea, and they in turn were compressed and turned into stone, in this case sandstone. As the sea receded further, other sediments were added to the mix and they too eventually turned to rock. Gradually, the various sediments and depositions began to resemble a multi-layered cake, with older sediments buried by younger.

When the Rockies were being built in earnest about 55 million years ago, extremely large rivers eroded the new mountains and rushed onto the plains to the east, carrying with them erosive debris. Over a long time, gravel and cobbles were pushed out from the mountains and began to form a conglomerate rock that became the uppermost sedimentary layer of the Cypress Hills. The gravel was hard and contained well-rounded quartzite and chert pebbles and cobbles. These were laid down in such a fashion that they became a sheet-like cap over unconsolidated sands, silts and clays from earlier depositions. The gravel thus formed an erosion-resistant covering over the underlying sediments. The conglomerate rock looks for all the world like rather poorly mixed concrete. The influx of eroded materials was exacerbated (assuming one can use that word when speaking about millions of years) about 45 million years ago by the formation of the Sweetgrass Hills to the south. With the magma dome uplifting, water flows were altered in the area and more runoff was directed at the fledgling Cypress Hills. With that runoff came more material from the now eroding overburden covering the dome.

As the erosive deposits built up on what was to become the Cypress Hills, the rivers were forced to move around the hills. In the process, they eroded and lowered the land adjacent to the hills – that is, in places where gravel sheets were not deposited, the soft sediments were eroded by moving water and slowly the plains surrounding the Cypress Hills were ground down. The hard conglomerate rock protected the plateau from erosion, so the upland remained. Then came the ice.

The last glacial period (what we laypeople might incorrectly refer to as an "ice age") occurred during the Late Pleistocene epoch, beginning about 126,000 years ago and ending between 10,000 and 12,000 years ago. That glacial period, as it occurred in present-day Alberta, is known as the Wisconsinian glacial episode. During that episode the Laurentide ice sheet came west from the Canadian Shield and the Cordilleran ice sheet came east from the Rocky Mountains. Together they extended to cover virtually all of Canada and most of the northern United States. Where the two ice sheets met is said to be a "suture zone," and in that zone lay the Cypress Hills. Indeed, as the ice sheets slowly covered most of the North American continent, they flowed around the plateau but never completely engulfed it. The top of the plateau became somewhat of an island in the ice – a nunatak. Indeed, the southern slopes of the Cypress Hills became the northernmost point on the continent that remained south of the continental ice sheets. The implications of this are profound because it means that those slopes of the plateau are among the only unglaciated lands in Canada. It also means that the Cypress Hills formed a major drainage divide separating rivers draining to the Gulf of Mexico by way of the Missouri and those draining to Hudson Bay by way of the Saskatchewan system.

While the top of the plateau was not eroded by the ice, the rest of the landscape on the plains at the base of the plateau was altered dramatically by the ice. In addition, the ice acted as a dam for an extended period of time, diverting meltwaters to the south and east, draining out the Milk River valley south of the Cypress Hills. As the ice sheets began to melt about 15,000 years ago, the ice started to recede, and eventually the ice dam was overcome. Meltwaters then began to flow around the Cypress Hills, in the process further eroding the landscape on the plains. All of this acted to accentuate the elevation differences between the plains and the hills themselves. It was about this time that the meltwaters began to run inside the plateau, cutting valleys that dissect the Cypress Hills today. By about 10,000 years ago the glacial episode was at an end, and the "heavy lifting" that built the Cypress Hills was over. Changes still persist, but most of them are less dramatic in terms of altering the landscape. Further erosive effects from spate conditions in waterways, slumping and landslides will be with us henceforth, but such alterations are minor by comparison with what had gone before.

CLIMATE, WEATHER AND PLANT LIFE

Because of their higher elevation, the Cypress Hills are generally a few degrees cooler than the surrounding area, and they receive more precipitation than the prairies. As air masses approach the plateau, they are forced upward and over the hills, which typically drops the temperature about 5°c per 100 m gained. As the air cools, clouds often form and precipitation begins. The top of the plateau receives about 100 mm more precipitation per year than the bottom does. Thunderstorms are also more common at the top of the plateau. The higher precipitation directly impacts the floral community in the hills, where the flora is more in keeping with what might be expected in the mountains. It is also noteworthy that the top of the plateau was not glaciated, and, as a consequence, plants that existed there prior to the last glacial episode might still be in evidence. The plateau is said to be home to over 750 species of plants, including trees, shrubs, wildflowers, grasses, sedges, lichens and others. Fauna is likewise diverse, and includes a spectrum of animals from large ungulates to rodents to over 200 species of birds.

HUMAN HISTORY

Archaeological sites in the park indicate some human occupation of the area as far back as 7,000 years ago. The earliest occupants were undoubtedly nomadic Native peoples who followed and hunted the bison herds on foot. By the 1730s the horse was introduced to the plains Natives, and that was a watershed in the relationship of the Natives to their environment and their relationships with each other. The addition of firearms further complicated the balance of power, but by the late 18th century the Blackfoot Confederacy had solidified its hold over much of present-day southern Alberta, as well as northeastern Montana. The Cypress Hills themselves were primarily controlled by the Assiniboine, but the hills were a meeting place – and at times a fighting place – for a wide diversity of Native peoples, including the Cree, Assiniboine, Atsina (Gros Ventre), Blackfoot, Saulteaux, Sioux, Crow, Nez Percé and others. It would appear that the hills were important wintering grounds for a variety of peoples. By the 19th century the Métis settled in the hills, particularly as a wintering ground. As time went by, the bison herds were being decimated, and as the bison numbers declined, so did the Natives' visitations to the hills. By 1880 virtually all of the plains Native peoples had taken treaty and were moved to reservation lands.

The Palliser Expedition visited the Cypress Hills during its first summer in British North America. Palliser took the party south from the South Saskatchewan River directly into and across the lands controlled by the Blackfoot. It was Palliser's intention to investigate the Cypress Hills, then move farther south to the 49th parallel, then turn west and make for the Rocky Mountains. During the trip to the hills, Palliser's party found the country to be poor, dry and desolate. They were bothered by some of the Natives they encountered, but no real troubles arose. On arriving at the Cypress Hills, however, Palliser proclaimed them a " perfect oasis in the desert." After a short sojourn there, the party moved west and the description of the Hills as oasis was reinforced. The lands to the west were, by comparison, completely without merit until the expedition arrived in the foothills of the Rockies. It was on this exploration that Palliser made the determination that the area of southwestern Saskatchewan and southern Alberta was unsuitable for settlement and agriculture because of unfavourable climate and soil conditions. Those lands came to be called the "Palliser Triangle."

Parenthetically, Palliser's recommendations ultimately were ignored by government officials, who were significantly influenced by a man named John Macoun. Macoun was Irish by birth but his family immigrated to Canada in 1850 to escape the worsening economic disaster that was playing out in Ireland. After his arrival in Canada, Macoun became a school teacher and a self-taught botanist and naturalist of some repute. A number of plants in western Canada bear his name. In 1872 Macoun met Sandford Fleming, the chief engineer for the fledgling Canadian Pacific Railway. Fleming recruited Macoun to explore the western lands through which the railway would be built, with a view to determining the agricultural potential of the lands. Macoun happily took up the assignment, and his travels coincided with a period of particularly higher than normal rainfall in the "triangle." Macoun's recommendations to

Fleming were bullish, and those recommendations certainly contributed to the selection of the final routing for the railway. Prairie settlement was encouraged and the coming of the new century saw a significant influx of aspiring farmers. Things went well for a time, but a combination of poor farming practices and the normal climate of the area reasserting itself led to dust bowl conditions by the 1930s. Successful agriculture in the area is precarious at best.

By the Deed of Surrender signed in 1869, the Hudson's Bay Company transferred its ownership in Rupert's Land to the new country of Canada. The lands in western Canada that were to become the prairie provinces were designated as the North-West Territories, but the newly formed country of Canada was ill-prepared to exert its sovereignty over those lands. Indeed, even getting to the lands posed some significant difficulties. In truth, they were more easily reached from eastern Canada by travelling through the United States than through Canada. The territories were only sparsely settled by white men, and little or nothing in the way of law and order existed. Indeed, after the Hudson's Bay Company was gone, so called "free traders" from Montana Territory rushed in to fill the void and capture the trade in buffalo hides and furs with the Blackfoot. The War between the States (the US Civil War) had ended in 1865, and former soldiers from both sides began to drift into the western territories. Many of them were little more than common outlaws and they were well armed. All of them appeared to be looking for a way to make quick and easy money.

By this time, Fort Benton was a commercial centre in the Montana Territory, and it was serviced by steamboats that brought trade goods up the Missouri River. Consequently, Fort Benton was the supply point for traders in the whole area, whichever side of the international boundary they were on. Indeed, the international boundary did not count for much. Trading forts were established throughout the area that comprises present-day southern Alberta and Saskatchewan, and all of them were serviced by merchants from Fort Benton. The trail from Fort Benton northward and eastward became well travelled by freighters taking trade goods to the forts and returning with hides. One of the primary items of trade was whisky, or what passed for it. The trail north from Fort Benton quickly became known as the Whoop-up Trail, and it boasted such ports of call as Fort Slideout, Fort Standoff, Fort Robber's Roost, Fort Whisky Gap and of course, Fort Whoop-up. Most of these "forts" were little more than log huts. Most historians say the name Whoop-up is a shortened form of "whoop it up," meaning to celebrate boisterously. There is another school of thought, however. Some historians argue that the term may have arisen from the process of getting a bull team moving along the track. To accomplish that, the bull whacker would walk alongside the train and crack his whip at the animals, a process called "whooping it up." However the term came to be coined, it was soon to be synonymous with the illicit whisky trade and the lawlessness that went hand-in-hand with that trade.

Quite conceivably the single most important event to occur in the hills in modern history was the Cypress Hills Massacre, which took place on June 1, 1873. A group of American wolf hunters (wolfers) lost a number of horses to horse thieves in Montana Territory, just across the international boundary from the Cypress Hills. Most historians say the thieves were Crees, but that matter is of little consequence. The wolfers were greatly angered by their loss and attempted to track the thieves, without success. The trail of the thieves led north toward the North-West Territories, and the wolfers continued in that direction, soon arriving in the Battle Creek valley of the Cypress Hills, where two trading posts, operated by Abel Farwell and Moses Solomon, were located. Some Métis freighters were also in residence when the wolfers arrived. Camped nearby the posts was a group of 200–300 Nakota Indians, a Siouan-speaking people that were a part of a larger cultural group that includes the Assiniboine. The winter of 1872/73 had been hard, and food was in short supply. The Nakota had attempted to trade with the white men but had met with little success. Indeed, the Natives had recently accused Moses Solomon of cheating them in their dealings. Shots had been fired into his trading premises and threats had been made. To say the least, tensions were already high when the wolfers arrived on the evening of May 31.

The wolfers soon began a search for their missing horses, but Abel Farwell assured them that the Nakotas were poor and certainly did not have the stolen horses. That seemed to smooth the matter for a time, but the flames of animosity were soon fanned by whisky, and an explosive atmosphere returned. The next morning, with the addition of still more whisky, there was a misunderstanding over another missing horse, and drunken accusations were hurled at the Nakotas. Before that matter could be sorted out, a group of wolfers, in company with Métis freighters, closed in on the Nakota camp. In the fog of battle and whisky, the exact sequence of events is not accurately known, but shots were fired and the aftermath was unmistakable – a number of dead Nakota men, women and children, and one dead wolfer, plus reports of rapes and dismemberments. Estimates differ wildly as to the exact number of dead among the Natives: some say 16, some 23, some 36, to as many as 80. Whatever the accurate number, there is no doubt that the massacre was one of the most violent episodes in the annals of the Canadian West, and it was a grave turning point in how the West would be governed in the future.

As word spread about the incident, the whole affair was met with outrage by citizens north of the international boundary, who universally condemned the matter as an affront to Canadian sovereignty. Most history books relate that the creation of the North-West Mounted Police (NWMP) was a direct result of the massacre, but strictly speaking, that cannot possibly be so, because the enabling legislation that established the NWMP had already passed in the Canadian Parliament just prior to the massacre. It is fair to say, however, that the massacre probably prompted the Canadian government to "fast track" the recruitment of the force and deployment of it to the North-West Territories in the year following the massacre.

As a footnote, following the Cypress Hills Massacre, the traders, wolfers and Métis fled the area, most of them scattering to the Montana Territory. The two trading forts were burned to the ground, quite possibly by their owners in an attempt to keep any supplies out of Native hands. In 1875 the NWMP went to the Montana Territory to begin extraditing the perpetrators of the massacre to stand trial in Canada. Warrants for arrest were duly issued, but the Montana authorities were little interested in the matter and reluctant to assist the NWMP with their activities. Eventually, seven persons were arrested and delivered before an extradition hearing in July 1875 in Helena, Montana. At the hearing the respondents were characterized as "Belly River wolfers, outlaws, smugglers, cutthroats, horse-thieves and squawmen," and the proceedings quickly deteriorated into a farcical circus. The chief witness for the applicant seeking extradition was Abel Farwell, one of the traders from the Cypress Hills. The evidence adduced by Farwell was so confused and contradictory that the judge took little time in dismissing the application and set the respondents free. Later that year, three other accused were arrested in Canadian territory and sent off to Winnipeg for trial for "the wanton and atrocious slaughter of peaceable and inoffensive people." At that trial, Farwell was once again called upon as the Crown's principal witness, and once again he so confused and garbled the evidence that the accused were acquitted. In 1882 the Canadian government dismissed the last of the outstanding indictments against the alleged perpetrators and the matter was laid to rest, judicially speaking. In the final analysis nobody was ever convicted of any crime whatsoever arising from the Cypress Hills Massacre. Some would say this was a poor advertisement for Native peoples accepting "white man's justice." Others opine that the lack of convictions was immaterial in the face of what other important principles were advanced as a result of the massacre – e. g., that the Canadian government would indeed attempt to prosecute white men accused of crimes against Natives.

A fictionalized account of the massacre is told in Guy Vanderhaeghe's acclaimed novel *The Englishman's Boy.*

As discussed earlier, the NWMP troop led by Commissioner George Arthur French and Assistant Commissioner James Farquharson Macleod eventually made its way west and established a permanent post on the Oldman River. The place was named after the assistant commissioner: Fort Macleod. One year later Macleod divided his force, sending Inspector E.A. Brisebois north to the confluence of the Bow and Elbow Rivers to establish Fort Calgary, and Inspector James Morrow Walsh east to the Cypress Hills to establish Fort Walsh.

Fort Walsh was constructed just north of the scene of the massacre. The fort was located on the floor of a deep valley, surrounded by hills. The location was quite deliberately selected to give the impression to the Native peoples that this was not a place to be feared, but a place to be approached with confidence and in the spirit of co-operation.

Undoubtedly, one of the most momentous happenings at Fort Walsh during its abbreviated existence involved the arrival in Canada of Sitting Bull, the Hunkpapa Lakota Sioux holy man who had figured prominently in the annihilation of George Armstrong Custer and his 7th Cavalry at the Little Big Horn on June 25, 1876. After the defeat of Custer, Sitting Bull led his Sioux band, almost 5,000 strong, northward, eventually crossing into Canada and settling near Wood Mountain, Saskatchewan, east of Fort Walsh. The boundary between the United States and British North America was known to the Native peoples as the "medicine line." The concept of an imaginary line separating the two countries was a completely foreign construct to the Native peoples. It was very big "medicine" indeed that the imaginary line had the ability to prevent the American soldiers – the "long knives" – from crossing it in pursuit of the Native tribes.

Soon after the arrival of the Sioux in the "Great White Mother's" (Queen Victoria's) country, Major Walsh met with them and explained that sanctuary could only be had if they obeyed the laws that applied to all people living in the country. Walsh told them:

> First of all, it is against the law for anyone to take the life of another – to kill any man, woman or child. You must not injure any person, nor steal from – nor give false testimony against – another. You must not take another person's horses, guns, robes, lodges, wagons or anything else. You must not damage, injure, destroy, burn or remove anything from anyone else without their permission. No woman or female child shall be violated, and it is the duty of every man to protect them. You must not cross the international boundary line – what the Indian people call the medicine line, or some of you call "the big road" – to run off horses from other Indian tribes or to raid them or anyone else, or to make war

on American soldiers or the American people. The Great White Mother lives at peace with the Americans.

Walsh continually stressed that only on the basis of abiding by the law would the Sioux enjoy peace. Walsh became responsible for Sitting Bull and his people obeying Canadian laws, a duty that he embraced wholeheartedly and carried out splendidly. Indeed, it is said that Walsh and Sitting Bull became good friends. It is certainly apparent that the two men were very respectful of each other and a deep trust was forged between them. In fact, Walsh was probably the first white man that Sitting Bull ever trusted.

Sitting Bull would have liked to have been offered permanent status in the new country, and he made a compelling case for sanctuary and a grant of land, maintaining, among other things, that his people had been consistently loyal to the British Crown since the days of the battles for New France. The Canadian government, however, rebuffed the Sioux leader and offered him neither land nor food nor support. The government viewed the Sioux as American Indians who had no particular rights in Canada, and indeed made it clear that they would prefer the Sioux return to the United States at the earliest opportunity. The Canadian government was also fearful that the Sioux might launch raids into the US from Canadian territory, an eventuality that was completely unacceptable because such acts would almost certainly result in an international incident. United States policy accorded completely with that of Canadian officials. It is also correct to say that the indigenous tribes on the Canadian side of the medicine line were not happy to have the Sioux in Canadian territory. The Blackfoot and Cree had long been at odds with the Sioux, and suspicions ran high on both sides.

For the most part, the Sioux in Canada kept the peace, obeyed the laws and enjoyed their sanctuary. Perhaps the nearest they came to a major breach was in the summer and fall of 1877 when elements of the US Army led by General Nelson Miles were harrying the Nez Percé Indians as they made a run for the medicine line. The Nez Percé, led by Chief Joseph, was the last great Indian nation to be "pacified" by the army, and the tribe had fought numerous battles during a 2900-km-long strategic retreat to reach Sitting Bull in Canada. The trail for them ended in surrender less than 60 km from the boundary on October 5, 1877. A few of the Nez Percé under Chief White Bird made it over the border to join the Sioux, but many in his party were injured. Walsh was to later describe White Bird as "the greatest Indian soldier that ever lived." At the time, it was all Sitting Bull and Walsh could do to keep the warriors of the Sioux nation from riding to the assistance of the Nez Percé during the final stages of their flight. As one anonymous US officer put it: "I think that in his long career, Joseph cannot accuse the government of the United States of one single act of justice." The actions of the Great White Father, again, were certainly not lost on Sitting Bull.

Quite by coincidence, less than two weeks after the surrender of the Nez Percé, a meeting was brokered at Fort Walsh wherein Commissioner Macleod, Major Walsh and a delegation headed by US General Alfred H. Terry sat down with Sitting Bull to try to convince the Sioux to return to the United States. It took several days of negotiations between Sitting Bull and Walsh to even get the Sioux leader to appear for the meeting. The United States offered a pardon to the Sioux if they would lay down their guns, give up their horses and move to a reservation in the Dakota Territory. Sitting Bull declined the offer, saying:

For 64 years, you have kept and treated my people bad; what have we done that caused us to depart from our country? We could go nowhere, so we have taken refuge here ... We did not give you our country; you took it from us; see how I live with these people; look at these eyes and ears; you think me a fool; but you are a greater fool than I am; this is a Medicine House – a place of truth; and you come to tell us lies, and we do not want to hear them; I will not say any more. I shake hands with these people; you can go back where you came from; take your lies with you; I will stay here; that part of the country we came from belonged to us, now we live here.

MAJOR J.M. WALSH
of N.W.M.P.
FIRST GOVERNOR OF
YUKON TERRITORY
DIED 25TH JULY 1905.

Above: James M. Walsh
Left: Sitting Bull

In 1879 the bison did not appear, and the Sioux began to starve. Little by little they began to drift south across the border and onto reserves in the Dakotas. Sitting Bull, with Walsh as his friend and confidant, remained in Canada until July 1881. At that time, he returned to Fort Buford, his guarantee of safe conduct having been arranged by Walsh with the US Army. By that time Sitting Bull's followers still in Canada numbered a mere 187. A few years after his repatriation, Sitting Bull became involved in the Ghost Dance movement, a messianic resurgence of Native peoples' dominance of North America. The United States government feared Sitting Bull's influence in the movement and acted to have him arrested. During the arrest an altercation broke out and Sitting Bull was fatally shot. Within two weeks of Sitting Bull's death, General Nelson A. Miles, an army commander who played a role in virtually all of the campaigns against the Native peoples of the Great Plains, precipitated a massacre of over 300 Sioux – men, women and children – at Wounded Knee Creek in South Dakota. The action was conducted by the 7th Cavalry. It would prove to be one of the last military actions against the Natives in the United States.

Fort Walsh was to become the headquarters for the NWMP from 1878 to 1883, and its namesake, James M. Walsh, was to become the superintendent of the force. The fort's importance waned considerably when the Canadian Pacific Railway chose to build its line some 50 km north of the fort. Eventually the headquarters of the force was moved to Regina and Fort Walsh was abandoned. The Fort Walsh National Historic Site, an interpretive reconstruction of the original fort, now sits on the site.

Major Walsh retired from the NWMP on September 1, 1883, after ten years of service. Following his departure from the force, he established the Dominion Coal, Coke & Transportation Company in Brandon, Manitoba, and became wealthy selling coal to the CPR. Walsh spent his last years in Brockville, Ontario, in his home, which he named "Indian Cliff." The house was named after Walsh's favourite rock outcropping in the Cypress Hills.

Cattle ranching commenced in the Cypress Hills area in the late 1800s, following the disappearance of the bison and the removal of the Native peoples to reserves. That activity continues to the present day.

In 1906 the Cypress Hills Forest Reserve was created under the Dominion Forest Reserves Act. That reserve was later expanded in size, and the whole of it was turned over to the provinces in 1931. The Centre Block in Saskatchewan was designated as Cypress Hills Provincial Park at that time. In 1945 the Alberta government dedicated Elkwater Provincial Park, and it became Cypress Hills Provincial Park in 1951. The parks expanded from time to time, and in 1989 the two provinces signed an agreement stipulating that the two parks would henceforward be operated as one under the name Cypress Hills Interprovincial Park.

There are several natural ecoregions represented in the park. The Beaver Creek/Horseshoe Canyon Loop trails will give you a very good view of all of these regions. What follows is a description of that loop trail.

BEAVER CREEK/HORSESHOE CANYON LOOP

NTS Map O72E/09 (Elkwater Lake)

total distance: 9 km
elevation gain: 230 m

This loop trail starts at the southwest corner of the Beaver Creek campground, at coordinates 12U 0550798 5500848. Elevation at trailhead is approximately 1225 m. The trail meanders through the forest, following Beaver Creek uphill to Nichol Springs, about 4.1 km from the trailhead. The trail is mostly closed in by the tree canopy, but shade-tolerant wildflower species abound along the route. If the trail is wet, footing can be somewhat tricky owing to the many exposed roots, which get quite slick when wet. Trekking poles are highly recommended in such conditions.

There is one junction that hikers should look for, at coordinates 12U 0550628 5500181. At that point the main trail appears to turn right and

PHOTOGRAPH: LINDA JENNINGS

View from lookout

cross a bridge over the creek, but in fact the trail to Nichol Springs continues straight on uphill on a much narrower track. The bridge will return you toward the Beaver Creek campground.

After that junction, the trail continues to meander uphill, reaching Nichol Springs at coordinates 12u 0549208 5498548 and an elevation of 1450 m. There is a biffy and a shelter at the springs. The shelter contains a wood-burning stove and can be a welcome place to rest and eat lunch or a snack. Nichol Springs was once a campground but that use ended in 2002 when it became a "day-use" area only.

From the shelter the hike continues by climbing the stairs to the west, moving through a V stile in the fence at the top and continuing a short distance west to a signed junction at 12u 0549215 5498439. Turn right and continue 1 km to the meadows atop the plateau adjacent to the viewpoint overlooking Horseshoe Canyon.

From the viewpoint, turn north and follow along the meadow to the start of the Horseshoe Canyon Trail beside a kiosk at 12u 0548405 5498545. From that point the trail tracks north through meadows along the top of the plateau, essentially following the route of an old logging road. The meadows are resplendent with a variety of wildflowers. There are a couple of good viewpoints along the way, looking to the east toward Elkwater Lake. Continue on the trail to its end at 12u 0550715 5500912. At trail's end, simply cross the road and return to the parking area for the Beaver Creek campground. The loop should take about four hours to complete, depending on how often you stop.

ORCHIDS IN THE PARK

It is said that the Cypress Hills host the largest diversity of orchids of any place in the prairies. It is certainly fair to say that of all the plants found here, the orchids attract the greatest amount of interest and attention. The orchids are the largest family of flowering plants on earth, with estimates ranging from 22,000 to 35,000 species in almost 900 genera worldwide. To put that into perspective, that is about four times the number of species of mammals on earth, and twice the number of birds. The overwhelming majority of orchid species are found in warm, humid tropical areas, so it is quite understandable that some visitors may be surprised by their presence here. Of the orchids in the park, some are relatively common, some are rare, and a couple are extremely rare. Mid-June is usually a good time to look for orchids in the park. Please remember that it is illegal to pick any flowers inside a park, whether provincial, interprovincial or national.

Most authorities will tell you that the name "orchid" is derived from the Greek *orchis*, which means "testicle," referring to the resemblance between male genitalia and the paired subterranean tuberoids of many species of orchids. To be slightly more expansive, however, in Greek mythology Orchis was the offspring of a nymph and a satyr. During a feast for Bacchus, the god of wine, Orchis attempted to rape a priestess, an act that so enraged Bacchus that he directed wild beasts to tear Orchis into tiny pieces, which they did. The gods were hugely offended by Orchis's behaviour and refused to put him back together. Instead, they broadcast his parts into the world, and where each piece landed, it became a beautiful flower. Orchis's testicles were the last pieces cast out. When they were thrown into the sea, they united with sea foam to produce Aphrodite, the goddess of love. Orchids were once thought to be a powerful aphrodisiac for both people and animals.

Orchids are primitive plants and the tiny seeds lack stored food. Because of this, each seed depends on the presence of a specific fungus for

germination and development, and further depends on the fungus to transfer water and nutrients from the soil to the seedling. For these reasons, attempts to transplant orchid species virtually always end in failure. Enjoy these treasures where you find them, and take extra care not to damage the delicate plants or their environment. Do not pick these flowers – doing so will kill the plant. What follows is a brief description of several of the orchid species found in the park.

Round-leaved Orchid
Amerorchis rotundifolia (also *Orchis rotundifolia*)

The smooth flowering stem on this tiny species usually stands no more than 30 cm tall. It occurs in well-drained parts of bogs and swamps, along streams and in cold, moist, mossy coniferous forests. The flowering stem supports 2–15 flowers, occurring in an open cluster scattered along the upper one-third of the stem. The flowers are irregular, with three white to pink sepals. The upper sepal combines with the upper two purple-veined petals to form a hood. The two lateral sepals are wing-like. The lowest petal forms a white to pink, oblong lip, spotted with dark-red or purple markings. The solitary leaf is basal, broadly elliptic and up to 9 cm in length.

In addition to this species, the park is home to a very rare variety in which the spotting on the lip is absent, replaced by a purple striping.

This lovely small orchid is fairly common and widespread in Alberta. The greatest profusion of the plant that I have ever witnessed is in Griffith Woods Natural Environment Park, along the Elbow River in Calgary, adjacent to the community of Discovery Ridge. The bloom usually occurs there in mid- to late June and almost needs to be seen to be believed.

Venus Slipper
(Fairy Slipper, Calypso Orchid)
Calypso bulbosa

This sweetly scented Orchid is found in shaded, moist coniferous forests. The flowers are solitary and nodding atop a leafless stem. The flower has pinkish to purplish sepals and mauve side petals. The lip is whitish or purplish, with red to purple spots, stripes or mottling and is hairy yellow inside. Interestingly, the flowers contain no nectar, and their pollen is inaccessible to visiting insects, but their scent "tricks" insects to visit. The markings on the lip vary subtly to greatly from flower

to flower, causing insects to visit a number of individual flowers, probably "thinking" they are somehow different. Eventually the insects catch on to this deception and quit frequenting the flowers, by which time the flowers have been cross-pollinated. This small but extraordinarily beautiful flower blooms in the early spring, often occurring in colonies.

The genus name, *Calypso*, is derived from Greek mythology, Calypso being the daughter of Atlas. *Calypso* means "concealment," and is very apt, given that this flower is very easy to miss, being small, delicate, and growing in out-of-the-way places. The species name, *bulbosa*, refers to the bulb-like corm from which the flower grows. Venus was the Roman goddess associated with love, beauty and fertility – the Roman equivalent of Aphrodite in Greek mythology. The plant goes by many locally common names, including Fairy Slipper and Calypso Orchid.

Venus Slippers are fairly common and widespread. They usually bloom early, starting in mid-May. They prefer shady habitat, often among Lodgepole Pines.

THE CORALROOTS

There are three Coralroots found in the park, all preferring moist woods and boggy areas. They grow from extensive rhizomes which resemble coral. Indeed, the genus name, *Corallorhiza*, is derived from the Greek *korallion*, meaning "coral," and *rhiza*, meaning "root," a reference to the rhizomes. The plants are leafless but do have two or more bracts that sheath the flowering stem. Each plant produces a number of flowers arranged in a raceme toward the top of the stem. All Coralroots are saprophytes, i.e., a plant that absorbs its nutrition from decaying organic matter and lacks any green pigment (chlorophyll) used by most plants for food production. They may have some chlorophyll, enabling them to capture solar energy through photosynthesis, but they supplement that by parasitizing fungi in the soil. The Coralroots depend on a complex relationship with fungi in the soil for germination and survival. The plants are fairly common and widespread.

Pale Coralroot
Corallorhiza trifida

Grows to heights of about 15 cm and the yellow or greenish-yellow flowers are spread out along the thick, yellowish-green stalk, in a raceme. The flowers often have pale red dots on the lip.

The species name, *trifida*, is a reference to the three-lobed lip on the flower.

Striped Coralroot
Corallorhiza striata

This plant is usually taller than Pale Coralroot, and the pink to yellowish-pink flowers have purplish stripes on the sepals. The lowest petal forms a tongue-shaped lip. The stem is purplish, and the plant looks like purple asparagus when it comes out of the ground in the spring.

The species name, *striata*, refers to the striped markings on the flower. Of the coralroots, the Striped Coralroot has the largest flowers. Striped Coralroot is sometimes referred to as Madder-Stripes or Hooded Coralroot. There is also

an extremely rare variety of this orchid that has been reported in the park. It is like this species, but does not have the stripes on the sepals.

Spotted Coralroot
Corallorhiza maculata

This plant is usually about the same size as Striped Coralroot and has a purplish to brownish stem, closely resembling Striped Coralroot when young. The sepals and upper petals on the flowers are reddish purple, while the lip petal is white with dark-red or purple spots. The species name, *maculata*, means "spotted," a reference to the markings on the lip.

THE LADY'S SLIPPERS

These orchids occur in a variety of habitats but most commonly are found in boggy ground, damp woods and along stream banks. They take their common name, Lady's Slippers, from the fact that the lower petal forms a prominent pouch-shaped lip, resembling a small shoe. These plants can occur as solitary or may be found in bunches. There are four different Lady's Slippers that occur in Alberta, three of them in the park. Two of these are fairly common, while the third is relatively rare province-wide. The genus name, *Cypripedium*, is derived from the Greek *kupris*, meaning "Aphrodite," the Greek goddess of love and beauty, and *pedilon*, meaning "foot" or "slipper," thus "Aphrodite's slipper." Bees enter the opening of the "slipper" and cannot exit without being covered in pollen. All of these lovely flowers have suffered significant range reductions as a result of land development, picking and attempted transplantation, which virtually always fails.

Yellow Lady's Slipper (Yellow Moccasin Flower)
Cypripedium parviflorum (formerly *C. calceolus*)

The flowers are bright yellow and usually occur one per stem. The sepals and lateral petals are similar, greenish-yellow to brownish, with twisted, wavy margins. The "slipper" has purple dotting around the puckered opening. Yellow

Lady's Slipper was originally known as *Calceolus mariae*, which translates from the Latin into "St. Mary's little shoe." The species name, *parviflorum*, translates from the Greek as "small-flowered," which is rather confusing given that the flowers on this species are as large or larger than those of other members of the genus.

Sparrow's-Egg Lady's Slipper (Franklin's Lady's Slipper)
Cypripedium passerinum

This species has white flowers that are smaller than the other species of Lady's Slippers. The flowers have purple markings inside the lip, said to resemble the markings on the egg of a sparrow, thus the common name. The species name, *passerinum*, means "sparrow-like." The stems and leaves are covered in soft hairs, and the sepals opposite the "slipper" are short, stubby,

greenish-white and not as twisted as those on the Yellow Lady's Slipper.

Both the Yellow Lady's Slipper and the Sparrow's-Egg Lady's Slipper are relatively common in the province. Blooming time is usually mid-June.

Mountain Lady's Slipper
Cypripedium montanum

This plant is somewhat rare, and, as its species name would suggest, it usually appears at higher elevations. It usually has two or more white flowers per plant. The flowers are similar in size to those of Yellow Lady's Slipper.

The sepals and lateral petals are similar, greenish-yellow to brownish, with twisted, wavy margins.

THE TWAYBLADES

These small orchids prefer a cool, damp, mossy habitat. Their small size and preferred location make them easy to overlook. All members of the genus have flowers that appear in an open raceme scattered up the flowering stem. The distinguishing feature of Twayblades is the leaf structure. There are only two leaves and they appear opposite to each other part way up the stem. It is from this arrangement that the name Twayblade arises. In the park there are two members of the genus present: Heart-leaved Twayblade (*Listera cordata*) and Northern Twayblade (*L. borealis*). Heart-leaved Twayblade has white flowers on which the lip is deeply split, almost in two. Northern Twayblade is a more common species which has larger greenish-brown flowers that are oblong and only slightly cleft into two rounded lobes.

Rattlesnake Plantain
Goodyera oblongifolia

This orchid grows in shaded, dry or moist coniferous woods in the park. It is a single-stemmed, stiff-hairy perennial that grows up to 40 cm tall. The basal leaves are distinctive, with a white, mottled mid-vein and whitish lateral veins. The robust downy spike bears small, greenish-white flowers in a loose, one-sided or twisted raceme, with the lower flowers blooming first. The lip of the flower has a wide open mouth, pressed up against the overhanging hood.

The genus name com-memorates the 17th-century English botanist John Goodyer. The genus name, *oblongifolia*, refers to the shape of the leaves. Plantain comes from the Latin *planta*, meaning "foot," a reference to the broad, flat, foot-like leaves. The common name, Rattlesnake Plan-tain, originates from the mottled white markings on the leaves, which reminded early European settlers of the markings on a rattle-snake. Indeed, some Native peoples chewed the roots of the plant and applied the masticated substance to the bite of rattlesnakes and other venomous reptiles.

Northern Rattlesnake Plantain (*G. repens*), also known as Lesser Rattlesnake Plantain, has also been reported in the park. It is similar to this species, but it has a shorter inflorescence, smaller leaves with fewer white markings, and a more pronounced pouch on the lip of the flower.

Hooded Ladies' Tresses
Spiranthes romanzoffiana

This orchid is reasonably common in swampy places, meadows, open shady woods and lakeshores, and can stand up to 60 cm tall. The characteristic

feature of the plant is the crowded flower spike, which can contain up to 60 densely spaced white flowers that appear to coil around the end of the stem in three spiralling ranks. When newly bloomed, the flower has a wonderful aroma which most people say smells like vanilla.

The genus name, *Spiranthes*, is derived from the Greek *speira*, meaning "coil," and *anthos*, meaning "flower," referring to the spiral inflorescence. The species name honours Russian Count Nicholai Romanzoff, a 19th-century Russian minister of state and patron of science. The species was first discovered on the Aleutian island of Unalaska, when Alaska was still a Russian territory. The common name of the plant is a reference to the braid-like appearance of the flowers, similar to a braid in a lady's hair.

Tall White Bog Orchid
Platanthera dilatata,
(also *Habenaria dilatata*)

As the common name suggests, this plant favours wet ground, shaded woods, bogs, pond edges, and streamside environments. It grows up to 1 m tall and produces white to greenish, sweet-scented flowers in a spike-like cluster, with flowers distributed along the stalk. The flowers are waxy and small, with the lowest petal forming a lip that widens at the base. The flower also has a slender, curved spur. The lance-shaped leaves are prominently veined and fleshy, short at the base, longest in the middle of the plant and shorter at the top.

The genus name, *Platanthera*, is Latin for "flat anthers." The alternative genus name, *Habenaria*, is derived from the Latin *habena*, meaning "rein," a reference to the rein-like appendages on the lip, hence the source of the common name "rein orchid" often applied to members of the genus. The species name, *dilatata*, means "dilated," a reference to the expanded base of the lip on the flower. When blooming, this flower has a heavenly scent, variously described as of vanilla, mock orange and cloves. It is also commonly known as Fragrant White Orchid. Some Native peoples believed the plant to be poisonous to humans and animals, and used an extract from the plant to sprinkle on baits for coyotes and grizzlies.

Several related and similar orchids also occur in similar habitat in the park, including:

Northern Green Bog Orchid
Platanthera hyperborea,
(also *Habenaria hyperborea*)
Northern Green Bog Orchid has green flowers and fewer leaves than Tall White Bog Orchid.

Blunt-leaved Bog Orchid
Platanthera obtusata,
(also *Habenaria obtusata*)
Blunt-leaved Bog Orchid has greenish-white flowers, but no stem leaves. It has one or two rounded oval to lance-shaped leaves, but both are basal.

Bracted Bog Orchid
Coeloglossum viride ssp. *bracteatum,* (also *Habenaria viridis* var. *bracteata*)
This orchid was once included in the *Habenaria* genus. It differs from Tall White Bog Orchid by having a greenish flower, long bracts below each flower, and broader, oval-shaped leaves.

White Adder's Mouth
Malaxis monophylla
This orchid is one of the rarest in Canada, but it has been reported in the park. It is tiny, standing only 5–20 cm tall. The greenish-white flowers are also tiny. There

is usually only one ovate to linear leaf (sometimes two) and it is sheathing on the lower part of the flowering stem. Sorry, but no image available. I am still looking for it.

HOW TO GET THERE

Cypress Hills Interprovincial Park is 66 km southeast of Medicine Hat, Alberta. If you are travelling from Calgary, go east on the Trans-Canada Highway (Hwy 1) to Medicine Hat and then take the exit for Hwy 41 south. Hwy 41 will take you straight into Elkwater. If coming from Lethbridge, go east on Hwy 3 to Medicine Hat, connecting to the Trans-Canada and on to the exit for Hwy 41 south. If coming from Milk River, go east on Hwy 501 to its junction with Hwy 41 and then go north to Elkwater.

NTS map o72E/09 (Elkwater Lake).

Limber Pine

The Whaleback

Approximately 140 km south from Calgary, just north of the Oldman River, west of the Porcupine Hills and east of the Livingstone Range, lies an area known as the Whaleback. That name is applied because the ridgelines, which extend for approximately 20 km north/south, are said to resemble the silhouette of a recumbent whale when viewed from a perspective east of the area. The area comprises just over 200 km² and is important and unique because it encompasses one of the most extensive expanses of relatively unfragmented montane landscape in the whole of the Rocky Mountain region, if not in the whole of Canada. The area sits within the drainage basin of the Oldman River, and elevations range from 1250 m in the southeast to almost 1800 m at the top of the ridgelines. The Whaleback as a whole straddles the montane and subalpine natural subregions between the Porcupine Hills and the Livingstone Range, and is a transitional zone between the two. The habitat is diverse, with grasslands thriving at the lower elevations and on south- and west-facing slopes, and both deciduous and coniferous forest communities growing at higher elevations and on north- and east-facing slopes. The area is subject to a significant amount of chinook activity during the winter months, and those warm winds tend to blow away or melt snow for much of the winter, creating wildlife travel corridors and feeding areas that might not otherwise be available. The floral community in the Whaleback is very diverse and includes species normally associated with both montane and subalpine areas, as well as species found in the transitional areas between the two. Fauna in the area includes an estimated 150 species of birds (including long-billed curlew, short-eared owl, peregrine falcon, golden eagle and prairie falcon), 57 species of mammals (including elk, deer, moose, black bear, grizzly bear and cougar), ten species of fish, four amphibians and two reptiles.

The montane zone occupies only a very small area of the province, estimated to be only about 2 per cent of the total landmass. Most of the montane landscapes are located in major river valleys that lead east from the mountains. That being the case, most of the montane zone is occupied by human habitation and activities. The Whaleback is unique in that it does not have any human habitation, is not cut up by roadways and is still relatively intact. The forests here tend to be open and are interspersed with grasslands. Douglas Fir and Limber Pine are characteristic of the area, along with Lodgepole Pine, White Spruce and Aspen. Willows are locally common, particularly in the moister locations like streams, bogs and springs. The shrub community is diverse and includes Buffaloberry, Junipers, Wild Roses, Snowberry, Red-osier Dogwood, Saskatoon, Chokecherry, Bearberry, Honeysuckles and others.

The grassland communities in the Whaleback are dominated primarily by native rough fescue grasses. Of the fescue prairie that once existed on the plains of western Canada, only a mere 5 per cent remains today. The fescues are highly valuable forage for wildlife and domesticated livestock because they retain their high nutrient levels even during dormancy. As a rule, they are very hardy plants but they do have some downsides. They take a long time to become established and mature, they grow slowly, they are very susceptible to damage as a result of overgrazing, and they do not do well when competing with non-native grass species that have been introduced over the years. Once they are gone from an area, it is virtually impossible to replicate the previous regime by replanting. Protection and good husbandry are the best way of keeping fescue grasses viable.

The grassland community also includes a myriad of wildflowers. Common varieties include Blue-eyed Grass, Prairie Crocus in immense numbers, various Locoweeds, Brown-eyed Susan, various Beardtongues, Blue Flax, Buffalo Bean, Blue Clematis, Baneberry, Northern Bedstraw, Western Meadow Rue, Lupine, Yarrow, Geranium, Three-flowered Avens, Shooting Star, various Asters and Fleabanes, Paintbrush, Star-flowered Solomon's Seal and many others. Two of the more unusual wildflowers found on the Whaleback are Blue Camas (*Camassia quamash*) and Kittentails (*Besseya wyomingensis*).

The Whaleback represents the northernmost limit of the range of Blue Camas. It is not found in large numbers here, but it might be said to be locally common. The plant takes its genus name and common name

"Camas" from a Nootka or Chinook word, *chamas*, meaning "sweet." The species name, *quamash*, is the Native name for the plant. The bulbs of Blue Camas were an extremely important food to many Native peoples and early settlers, and they were also a much sought-after trade good. In fact, intertribal wars were fought over Camas gathering places. At one time, prior to the arrival of European farming practices, the plant was quite common in the northwest United States, and it remains so on Vancouver Island. Indeed, Victoria, British Columbia, was once known as "Camosun," which means "a place to gather Camas." The bulbs were gathered during or soon after flowering in the spring. Most often they were steamed in large pits for long periods to render them sweeter and more digestible. Following steaming, the bulbs could be eaten right away or they could be dried for storage or trade. Extreme caution must be exercised when gathering Camas as food. Blue Camas has two closely related plants – Death Camas (*Zigadenus venenosis*) and White Camas (*Zigadenus elegans*) – both of which are extremely poisonous if ingested and both of which often occur in the same habitats as Blue Camas. Without the flowers present, it is virtually impossible to distinguish Blue Camas bulbs from those of either of its poisonous relatives, and many Native peoples and early settlers paid the ultimate price for failing to properly distinguish one from the other.

Blue Camas was first collected for science by Meriwether Lewis and William Clark of the Lewis and Clark Expedition of Discovery, and they wrote more in their journals about this plant than all others. On September 20, 1805, Clark and an advance party were searching for food for the virtually starving members of the expedition when they came upon a group of Nez Percé Indians in the vicinity of the Lolo Trail in present-day Idaho. The Natives offered Clark and his men a "bread made of this root all of which we eate hartily." In June of the following year, on their return from wintering on the west coast, Lewis noted in his journal:

> ...the quawmash is now in blume and from the color of its bloom at a short distance it resembles lakes of fine clear water, so complete in this deseption that on first sight I could have swoarn it was water.

Kittentails is a small, early blooming plant that favours the dry, open grasslands and rocky slopes habitat in the Whaleback. The long-stalked leaves are mostly basal, oval to heart-shaped, and toothed on the margins. The stem has small, clasping leaves. The inflorescence is densely crowded in a spike atop the stem, resembling a bottle brush in shape and appearance. The individual flowers consist of two or three green sepals, two purple stamens, and a purple style with a button-shaped stigma. There are no

Clockwise from above: Blue Camas, blue grouse hen, blue grouse pair, Kittentails, Whaleback view, Whaleback view

PHOTOGRAPH: CHUCK MURPHY

153

petals. The whole plant is covered in fine, white hairs. The common name for the plant is said to arise because the flowering stalk was thought to resemble a kitten's tail. The genus name, *Besseya*, honours Charles Bessey, a 19th-century American botanist. The reference in the species name to Wyoming arises because the plant was first discovered there. Indeed, a locally common name for the plant is Wyoming Kittentails. Kittentails are relatively common on the Whaleback early in the spring, as they are in the Cypress Hills and on Jumpingpound Mountain.

As you move upward from the valley bottoms toward the ridgelines, copses of aspens are scattered in the grasslands. Higher on the ridges, particularly on the north- and east-facing slopes, are Douglas Firs, many of which are now old-growth trees up to 400 years old.

As you move higher toward the ridgetops on the Whaleback, you will encounter Limber Pines (*Pinus flexilis*) scattered among the rocky landscape. They are usually solitary, but if in groups, they present themselves as widely spaced among the rocks. The species is usually found on rocky ridges and slopes with southerly exposures. The trees are shade intolerant, frost hardy and drought resistant – all of which makes them well adapted to the ridgetops on the Whaleback. These extraordinary trees are most often gnarled, dwarfed, bent, windswept, deformed, contorted, twisted, misshapen and weathered – all of which imbues them with huge appeal as photographic subjects. This is particularly so when the lens places the pines in the broad landscape that they survey: rolling, grassy and forested hills with snowcapped mountains in the background and brooding, ominous clouds often scurrying across the sky.

Many of these trees are ancient. The oldest of this species on earth are more than 1,000 years old; the oldest on the Whaleback are said to be almost 600 years old. The trees grow very slowly, both by their nature and as a result of the harsh climate of their favoured habitat. The main stems or trunks seldom grow taller than 20 m; indeed, many never achieve even half of that on exposed slopes. Often the trunks are short, stout and deformed or crooked – more reminiscent of shrubs than trees. The bark is light grey and smooth when young, becoming dark-brown to black, checkered and roughly scaly with age. The limbs are thick, often appearing in whorls around the stem, and are spreading to ascending, with upturned tips. The lowest branches tend to be long and drooping, with ascending tips. The species name, *flexilis*, is a reference to the limbs. It is derived from the Latin *flexi*, which means "bent" or "pliable," and refers to the very flexible wood of the branches, an adaptation to allow the species to endure persistent high winds and to shed snow during the winter. The "leaves" are upturned, spreading evergreen needles that are triangular in cross-section. They occur in fascicles (bundles) of five needles bound together at the base by a deciduous sheath. The fascicles are densely crowded at the ends of twigs and branches. The needles themselves are entire – i.e., smooth to the touch when rubbed gently in both directions. The tree produces both male and female cones. The male cones produce pollen, and they are reddish and found in the spring at the bases of new growth. The female cones are the seed cones, and they are light green when young, turning brownish-yellow at maturity. The seed cones are 5–12 cm long and have no prickles, unlike virtually all other pine cones, which do have prickles. The seeds mature in their second year. When mature, the cones open in the autumn while still on the tree, spill the seeds on the ground and then fall off the tree during the winter. The seeds are eaten by a variety of birds and small mammals, as well as by grizzly bears. The cones are often stripped from the tree by Clark's nutcrackers, which play an important role in distributing the seeds.

THE WHALEBACK AND INDUSTRIAL DEVELOPMENT

While the Whaleback enjoys a certain amount of protection and special status today, that has not always been so. As a cautionary tale, a short review of some recent history is appropriate. In 1994 Amoco Canada Petroleum Ltd. (Amoco), as it then was, made an application to the Energy Resources Conservation Board (ERCB), the precursor to the present Alberta Energy & Utilities Board (EUB), for a permit to drill an exploratory sour gas well in the Bob Creek valley area of the Whaleback. The application was strongly opposed by local residents, the Canadian Parks & Wilderness Society and the Alberta Wilderness Association. Those intervener groups argued against the application on several fronts, maintaining, among other things, that:

- the Whaleback represents the largest intact part of the montane ecoregion remaining in Canada, and as such, it should be protected in perpetuity;
- manifest and cogent evidence exists to confirm the critical importance of the Whaleback as essential wildlife habitat and migration corridor for a number of species, including large ungulates and predators;
- the area has been traditionally used by local residents in a way that is sustaining its ecological value;
- the Whaleback provides unique and diverse habitats that support a variety of plants, birds and other species;
- the Whaleback is critical wintering range for one of Alberta's largest elk herds;
- the area has been sacred to local Native peoples for thousands of years; and
- the area is a spectacular wild place, and an industrial human presence should be excluded from such places.

Public hearings were held on the application, and after two weeks of presentations followed by three months of deliberations, the ERCB found that the application by Amoco was "deficient in key areas," and "inconsistent with existing land-use policies," and the application was denied. Following the decision by the ERCB, Amoco engaged in discussions with various interested parties, and those discussions eventually led to an assignment by Amoco of its mineral rights in the Whaleback to the Nature Conservancy of Canada. It was agreed that the Nature Conservancy would hold the rights until 2004, at which time they would be surrendered to the Crown and would never be re-offered for sale. At the time, Joseph H. Bryant, president of Amoco, said:

> We fully appreciate the national significance of this area. We are extremely proud to have played a role in ensuring that a living legacy, the Whaleback area, will forever benefit future generations. Creating this environmental legacy is the right thing to do. Our partnership with the

Nature Conservancy ensures that oil and gas activity will never occur in the Whaleback protected area.

Following this apparent victory in the fight to save the Whaleback, the Bob Creek Wildland Park and the Black Creek Heritage Rangeland were established in the Whaleback as protected areas.

However, as is often the case with issues involving sensitive environments, the dispute, like the opera, "ain't over until the fat lady sings." In 2003 Polaris Resources Ltd. of Calgary, acting as the lead partner of a joint venture consortium of oil and gas companies, acquired the freehold subsurface mineral rights to a half section (320 acres) of land that bordered on the protected areas of the Whaleback. According to regulations in force at the time, the proponent for drilling an exploratory sour gas well was required to hold the mineral rights to a full section (640 acres) prior to drilling. Polaris attempted to make a deal with the Nature Conservancy to obtain the subsurface rights assigned to the Nature Conservancy by Amoco, but the Conservancy turned them down flat. Not to be stopped by this refusal, Polaris then made an application to the Alberta Energy Utilities Board for a "forced pooling" of its lease with the one held by the Nature Conservancy – a mechanism that would force the Nature Conservancy to throw in its rights on 320 acres of land and become the very unwilling partner of Polaris et al. in their plans to drill the exploratory well. An order of forced pooling would almost inevitably lead to a licence to drill an exploratory sour gas well.

In the words of Yogi Berra, "this is déjà vu all over again." Opposition to Polaris's plans was swift, outraged and very vocal. In short order there were over two dozen interventions on the application and public hearings were held by the EUB. After the hearings and deliberations of the board, the application of Polaris was denied for various reasons, most of them dealing with the inadequacies of the company's plans on various fronts. Round two was settled in favour of the Whaleback. Will this be an end to the proposals for "development" of the Whaleback? It is probably best to never say never, while remaining attentive and alert.

In the meanwhile, you ought to plan a hike on the Whaleback. Be prepared to be awed, and make sure you bring the camera. As a suggestion, the area known as the Little Whaleback Ridge South is highly recommended. A hike on the Little Whaleback Ridge South involves an estimated elevation gain of 300 m, and once at the top there is a fair amount of up and down involved along the ridgetop. The hike starts in the valley of Bob Creek. During the hike you will be moving through a diversity of vegetation zones and will enjoy scenery that includes rolling grasslands, aspen woodlands, coniferous forests, limber pines and riparian areas. The map reference is NTS map 82G/16 (Maycroft).

The trailhead for the Little Whaleback Ridge South is at the end of the A7 access road (as described below) at coordinates 11U 0697109 5529913. From the trailhead, proceed north, cross Bob Creek at the ford and continue north, with the creek on your right-hand side. A short distance north, there is a trail junction. Stay straight. The right fork leads to the Beaverdam Creek Trail. Continue north as the trail climbs onto a bench covered with open grassland and patches of aspens. The wildflower community here can be quite diverse. As you go farther north, bear to the west and move gradually up the slope to the crest of the ridge. At the top you will be looking west over the Camp Creek valley. The Livingstone Fire Lookout is visible to the west. Once you reach the crest, you can move along it at will, enjoying the spectacular scenery in every quarter. If you are there in the early spring, keep an eye – and an ear – out for blue grouse which might be "dancing" on the ridge. The courting sound of the male blue grouse is often described as an owl-like hooting, but I have always associated it with a deep, almost moaning "oooomm" sound reminiscent of Asian holy men. When you are ready to return to your vehicle, move south on the ridgeline trail.

The ridgeline ends at 11U 0696010 5532093 overlooking a grassy slope that falls down to the southeast. Descend from here and in about 1 km the slope comes to the edge of a forested creek valley running east/west. Follow that edge down to Bob Creek and rejoin the trail back to the parking area, which is about 1 km south.

HOW TO GET THERE

There are two access points to the Whaleback. Both are approached over or through lands that are privately owned or are the subject of grazing lease dispositions to local ranchers. Stay on main roads only and park vehicles in designated areas only. Do not block gates or roadways and leave all gates as you find them. Do not smoke or light any fires, because fire risks are assumed to be always high in this remote area. Do not approach or harass livestock in any way.

From Calgary, travel south on Macleod Trail (Hwy 2) to its intersection with Hwy 22 (the Marquis of Lorne Trail) and turn west onto Hwy 22x. Continue west on 22x toward Priddis until you approach the intersection with Hwy 22. At that intersection, turn left (south) toward Turner Valley. Proceed south on Hwy 22 through Turner Valley, Black Diamond and Longview, then continue south from Longview. Three kilometres south of the intersection of Hwy 22 and Hwy 520 there is a small parking area on the right-hand side (west side) of the highway. Park there and hike along the gravel road heading west. This is the access to the North Whaleback area near Callum Creek.

If you wish to access the South Whaleback area, continue south from Callum Creek toward the bridge on Hwy 22 that crosses the Oldman River. The bridge is approximately 88 km south from Longview. Just before you cross the bridge, turn west on the Maycroft/A7 access road and proceed 13 km to road's end and the Bob Creek staging area. Park at the end of the road and proceed on foot. The road can be very slick in wet conditions, so be careful.

Note: Cattle are often grazing in the Whaleback area, so keep your distance and do not approach or disturb them. Hunting is allowed in the area in season, so if you are in the area during open hunting seasons, wear bright-coloured clothing and make some noise to make your presence known. Some of the roads are open to use by off-highway vehicles, so remain alert and cautious while hiking.

Red-tailed hawk

Ann & Sandy Cross Conservation Area

The Ann & Sandy Cross Conservation Area (ASCCA) sits just outside the southwest city limits of Calgary, and it is unquestionably one of the greatest gifts ever made to the people of Alberta. It is nothing short of astonishing that anybody would have the foresight, altruism, dedication and generosity to preserve this land. Without anything else, that makes the ASCCA unique.

Sandy Cross sprang from a distinguished line of Alberta pioneers. His mother was Helen Rothney Macleod Cross, the eldest of five children born to Colonel James F. Macleod and his wife, Mary Isabelle, née Drever. His father was Alfred Ernest (A.E.) Cross, who, among a myriad of other accomplishments, was a southern Alberta pioneer of repute who established the A7 Ranche and was one of the founders of the Calgary Exhibition & Stampede. Sandy Cross began accumulating ranchlands in the rolling foothills country southwest of Calgary in about 1945, and over the years his holdings became significant. He was a keen conservationist and was dedicated to the preservation of wildlife habitat from an early age, long before it might have been considered fashionable to be so interested. In 1987 Sandy Cross and his wife, Ann, donated 809 ha of their ranchlands to the Province of Alberta, stipulating that the lands would be held in perpetuity for the benefit of the public and would be operated as a nature conservation area. At that time the donation was the largest such gift of land in Canadian history, and it became the basis of the ASCCA. The Nature Conservancy of Canada was selected to be the operator of the lands. In 1991, following a successful fundraising campaign, Belvedere House was constructed on the property to be the education and administrative hub of the ASCCA. In 1996 Ann and Sandy Cross donated an additional 1130 ha to the ASCCA, and in that year created the Sandy Cross Conservation Foundation, recently officially renamed as the Ann & Sandy Cross Conservation Area, to manage the newly enlarged preserve. The foundation is a not-for-profit charity and is registered as such with the Canada Revenue Agency. Much of the ongoing work of the foundation is done by volunteers, who donate their time and talents to attend to such diverse duties as education, communications, area stewardship, general maintenance and habitat management.

The land that comprises the ASCCA is in a transition zone between the prairies and the rolling foothills. About half of the property is covered with aspen forest, about a tenth is native prairie and the balance is pastureland that is dominated by introduced grasses. There are a number of natural springs and small brooks in the valley bottoms. Approximately 40 per cent of the land is open to the public by appointment. The property is managed as a natural area, with some cattle grazing and hay farming practised on some of the lands. There is enormous biodiversity in both flora and fauna. It is said that the area is home to over 300 species of plants, including trees, wildflowers, grasses, sedges and others. The wildflower assortment in the ASCCA during the season is always impressive.

The bird population at the ASCCA is comprised of almost 150 different species, including one of the highest concentrations of red-tailed hawks in North America. The red-tailed hawk (*Buteo jamaicensis*), also known as red-tail, is one of the raptors – the birds of prey – which, with their hooked beaks, sharp talons and piercing eyes are perhaps one of the most fascinating groups of birds on the planet. The red-tailed hawk occupies a tremendously wide range of habitats from Alaska and northern Canada all the way to Panama and the West Indies. Indeed, about the only habitats it does not use are unbroken forests and the Arctic. The wide range of the bird is testified to by its scientific species name, *jamaicensis*, which is a reference to the island of Jamaica, where the bird was first described for science.

Hawks are classified based on their general body shape and flight habits. The most common groups of hawks are accipiters and buteos. The accipiters have long tails and short, rounded wings – adaptations that allow them to more easily move around in forested areas, chasing other birds, which are their primary prey. In Alberta the most common accipiters are the Cooper's hawk, the sharp-shinned hawk and the northern goshawk. The buteos, on the other hand, are broad-winged and broad-tailed – adaptations that are designed for soaring, the principal means of prey location among this group. Buteo species in Alberta include the Swainson's hawk, the broad-winged hawk, the rough-legged hawk, the ferruginous hawk and the red-tailed hawk. Interestingly, in Europe the buteos are generally referred to as "buzzards," and that term does not include the unrelated vultures, as it might in North America. What the Europeans call buzzards, the North Americans call hawks. It's one of those "you like tomato, and I like tomahto" things.

Red-tailed hawks typically are 45–65 cm in length, have a wingspan of 110–145 cm, and weigh between 690 and 1900 g. The females are the larger of the two sexes, outweighing the males by as much as 25 per cent. In the United States these hawks are often referred to by the colloquial name "chickenhawk," though they very seldom target chickens as prey. The plumage is highly variable and there are a number of colour variations in the red-tailed hawk population. Indeed, there are 14 recognized subspecies of the bird worldwide. Generally speaking, the underside of the bird is lighter in colour than is the back, and there is often a brown band across the belly. The tail is brick red above and pinkish below. The bill is short, dark and hooked. The legs and feet are yellow. Maturity is reached in three to four years. Mature birds have reddish-brown eyes, while immature ones have yellowish eyes. The voice of a red-tail is quite distinctive. It is described as a three-second-long, hoarse, rasping, wheezy scream of "kkeeeeer," which begins at a high pitch and slurs downward. The bird often vocalizes while soaring, and it will make a loud screaming protest when its territory is invaded by a rival hawk. As a general rule the red-tail is not aggressive toward other birds. Indeed, it almost has a Rodney Dangerfield "thing" going – "I can't get no respect" – and is quite often seen while being harassed by crows, magpies and even pesky songbirds. These hawks typically travel at speeds between 30 and 60 km/h, but might reach 190 km/h during a dive. Active flight is slow and deliberate, with deep wing beats. Much of its time is spent soaring. When doing so the wings are positioned in a slight dihedral, meaning to say that they are set at a slight upward angle from horizontal. In windy situations, the bird can also hover on beating wings above the ground.

Above: Western Wood Lily
Right: Crocus pair
Opposite: Prairie Gentian

165

The preferred habitat of red-tailed hawks is mixed forest and field, ideally with high perch sites like trees, bluffs and utility poles. Hunting is primarily done from such perch sites or by soaring, then swooping down to capture prey. Small mammals are the bulk of the diet, but red-tailed hawks are opportunistic feeders and will take reptiles and small birds on occasion.

These hawks are most often sexually mature at two years of age and they are monogamous for the most part. Courtship is aerial, with the birds flying in wide circles at great heights, performing dives and climbs as displays. Nests are made of sticks and most often are situated in trees. The birds use the same nesting territory for years, often returning to the same nest. Great horned owls are notorious for expropriating red-tailed hawk nests, and the owls start nesting much earlier in the year than do the hawks. If a new nest must be constructed, it is usually built within some close proximity to the old nest. The female will lay a clutch of one to three eggs, and incubation duties are shared.

In addition to birds, the ASCCA is also inhabited by a large variety of other wildlife, including occasional large predatory animals like bears and cougars, large ungulates like deer, moose and elk and an assortment of smaller mammals. In fact, the area is a very important habitat and wintering ground for an extensive herd of elk.

The ASCCA has a long involvement with research and educational programs focused on conservation and the environment. Many of the programs are directed at school-aged children, and it is common to see outdoor "classrooms" at work in the area. Outreach and continuing educational programs are also available for children and adults. Belvedere House is wheelchair accessible, as is a 2-km stretch of trails adjacent to the facility.

The public is welcome at the ASCCA, but that welcome is predicated on an agreement by the visitor to abide by the rules established to protect the area from being "loved to death." In that regard, all visitors are asked to pre-book their hikes by going to the foundation's website at www.crossconservation.org and clicking on the link "Book a Hike." Then just complete the simple form and submit it. From its inception until early in 2009 no admission was charged, but that policy has now changed in an ongoing effort to keep up with the administrative and operational overheads of the area. As of the summer of 2009 a modest admission fee of $2 per visit will be requested from all hikers in an effort to keep up with expenses. The procedure for paying the admission fee is explained at the entry kiosk beside the parking lot. Special arrangements can be made for large groups such as hiking clubs, so check with the administrative offices if you wish to book a group visit.

There are approximately 20 km of trails on the property, and they cover all of the ecozones contained within the area. Virtually all of the trails can be walked as loops, so the hiker is never called upon to double back on trails already covered earlier. There are also some lookout points along the way, with expansive panoramas of the Front Ranges of the Rockies to the west. A trail map of the ASCCA is available at the entry kiosk, and the trails are well signed on site. When you attend for a hike, come prepared. The trails are hilly and good hiking boots are recommended. Make sure you have a hat, warm clothing and raingear in the event of cold fronts and showers. The weather can change quickly here. Some of the trails take you well away from the parking lot and you may not be able to make a quick retreat to your vehicle. Carry water with you on the trail. Do not drink any surface water you might find during your outing. Make sure you have sunscreen and insect repellent. There are several available biffies in the area, so check their locations before setting out. There is a washroom available at Belvedere House. Should you have any questions before setting out, check with the staff at Belvedere House. Volunteers regularly walk the trails, so you may be able to direct questions to them should you encounter them while hiking. Bear in mind that this is a wildlife preserve and it is not maintained as a park. There are hazards in the area such as biting insects, fallen trees, holes and animal burrows, mud, ice, wild animals, water etc., as might be expected in any such preserve. Visitors use the area entirely at their own risk, and the ASCCA, as a condition of entry, disclaims any liability for injury or other damages that may occur or be sustained by anyone hiking any of the trails.

THE RULES FOR HIKES

When you arrive for your hike, park in the lot by the perimeter fence. Only vehicles performing official business for the ASCCA are allowed in the lot in front of Belvedere House. Step to the kiosk by the parking area, review the registration procedure outlined on the signage, complete the necessary paperwork for registration and user fee payment, and place the proper paperwork on the dashboard of your car. Volunteer Area Stewards are often on the land, so if you have any questions, please ask.

- All visitors must stay on the trails at all times. If you go off the trails you will be asked to leave the area.
- Do not approach or harass any wildlife. The animals you see here are wild, and you could be in danger if you approach them.
- Do not remove anything from the area. Do not leave anything in the area. Do not pick the flowers.
- No dogs, horses or other pets are allowed on site at any time.
- No fires or smoking are allowed at any time.
- No camping is allowed at any time.
- No hunting or discharging of firearms is allowed at any time.
- There are no food facilities on the site, so bring your own water and food for the day. There are no garbage receptacles on location, so be prepared to carry away anything you bring with you.
- The area is closed between 11 p.m. and 4 a.m.
- If you witness violations of the rules, please report them to the administration immediately.

The rules are intended to give the greatest amount of protection to the area while still allowing visitors to enjoy their experience. All of the rules are reasonable, and to my way of thinking they should not present any impediment to any visitor. In the final analysis the rules are really nothing more than a short canon of etiquette for all hikers, wherever they are visiting. You should plan to visit often, because each visit will be different from previous visits.

For further information on the ASCCA, you may want to consider obtaining a copy of *Paradise Preserved: The Ann and Sandy Cross Conservation Area* by local award-winning author Bruce Masterman. The book is available at local book stores or in Belvedere House. Royalties from sale of the book go to the Foundation for its ongoing works.

HOW TO GET THERE

Drive west on Hwy 22x (the Marquis of Lorne Trail) from Macleod Trail (or 37th Street) until you get to 160th Street, which is the first turn to the left after you pass the Calgary city limit sign. There is no sign on the highway marking the Cross Conservation Area. At 160th Street turn left (south) and carefully cross the eastbound lanes of Hwy 22x onto a gravel road leading south up a rise. Continue approximately 1.5 km to the end of the road and you will find yourself in the parking lot for the ASCCA. Walk south from the parking lot to get to Belvedere House and the start of the various trails. Only official vehicles are permitted past the parking lot. On leaving the parking lot at the conclusion of your visit, be aware that when travelling north on the access road there is a stop sign about halfway back to Hwy 22x.

Ann & Sandy Cross Conservation Area

Black-crowned night heron

Frank Lake

Approximately 50 km south from Calgary and 6 km east from High River sits Frank Lake, one of the best birdwatching venues in southern Alberta. The lake takes its name from Christopher E. Frank, who came to the area from Utah in the early 1900s and established a place nearby called Frankburg. Frankburg disappeared in the 1930s, but the lake lives on. The productive wetland, slough and shallow lake is of tremendous importance to a large number of species of birds, both resident and migrant. Indeed, it is considered by many to be one of the most important breeding areas in southwestern Alberta for water birds, marsh birds and shore birds. The margins of the lake are bordered by low-lying meadows and marshes. Most of the surrounding land has been cultivated and/or used for pasture, but there are some native grassland areas still surviving adjacent to the lake. The lake covers approximately 16 km^2 and has a meandering shoreline.

Frank Lake has had a history of becoming dewatered during times of prolonged droughts. For much of the 1930s and 1940s, and during the mid-1980s, the lake was dry for extended periods. In 1988 Ducks Unlimited Canada (DUC) became involved with a plan for revitalization of the lake. Working in conjunction with local industry and various levels of government, DUC put into place a remedial plan to assure adequate supplies of water for the lake so it could return to and remain at levels adequate to support breeding activities of birds who visited the area. The plan involved taking some water from the Highwood River, some treated wastewater from High River's wastewater treatment plant, and some effluent from the Cargill Foods Ltd. meat-packing plant located near High River. The water was sent to Frank Lake by pipeline. In addition to guaranteeing water levels in the lake, the wastewaters are being naturally treated by the production of wetland vegetation, which is taking up the nutrient loads found in the wastewaters.

While establishing stable water levels in the lake, DUC has also built other structures in and around the lake to enhance bird breeding habitat, including placement of nest boxes, construction of nesting platforms and building islands in the lake. The upland habitat adjacent to the lake is also being managed for the benefit and improvement of upland species of birds and other wildlife. Some of the land continues to be cultivated, some is still wild, and some is grazed in order to provide for a variety of habitats.

Over 200 species of birds have been recorded at Frank Lake over the years. Many are common and numerous, some are rare and elusive.

BIRD SPECIES AT FRANK LAKE

American Avocet	American Coot	American Crow
American Robin	American White Pelican	American Widgeon
Baird's Sandpiper	Baird's Sparrow	Barn Swallow
Black Tern	Black-billed Magpie	Black-capped Chickadee
Black-crowned Night Heron	Black-necked Stilt	Blue-winged Teal
Brewer's Blackbird	Brown-headed Cowbird	Bufflehead
California Gull	Canada Goose	Canvasback
Cinnamon Teal	Clarke's Grebe	Common Goldeneye
Common Merganser	Common Raven	Common Redpoll
Common Tern	Common Yellowthroat	Double-crested Cormorant
Eared Grebe	Eastern Kingbird	European Starling
Ferruginous Hawk	Forster's Tern	Franklin's Gull
Gadwell	Great Blue Heron	Great Horned Owl
Greater Scaup	Greater Yellowlegs	Green-winged Teal
Grey Partridge	Horned Grebe	Horned Lark
House Sparrow	Killdeer	Lapland Longspur
Least Sandpiper	Lesser Yellowlegs	Long-billed Curlew
Long-billed Dowitcher	Mallard	Marbled Godwit
Marsh Wren	Merlin	Mourning Dove
Northern Flicker	Northern Harrier	Northern Pintail
Northern Shoveller	Pectoral Sandpiper	Peregrine Falcon
Pied-bill Grebe	Prairie Falcon	Red-breasted Nuthatch
Redhead	Red-Necked Grebe	Red-tailed Hawk
Red-winged Blackbird	Ring-billed Gull	Ring-necked Duck
Ring-necked Pheasant	Rock Pigeon	Ruddy Duck

Savannah Sparrow	Short-eared Owl	Solitary Sandpiper
Song Sparrow	Sora	Spague's Pipit
Spotted Sandpiper	Stilt Sandpiper	Swainson's Hawk
Tree Swallow	Trumpeter Swan	Tundra Swan
Western Kingbird	Western Meadowlark	White-faced Ibis
White-throated Sparrow	Willet	Wilson's Phalarope
Wilson's Snipe	Yellow-headed Blackbird	

What follows is some more in-depth information on a short but diverse selection of some of the birds seen at Frank Lake.

American Avocet
Recurvirostra americana

It is commonly held that the American avocet is among the most elegant and handsome of birds. It is a large, long-legged, long-necked, long-billed wading bird that breeds in wetland habitat throughout the grassland and parkland regions of the province. The birds are 43–47 cm tall, with a wingspan of 72 cm. They have black and white underparts. The head, neck and chest are a beautiful rusty colour during mating season, reverting to grey during other times of the year. The wings are black on the outer half, white on the inner half, and crossed by black bars on the dorsal surface.

PHOTOGRAPH: RUSS AMY

173

The legs are greyish-blue, giving the bird the locally common colloquial name of "blue shanks." The bill is black and curved upward at the tip. The genus name, *Recurvirostra*, is derived from the Latin *recurvo*, meaning "to bend backward," and *rostrum*, meaning "bill," a reference to the shape of the avocet's bill. The eyes are dark brown. Females are slightly smaller than males, with a shorter, more curved bill. Their vocalization most often is a high-pitched, repetitive "kleek."

American avocets breed and live in shallow freshwater and saltwater wetlands in the western Great Plains during the summer months, extending from Alberta and Saskatchewan southward to New Mexico and the Texas panhandle. They can also be found along coastal areas in California and Texas. They winter mostly in California and Mexico. The nest is usually a scrape on the ground that is lined with grass or other vegetation, feathers, pebbles or other small objects. A clutch of four greenish-brown eggs with irregular dark spots are usually laid, and both sexes attend to the incubation of the eggs. Hatchlings are usually out of the nest within 24 hours of emergence, and the day-old chicks can walk, swim and dive to evade predators.

Avocets usually feed by wading in shallow water. They may locate food by sight or by sweeping their long bill from side to side through the water like a scythe. By this mechanism they capture insects, crustacea and seeds of aquatic plants.

Female American avocets have been known to lay one to four eggs in the nest of another female avocet, leaving them there to be incubated by the "surrogate" mother. This kind of behaviour may also extend to laying an egg in the nest of other species of bird. In turn, it has been known that other birds will sometimes lay eggs in an avocet nest, where they will be incubated as if they belonged there.

Avocets are usually quite aggressive when bothered by predators, often charging them, screeching a series of shrill calls that gradually change pitch, all the while approaching the interloper on a teetering gait with outstretched wings. They have been known to physically strike predator species. Other displays performed by American avocets include one where three to four individual birds face each other in a circle and stretch and weave their bills toward each other. At mating time, the male preens himself with water, gaining in intensity and energy to the point of frenzied splashing just before mounting the female. After coupling, the pair often intertwine their necks and run together as if in some kind of avian three-legged race.

Black-crowned Night Heron
Nycticorax nycticorax

The Black-crowned night heron is a stout looking medium-sized heron that is only rarely seen owing to its habits. It frequents ponds, lakes, streambanks, and other wet areas similar to the habitats used by other herons, only this one, as its name suggests, usually appears at dusk and hunts during the night. During the daylight hours the birds are usually asleep, perched in trees near their hunting territories. Many of the authorities say that the rather redundant genus and species name, *nycticorax*, means "night crow," or "night raven." My research has disclosed a subtle difference, however. *Nycticorax* is derived from the Greek *nyx* or *nyctos*, which means "night," and *korax*, which means "croaker," a reference, almost without doubt, to the harsh, crow-like nighttime squawking call of this bird. The confusion as to the etymology of the name may have arisen because the common raven is named *Corvus corax*, *corvus* being classical Latin for "raven," and, according to many authorities, perhaps incorrectly, *corax* is said to be ancient Greek for "crow" or "raven." In any event, it is quite clear that the night heron is not related to the corvids, which is a family of birds that includes crows, ravens, rooks, jackdaws, jays, magpies and several others.

The black-crowned night heron is the most widespread heron on earth, inhabiting North and South America, Africa, Asia and Europe. It stands 58–66 cm tall, with a wingspan of 115–118 cm, and a weight of 727–1014 g when fully mature. The sexes are similar, with the female being slightly smaller. As its name would indicate, it has a black head (crown) and back, grey wings and white body. In breeding plumage, it has two long, slender, white feather plumes that trail down from the back of its head, sometimes described as a "pony tail." This bird seldom stretches its neck to full extension, even while in flight. Its bill is black and stout and is used to grasp prey, as opposed to impale it. Its eyes are relatively large and bright red. Its legs are not terribly long, for a heron, and they are yellow most of the time, turning pink during courtship and nesting. Its call, like most herons, is a loud, harsh squawk, which puts one in mind of a noise made by somebody suffering a terribly painful sore throat. Indeed, one locally common name applied to the bird is "Quark," a name that suggests the sound the bird makes.

The bird hunts the water's edges, sometimes moving slowly, but more usually by standing still and waiting to ambush passing prey. It feeds mostly on small fish, crustaceans, frogs and other amphibians, small reptiles, aquatic insects, shorebird nestlings and the occasional small mammal. The nest is a platform made from sticks placed in a tree, where the female lays three to five greenish eggs. The chicks are born with their eyes open, covered with grey and white down. The nests are often found in colonies, and the roosts are communal. During courtship the male often displays by bobbing its head, vocalizing and shaking twigs in its beak. In many tropical areas of the world the birds do not migrate. North American populations usually winter in Mexico, the southern US, Central America and the Caribbean, then migrate to the great plains to breed.

Yellow-headed Blackbird
Xanthocephalus xanthocephalus

I don't suppose there is anything you could call a yellow-headed blackbird that would be more appropriate, what with its brilliantly yellow head and breast, black body, wings and tail and white wing patches. I would also guess that the taxonomist who gave it the rather redundant name *Xanthocephalus xanthocephalus* felt the same way, because *Xanthocephalus* is derived from the Greek *xanthium*, meaning "yellow," and *kephale*, meaning "head," ergo "yellow head." Take it as a given, this bird has a very yellow head.

Yellow-headed blackbirds are quite conspicuous in the reeds and cattails of the wetlands at Frank Lake and other such marshy areas in western North America. They breed in loose colonies, and their nests are attached to reeds and other upright vegetation at the margins of the water. The males are 21–26 cm long, have a wingspan of 42–44 cm, and weigh 44–100 g. The females are slightly smaller, with an irregular yellow colouring on the head and chest, and a dull grey-brown body, wings and tail. A male will aggressively defend a small territory in prime breeding habitat, and he may attract as many as six to eight females to nest in his area, though two or three is more the norm. The cup-shaped nests are constructed by the females from available vegetation, and the male will usually assist with nesting duties at only the first nest built in the area, ignoring all others after they are in place. The birds forage on the ground or in waterside vegetation, eating miscellaneous aquatic and terrestrial invertebrates, seeds and grains. After the breeding season the birds can usually be found in mixed-species flocks. They migrate to the southwestern United States and Mexico for the winter.

The yellow-headed blackbird is classified as a songbird, but one must have a very open-minded approach to such things to call the voice of this bird a song. The vocalization in the reeds is a harsh, scratchy cacophony of raucous, discordant noise that puts most people in mind of the squeaking made by a large, rusty metal hinge. Indeed, the noise is so bad that it is quite noticeable and distinct among the other more pleasant calls and songs in the wetland. The first time you hear this croaking coming from such a beautiful bird it will probably give you quite a surprise. It simply does not fit, sort of like a burly football lineman opening his mouth and having a high, reedy falsetto whining escape. And hear it you will, as the male yellow-headed blackbird stridently defends its territory not only against others of its ilk, but also against several other species it considers unwanted neighbours, such as red-winged blackbirds and marsh wrens.

Trumpeter Swan
Cygnus buccinator

The trumpeter swan is the largest North American waterfowl. The genus name, *Cygnus*, is the classical Latin word for "swan," and it in turn is derived from the ancient Greek *Kyknos*, who, in Greek mythology, was the king of a group of people called the Ligurians. The king was transformed into a swan by the gods and was placed in the sky as a constellation. The scientific species name, *buccinator*, refers to the call of the bird. A buccinator was a person in the ancient Roman army who played the buccina – a brass instrument used in encampments to announce watches and other significant events. The buccina is an ancestor to both the modern trumpet and trombone. In truth, the trumpeter is appropriately named. Its call is raucous, brassy, resonant and very reminiscent of somebody blowing random notes on a trumpet or bugle. When I hear it, I am put in mind of an old-fashioned bicycle signalling horn, which was operated by squeezing a large rubber bulb to force air through a reed mounted between the bulb and the mouth of the horn. Once heard, the call will not be forgotten and it will not be confused with any other bird species.

Trumpeter swans are easily identified by their large size, long neck, completely white plumage and black bill, legs, and feet. The adult males (cobs) are 145–163 cm long, have a wingspan of up to 3 m, and might weigh 15 kg or more – making trumpeters the heaviest of all North American birds. The females (pens) are somewhat smaller. Trumpeters only exist in North American, and most of them are found in the western parts of the continent. Some populations are migratory and others not. The Rocky

PHOTOGRAPH: RUSS AMY

Mountain population is only in Canada during the summer; they winter in Idaho, Montana and Wyoming. The Pacific Coast population summers in Alaska and winters in British Columbia. The population in Yellowstone National Park stays there year round. They have a particularly thick layer of down which makes them virtually impervious to cold.

In the early history of settlement in North America the birds were relentlessly hunted for their meat, feathers and skin. The primary flight feathers were said to make the very finest of quill writing instruments, and the down was sought after for its insulating properties. Owing to over-hunting and habitat degradation, the trumpeter came dangerously close to extinction early in the 20th century. In 1933 breeding populations of trumpeters were reduced to 77 in Canada and 50 in the United States. Since then, hunting trumpeters has been absolutely prohibited. Captive breeding and reintroduction programs have worked very well over the intervening years and have now restored the species to much of its traditional range. Estimates of the populations in North America now range to over 30,000.

Trumpeters favour large, shallow water bodies with abundant vegetation, so they are most often found in lakes, ponds and riverine areas. In some wintering areas, such as coastal British Columbia, they will also use shallow saltwater bays. They feed primarily on aquatic plants but may also eat terrestrial grasses and grains. Foraging is done most often by swimming, though they will also occasionally feed on dry ground. The birds will take food items off the water's surface but will also tip and extend their long necks to grab food below the surface. While feeding, the adults will often pump their large feet to create a current that dislodges edible roots from the lake bottom.

At the age of three to four years trumpeters will form breeding pairs, and the pairs often stay together for life. The life span in the wild is about 12 years, though they may live to 35 in captivity. Nests are built near a water body, often on small islands or on top of beaver or muskrat lodges. Nesting sites are reused from year to year, often by the same pair. The female builds or repairs the nest and then lays four to six eggs, which she incubates for about a month. The cob defends the nest from predators, though in truth the birds have few natural enemies other than *Homo sapiens*. The hatchlings are referred to as cygnets, and they stay with the parents for up to four months. The cygnets have grey plumage and yellowish legs and feet until about two years of age.

Trumpeter swans can easily be confused with tundra swans (*C. columbianus*), another large, white-plumed, long-necked, black-billed waterfowl that may frequent similar habitat. On close examination the tundra swan may be seen to have a small yellow patch or "teardrop" just in front of its eye, a more sloping bill and a habit of holding its neck straightly erect. The trumpeter has no yellow patch and its neck appears to kink slightly at the base. If you see a tundra swan that does not exhibit the yellow patch, it can be very difficult to distinguish from a trumpeter, unless it vocalizes. The call of the tundra swan is quite distinctive from that of the trumpeter. Its call is softer and more melodious, more like that of a goose. Parenthetically, tundra swans were formerly known as whistling swans, but that name did not refer to its vocalizations, but to the sound of its slow, powerful wing beats during flight.

Short-eared Owl
Asio flammeus

This medium-sized owl is often seen at Frank Lake because it frequently flies during the daylight, especially at dawn and dusk. Such animals are said to be crepuscular, as opposed to diurnal (active during the daytime) or nocturnal (active during the night). *Crepusculum* is Latin for "twilight." The genus *Asio* is a group of owls that are called "eared owls" because they have feathered tufts on the head that resemble ears. In the case of the short-eared owl, as one might expect from the name, these tufts are quite small and might be difficult to see

PHOTOGRAPH: RUSS AMY

from any distance. This owl is the most widely distributed of the genus, with a range that includes all of the continents except Antarctica and Australia. The species name, *flammeus*, is Latin meaning "flaming" or "the colour of fire," said to be a reference to the brownish-orange feathering on the bird.

The short-eared owl is a bird of the grasslands, marshes, meadows and open habitats. They are quite nomadic and seem to select their breeding location based upon the population numbers of favoured prey species. The birds are 33–43 cm long, have a wingspan of 105–107 cm, and weigh 200–500 g. The females are slightly larger than the males. These owls are tawny coloured overall, generally spotted above and streaked below. The tail and wings are barred. The eyes are large and yellow, and set in dark eye patches in broad whitish facial discs. The bill is black. The wings are long and narrow, and the primary feathers are modified to eliminate the noise of air flow, thereby allowing silent flight during hunting. The underside of the wings display dark patches at the elbow. During flight the birds exhibit deep, slow, stiff and somewhat erratic wing beats, a pattern that is often compared to the flight of a butterfly. Hunting is done primarily on the wing, flying low to the ground and swooping down on prey, but hunting from a perch in the manner of hawks is not uncommon. Prey items are usually small mammals but may also include songbirds and insects. The vole appears to be a favoured prey. These birds are usually silent except during nesting. Their natural enemies include other raptors like bald eagles, gyrfalcons, red-tailed hawks and snowy owls, as well as mammals like skunks, coyotes and foxes.

During courtship, the male will put on aerial displays of agility and manoeuvrability, swooping and diving to impress the female. At the beginning of each dive he extends his long wings under his body and slaps the wing tips together, producing an audible noise similar to that made by a flag being buffeted by the wind.

This is the only owl that actually builds its own nest. All of the other owls expropriate nests built by other birds or burrowing animals. The short-eared owl's nest location is chosen by the female. It is on the ground in a small depression that is excavated by the female. The nest may be sparsely lined with vegetation and feathers or it may be plain. The nests are concealed by low-growing vegetation, and the female may lay four to fourteen eggs, the number apparently being a function of the availability of food. The female attends to the incubation duties and the male feeds her during the process. Both parents attend to the hatchlings. The eggs are not all laid at one time, but the female begins incubation after the arrival of the first or second egg. This behaviour is referred to as asynchronous, meaning the hatching is not synchronized and the earliest laid eggs usually hatch before the eggs laid later. As a consequence of this behaviour, the later-hatched owlets are often killed – and sometimes eaten – by their older, larger siblings.

American White Pelican (Rough-billed Pelican)
Pelecanus erythrorhynchos

For many people, it seems to come as a shock that we actually have a migrating population of pelicans in Alberta. Over the past 35 years I have consistently floated and fished the Bow River downstream from Calgary. On too many occasions to remember I have been with companions, clients and acquaintances who are absolutely flabbergasted to see American white pelicans on the river. Some people express concern that the pelicans might have a detrimental impact on the gamefish populations in the river, but in my experience these birds are not a threat to the recreational fishery because they do not consume large numbers of gamefish, and they certainly do not target gamefish in their foraging. Indeed, in my view, their presence here is a positive indicator as to the health of the fishery. These birds are not fishing for fun, they are fishing for a living. If they could not get a meal here, they would leave.

The American white pelican is one of the largest birds in North America. It typically is 130–180 cm long, has a wingspan of up to 3 m, and weighs 5–8.5 kg. The males and females are virtually identical, except the males are larger. The birds have large bodies, short legs, short tails and webbed feet. They seldom vocalize except when nesting. The most distinctive feature about the pelicans is their huge beak, which can be 26–32 cm long in females and 32–37 cm long in males. Beneath the beak is a large throat sac which can hold up to 20 litres, giving credence to the old riddle about "what animal's beak can hold more than his belly can." The plumage is all white except for black primary and secondary feathers on the trailing edge of the wings. The black feathers are all but invisible when the birds are at rest with their wings folded, but they are clearly visible when the birds are in flight. Immature birds have light grey plumage and a brownish head and primary feathers. Typically, pelicans can live for up to 16 years in the wild or double that in captivity. Most of the American white pelican population winters on the Pacific Coast from California to Guatemala, on the Gulf Coast of the US, and along the lower Mississippi River. They migrate north to breed in the spring and return south in the early autumn.

In the breeding season, the throat sac, a patch of bare skin around the eye (the lore), and the feet of the breeding birds turn from a pale yellow to a vivid orange colour. This alteration is referred to in the scientific species name for the bird, *erythrorhynchos*, which is derived from the Greek *erythros*, which means "red," and *rhynchos*, which means "bill." Other changes include development of a pale yellow crest of feathers on the back of the head, and growth of a flat knob, or "horn," on the dorsal surface of the beak about one-third of the way back from its tip. This knob is shed after mating and egg-laying occur.

Nesting takes place in colonies, usually on isolated islands in both freshwater and saltwater lakes throughout the Great Plains and Mountain West. Nesting areas are used year after year. Individual nests are not much more than shallow depressions scraped in the ground, into which two to three eggs are deposited. Both parents share incubation duties. Usually only one chick survives. Pelicans are exceedingly intolerant of humans, even to the extent of abandoning a nesting colony if harassed. A number of breeding areas in Alberta have been designated as Seasonal Wildlife Sanctuaries and it is illegal to enter or approach within 800 m of such places.

American white pelicans have a diet that consists mostly of fish, but they will also eat the occasional amphibian and crustacean. Unlike their cousin the brown pelican, (*P. occidentalis*), American white pelicans do not plunge dive when feeding. They feed while swimming by dipping their large pouched bill under the surface of the water and scooping up their prey. American white pelicans are often observed hunting co-operatively in groups by lining up and driving prey fish into shallow water for capture.

On land, American white pelicans can look quite awkward, but they are real stars when it comes to flying. When in flight, they double their necks back against their shoulders. They are gregarious birds and usually fly in groups, sometimes in evenly spaced lines or "strings," and sometimes in V-shaped formations like geese. The are exceptionally graceful when in flight and are often seen soaring and gliding at great heights. If an anthropomorphism be allowed, it seems like they glide around just because it is so much fun – and they can do it.

Black-necked Stilt
Himantopus mexicanus

The black-necked stilt is an intriguing bird to watch as it struts around the mudflats and shallow water of Frank Lake. It is a relatively common shorebird across North America from Atlantic to Pacific to Gulf Coast, and it frequents both freshwater and saltwater marshes, flats, flooded fields and shallow ponds. It wades in the water to catch its food, and the red to pinkish legs seem ridiculously long and gangling when compared to the body size they carry. Indeed, it is said that this bird has legs that are longer in proportion to their bodies than any other bird, with the single exception being the flamingo. Not surprisingly it is also known by the locally common names daddy-long-legs and longshanks. The genus name, *Himantopus*, is also a reference to the legs of the bird. The name is derived from the Greek *himantos*, which means "strap" or "thong," and *pous*, which means "foot," the reference said to be that the legs of the bird are long and thin, like a strap or thong.

PHOTOGRAPH: RUSS AMY

Stilts are handsome birds. The adults stand 33–43 cm tall, have a wingspan of 68 cm, and weigh 136–220 g. The male has white underparts, throat and chin and is black on the wings and back. The black feathering extends upward from the back, along the hind portions of the rather long neck, and forms a cap on top of the head. The cap extends downward to surround the eye, except for a small white patch immediately above the eye. The bill is black, long and slender. During the mating season the black feathers often display a greenish gloss. The females are similarly marked, but their backs tend to be brownish, not black. Both sexes have long, pointed wings. Their feet are somewhat webbed, but these birds are far more often seen walking rather than swimming.

The black-necked stilt persists on a diet comprised mostly of crustaceans, small fishes, tadpoles, insects and seeds. It gathers food by picking it off the surface of the water or occasionally by probing with its long bill. Its enemies include foxes, skunks, coyotes and some other birds, most particularly the gulls.

The stilt is sexually mature by the age of one, and it nests on the ground near water. The nest is rudimentary at best, often consisting of not much more than a scrape on the ground that may or may not be lined with grass and twigs. A typical clutch consists of three or four tan-coloured eggs that exhibit irregular dark spotting. The chicks are able to walk, run and swim within a day of hatching. Both parents share in nesting duties. After the chicks are hatched, the parent birds remove all shell fragments from the nest. It is speculated that this is done to promote camouflage for the nest's location. The birds will often form nesting colonies of six to ten nests. The males in the colony co-operate to defend the nests from interlopers by mobbing or swarming intruders to drive them away. When the birds are agitated or disturbed they make a repetitive, continuous, sharp yipping noise.

The black-necked stilt is quite prepared to use man-made structures for habitat and they are often seen in places like ditches, evaporation ponds and sewage treatment lagoons. As a consequence, their range is increasing.

Western Meadowlark
Sturnella neglecta

This familiar songbird is a harbinger of spring in Alberta. The birds that nest here usually overwinter in Mexico, returning to the province in late March or early April. The western meadowlark is in the same family as blackbirds, and it inhabits open country in the western two-thirds of North America. It can often be seen perched on fence posts in grassland country, singing its distinctive and beloved, melodic, flute-like song, so familiar and popular with human inhabitants of the prairies. As testimony to its popularity, it is the official state bird of no fewer than six of the United States – North Dakota, Kansas, Nebraska, Montana, Wyoming and Oregon – second only to the cardinal, which is the official bird of seven states. It was noted in the journals of the Lewis and Clark

PHOTOGRAPH: RUSS AMY

Expedition, but was mistakenly thought by Meriwether Lewis to be the same bird he knew as the eastern meadowlark (*S. magna*). That mistake persisted for some time, and when corrected, attracted the scientific species name *neglecta*, which, of course means "neglected" or "overlooked."

The western meadowlark is a stocky bird, 16–26 cm long, with a wingspan of 41 cm, and weight of 90–115 g. Its throat, chest and belly are yellow, with a distinctive, black, V-shaped patch stretched across its upper chest like a bib. Its head is black-and-white striped, and its bill is long and pointed. It has a short tail and the outer tail feathers are white. Its back is speckled in tones of brown, white and black. The sexes are similar in appearance, but the female is not as strongly marked. Meadowlarks forage on the ground picking up a cornucopia of invertebrates including beetles, worms, caterpillars, grasshoppers, crickets, spiders and sowbugs, as well as plant seeds and grains. Nests are on the ground and are constructed in a cup shape from dried grasses, barks and other vegetative materials woven into the surrounding vegetation. The nest may be open at the top or it may have a partial or full roof made from woven grass. Indeed, it is not unheard of to find a nest that has a grass entry tunnel several feet in length. It is not unusual to have more than one nesting female in a male's territory. The female attends to the nest and the incubation duties. She always walks away from the nest before flying, as a strategy to keep the nest's location a secret. The bird's predators are numerous and include hawks, falcons, crows, skunks, foxes, weasels, coyotes and raccoons.

The western meadowlark is very similar in appearance to the eastern meadowlark, but the eastern version has a simpler vocalization and its song is not warbled. Where the two birds have overlapping ranges, hybridization between the two species is rare. Interestingly, where both species nest in the same area, the western meadowlark male will defend the territory against all meadowlarks of either species.

Prairie Falcon
Falco mexicanus
The genus name, *Falco*, is said to be derived from the Latin *falx*, which means "sickle," and is thought to be a reference to the shape of either the

talons, the beak or the spread wings of birds in the genus. The specific epithet, *mexicanus*, refers to Mexico, one of the places, along with the western United States and southwestern Canada, where this falcon is commonly found. The prairie falcon is about the same size as the peregrine falcon, and those two species are the largest falcons in North America. The prairie falcon has a reputation of being the most aggressive of the falcons.

The prairie falcon is primarily found in arid to semi-arid open areas like grasslands and rangelands, but can also thrive nicely in desert and high alpine environments. It is 40 cm in length, has

PHOTOGRAPH: RUSS AMY

a wingspan up to 1 m, and weighs about 700 g. The females are slightly larger than the males. The birds have large, dark eyes, a dark-bluish bill that is yellow at the base, a pale face and throat and a white line over the eye. Its back is brown with paler fringes, and its tail is brown with faint dark bands. The wings are long and pointed, dark above and light underneath, with a distinctive dark, triangular-shaped marking in the "armpit" area of the underside. When the bird is at rest, the wingtips do not extend to the end of the tail. The whitish underparts have a few dark streaks on the breast and spots on the belly. The voice is a high-pitched, repetitive "kree" or "kik" sound.

The prairie falcon's diet consists mainly of small mammals like ground squirrels, chipmunks and rabbits, as well as songbirds, shorebirds, pigeons, waterfowl and gallinaceous birds like grouse, pheasants and grey partridge. The birds are usually solitary except during courtship, but have been known to congregate near ground squirrel colonies during the summer months. It is not unknown to have a prairie falcon become adapted to urban environments, particularly during the winter months when it can catch overwintering songbirds. Hunting may be done from a perch, swooping down to capture prey, or by flying low over the ground and surprising prey. Cruising speed is usually about 70 km/h, accelerating if in chase. In flight, the wing beats tend to be quick, shallow and stiff. Most avian prey are caught in flight. It is not unusual for these birds to cache food for later use.

Nesting is done on scrapes on cliff ledges, with little nest-building involved. The clutch typically consists of four eggs. The female attends to most of the incubation and brooding duties, with the male delivering most of the food during nesting. Prairie falcons are sometimes seen to share nesting cliffs with ravens, golden eagles and red-tailed hawks.

Eared Grebe (Black-necked Grebe)
Podiceps nigricollis

When in breeding plumage, the eared grebe is quite a handsome small water bird, with its dark bill, jet black head, neck and back, a spray of yellow feathers flowing backward from behind the bright red eyes, and its chestnut-coloured flanks. The sexes are similar in appearance, but are seasonally dimorphic, which means their appearance changes dramatically from breeding to non-breeding stages. In non-breeding plumage the birds

PHOTOGRAPH: RUSS AMY

are a rather drab black, white and grey, with a poorly defined black cap. The birds are 28–34 cm long, and have a wingspan of 58 cm.

The eared grebe is considered to be the most abundant grebe in the world, with at least three subspecies distributed on all continents of the globe, with the exception of Australia and Antarctica. The North American subspecies is *P. n. californicus*, and it breeds in shallow ponds, lakes and marshes in the western parts of the continent. It is a common sight on prairie sloughs. It winters in the southwestern US, Mexico and Central America.

Eared grebes breed colonially in vegetated areas at water's edge. The nests consist of floating platforms of decaying vegetation. A clutch is usually two to four eggs, and the hatchlings are often seen riding on the back of a parent bird. Eared grebes are excellent swimmers and divers, often pursuing prey underwater. Their diet consists of small fish, crustaceans and aquatic insects and larvae. They usually escape danger by diving rather than flying. They seldom vocalize except during the breeding season.

The genus name, *Podiceps*, is derived from the Latin *podex*, which means "vent" or "anus," and *pes*, which means "foot." The reference is to the point of attachment of the bird's legs, which is at the extreme back end of the body. As a result of this placement of the legs, grebes generally are awkward when on land and do not walk well. Indeed, grebes, along with loons, are unable to achieve flight from land; they must start from the water. This condition can become problematic in the extreme if the birds get surprised, as they often seem to, by an early freeze-up on the pond where they are sitting. The specific epithet, *nigricollis*, is derived from the Latin *niger*, meaning "black," and *collis*, meaning "neck," an appropriate description of the bird when in breeding colours.

White-faced Ibis
Plegadis chihi

This medium-sized, long-legged, long-necked wading bird takes its genus name, *Plegadis*, from the Greek *plegas*, which means "sickle," and is a reference to the sickle-shaped, downward-curving bill of the bird. Such bills are referred to as "decurved." The birds nest in the Great Plains of

PHOTOGRAPH: RUSS AMY

central and western North America, and winter in the southern United States and Central America. They have a close relative in the glossy ibis (*P. falcinellus*), and the two birds are very difficult to tell apart when not in breeding plumage. The glossy ibis is a bird of eastern North America, however, and it does not frequent the West.

The white-faced ibis stands 46–56 cm tall, has a wingspan of up to 1 m and weighs 450–525 g. The sexes are similarly coloured. The breeding plumage sees the head, neck, back and belly coloured an iridescent purplish-red chestnut hue that might appear dark or even black in low light or at a distance. The wings and tail are bronze and iridescent greens. The legs and eyes are red. On a bird, the small patch of skin between the eye and the bill is called the "lore." On a white-faced ibis in breeding colours, the lore is bright red and it is ringed entirely by an evenly wide, unbroken band of white feathers, which makes its face look white and is the source of the bird's common name. When the bird flies, it does so with its neck outstretched, and its long bill is distinctive. The birds feed on insects, amphibians, worms, snails, small fish and crustaceans.

The ibis breeds colonially in marshy areas, nesting on roosts on low platforms, mud banks, short bushes or low trees near the water. The nest is a deep, cup-shaped affair lined with grasses. The female lays three or four greenish-blue eggs, and the nesting duties are shared by the parent birds. Ibises are usually quiet, though they will sometimes give a series of low, duck-like croaks or rattles.

DUCKS

The word "duck" is said to be derived from the Anglo-Saxon *ducan*, which means "to dive," a reference to the way many species of waterfowl feed, either by tipping or upending, or indeed by completely submerging. At Frank Lake, several broad categories of ducks are present in the population, including divers, dabblers, fish-eaters and one species of stiff-tailed ducks.

Diving ducks are sometimes referred to as "bay ducks," because they tend to inhabit large bodies of water like lakes and bays. Most of them have short tails and large feet, and they can only take flight by running along the water before becoming airborne. They feed by diving completely beneath the water's surface and then swimming down to food items. They also will use diving as an escape technique when danger presents itself. They submerge and go long distances underwater before emerging, sometimes coming up only to take a quick, needed breath of air, then disappearing again to continue fleeing. Diving ducks at Frank Lake include redheads, canvasbacks, ring-necked ducks, greater scaup, common goldeneye and buffleheads.

Dabbling ducks are sometimes referred to as "surface feeding ducks" or "puddle ducks," because they usually feed by dabbling rather than submerging. Dabbling is a feeding technique wherein the head and neck are submerged by tipping, while the body and tail remain above the surface of the water. Dabbling ducks can usually walk on land with some ease, and they can take flight without the necessity of first running. Most of these ducks also have brightly coloured, iridescent patches on the wings, called speculums. The dabbling ducks at Frank Lake include mallards, pintails, gadwalls, widgeons, shovellers, blue-winged teal, cinnamon teal, and green-winged teal.

Fish-eating ducks are represented at Frank Lake by the common merganser (*Megus merganser*). The male of this species has a glossy, dark-green head, a black back and white sides. He looks quite dapper. The female has a dull grey body with white neck and chin, and a rusty red head that looks like it is experiencing a permanent "bad hair day." Both sexes have long, red to orange, tapered bills that have toothy projections along the edges to assist in holding on to slippery fish. These birds feed by submerging and pursuing fish underwater. Interestingly, the young of this species leave the nest within a day or so of hatching, and they catch their own food of aquatic invertebrates immediately. The parent mergansers are not called upon to feed the young at all after hatching.

The ruddy duck (*Oxyura jamaicensis*) seen at Frank Lake is the only North American member of a group called the "stiff-tailed ducks." Indeed, the genus name, *Oxyura*, is derived from the Greek *oxys*, which means "sharp," and *ura*, meaning "tail." It is a small, stubby, short-necked, large-billed bird that has stiff tail feathers that are usually held straight up or at a jaunty angle as it swims. If ducks could be said to have personalities, this one, by common agreement, would be called a class clown. It has a dark head, white cheeks, and a sky-blue bill. It is very enthusiastic in its displays,

PHOTOGRAPH: RUSS AMY

often pattering quickly across the water, pumping its bill faster and faster, slapping it against his inflated breast generating a hollow, thumping sound, all while water is strewn around. Another conspicuous activity is when it races across the surface of the water toward a potential mate, its feet making a popping sound on the water, then abruptly stops, skidding to a halt near the female – all as if to say "what do you think of me now?" Many times the females seem unimpressed, leaving the unrequited Lothario with nothing to show for his troubles.

HOW TO GET THERE

From Calgary, go south on Hwy 2. From the intersection of Hwy 2 and Hwy 22 (the Marquis of Lorne Trail), continue south for 41.3 km to the junction of Hwy 2 and Hwy 23. Take the exit off Hwy 2 and proceed east on Hwy 23, following the signs to Blackie and Vulcan. Approximately 5.5 km east of the junction, slow down. The highway starts a decided left-hand bend to the north. Just before that bend, turn onto a dirt track on the right-hand side of the highway and follow that track to a gate which is signed for Frank Lake. You can park near the gate and proceed on foot or travel the narrow lane in a southerly direction to another parking area beside the lake.

There is also an access on the opposite side of the lake. To reach that access, return to Hwy 23 and turn right. Follow the highway as it bends to the north, then east and then south. After travelling 8.7 km, turn right to exit the highway going south onto 232 St. E., a gravel road. Follow that road south for 3.2 km and turn right (west) onto 562 Ave. E., beside a "No Exit" sign. Follow that roadway west for 2.3 km to the shoreline of the lake. Note: if conditions are wet, be very cautious on the narrow laneways around the lake. They can become extremely slick during wet weather, and getting stuck is a decided possibility.

There is also an access on the south end of the lake. To get there, travel 6.4 km south on 232 St. E. to its intersection with 594 Ave. E. and turn right. Proceed 1.7 km to a parking lot on the right-hand side of the road, just west of a canal crossing. Park in the lot and walk north to reach the shoreline. There is a Ducks Unlimited sign at the parking lot.

To return to Hwy 2, retrace your steps.

PHOTOGRAPH: RUSS AMY

Middle Lake looking west

Bow Valley Provincial Park

People often ask me for recommendations as to places they should investigate for wildflowers. What they usually want is a place to have a pleasant outing, that they can get to reasonably quickly, that is not too physically rigorous or demanding, and where they may see some interesting and beautiful things. One of my first suggestions is always Bow Valley Provincial Park. When I make that suggestion, the almost universal response, even from long-time Alberta residents, is: "Oh really? Where is that?" That response always confounds me, given that Canmore and Banff are regular ports of call for many southern Albertans, and you cannot get to those places without literally driving right through Bow Valley Provincial Park. The park seems to be a well-guarded secret, but more probably its prospects are discounted because it may appear to be *too* easy to get to – a sort of "too good to be true" thing. But believe me, this one is good and it is true.

Bow Valley Provincial Park covers just over 930 ha at the confluence of the Bow and Kananaskis rivers, just east of the Front Range of the Rocky Mountains. It is crammed with a tremendous diversity of mountains, meadows, forests, foothills, springs, lakes and rivers. The scenery throughout is spectacular, with mountain vistas in every quarter. The trails are well signed and maintained, they are easily accomplished by hikers of whatever age, experience and physical condition, and they provide an opportunity to walk a series of easy loops through different habitats. During spring and summer, particularly the last half of June and first half of July, the wildflowers are numerous and diverse, including some unusual and rarely seen species. The birdwatching is spectacular anytime, with everything from bald eagles to hummingbirds inhabiting the park. Wildlife is abundant and sightings are relatively common. Pleasant picnic areas are comfortably and conveniently located. Camping is available if you are so inclined. If there is a downside here, it would have to be that this park does not have the feel of the "wilderness" or isolation that one gets when several kilometres up a trail in the backcountry. Yes, people do frequent the area, but you never get the feeling of being crowded when you are on the trails. And perhaps best of all, if your time is limited, this venue gives you the best "bang for your buck" of anyplace in the Kananaskis region.

If you are not in a rush, try the following loop. Enter the park and follow the meandering main road to the parking lot at Middle Lake. Park in the lot and walk west toward the lake on the Moraine Trail. At the T intersection beside the lake, turn right and wind around a portion of the east and then the north perimeter of the lake. Take the next right turn and move up a short incline to cross the main park road and head north across a rocky, open meadow. You will soon come to a T junction with a trail coming in from the left. Stay straight. You will return to this junction later, approaching on the trail on the left.

Check out the interpretative signs as you go and you will find that a moraine is a landform composed of an accumulation of sediment and debris deposited by a glacier. Glaciers were no strangers to this part of the world, and their periodic advances and retreats had a lot to do with how the landscape appears today. In this case, the moraine was formed from debris carried by an ice sheet that broke off the Bow Glacier thousands of years ago. As it melted, the debris entrained on and in the ice was deposited, forming long winding ridges, terraces and depressions. Because the ice was stagnant, the landforms here are referred to as a dead-ice moraine. As you walk along the trail, depending on the time of the year, you will be treated with a myriad of wildflowers including Early Yellow Locoweed, Prairie Crocus, Brown-eyed Susan, Harebell and many others.

If you pause briefly in a clearing and look to the north, you will see a mountain with a very distinctive flat face. If you are unfamiliar with the area, this mountain is unofficially called Yamnuska, a name that is derived from the Stoney word *Îyâmnathka* and means "wall of stone." Officially the mountain is known as Mount Laurie, it having been renamed in 1961 at the request of the Stoney Indians. It's official name honours John Laurie, an educator and political activist who came to Alberta in 1920 and became a lifelong outspoken advocate for local Indians. Laurie was one of the founders of the Indian Association of Alberta, and he is fondly remembered for his efforts. On a stone monument on the nearby Stoney Reserve the inscription reads in part:

"...His efforts improved the condition of the Indian, and created friendship, equality and understanding between Alberta Indians and other citizens. Over the boundaries of colour and race swept the will of the Great Spirit."

"The Yam," as it is affectionately known to local rock climbers, is the most easterly mountain in the Bow Valley, and it is composed of 600-million-year-old Paleozoic limestone thrust over 100-million-year-old Mesozoic sandstone. The mountain face is mostly vertical or even overhanging, and it stands 350 m tall and extends for almost 2 km side-to-side. Rock climbers started using the mountain in the 1950s to hone their skills, and there are now over 100 different recognized routes on the cliff face. Yamnuska is a dominant fixture in the mountain vistas seen from the park. Should you be interested in doing so at some other time, there is a hike that takes you up to the eastern shoulder of the mountain, where the view of the Bow Valley is spectacular.

As you continue along the meandering Moraine Trail you will soon see a powerline right-of-way in front of you. Stay on the trail, bearing downhill to the left and continue past a large amphitheatre on your right. Stay on the trail through the campground and you will soon arrive at the Bow River. Turn left and head upstream on the trail. If the river is in spate, carefully avoid getting too close to the edge. The banks are subject to erosion from high water, and they could crumble under your feet, depositing you in the cold, fast water. As you move upstream, look for waterfowl, ospreys and eagles, all of which are regular visitors to the area. Before long you will arrive at the Whitefish day-use area parking lot. There are picnic tables and biffies at Whitefish, so if a break is needed, this would be a convenient place to rest.

From the east end of the Whitefish parking lot, you can pick up the trail and follow it up the hill moving south. After going about 400 m you will come to the park road once again. Cross the road and turn right into the parking lot for Many Springs. In this area it is best to keep to the established trails because much of the environment is delicate and can be easily damaged. The trail from the Many Springs parking lot leads generally west for a short distance, then splits. Go right and follow the path around the springs in a counter-clockwise direction. As you move down the gentle incline, keep your eyes open for orchids such as Yellow Lady's Slippers, Round-leaved Orchids and various Coralroots. Blue Columbine, Yellow Hedysarum and Western Wood Lily also bloom along this trail, so be alert. At the bottom of the incline the trail curves away to the left and approaches the springs. At high water the trail may get wet, but there are usually some boards to walk on to keep you out of the water. Along this stretch of trail you may be fortunate enough to spot Sticky False Asphodel, a member of the Lily Family that produces a sticky substance on its flowering stem that acts as natural flypaper, trapping unwary insects. The Sparrow's-Egg Lady's Slippers are often found along this stretch too. You will soon come to a bridge over the outlet stream from the pond. From there on, some of the trail is narrow and somewhat overgrown with willows and honeysuckles; some of it is on a boardwalk adjacent to the ponds. If the water is high you may want to gently test the boardwalk to make sure it will support your weight above the water before you commit to crossing it. If it looks dodgy, co-operate with other visitors by spacing everybody so the weight is distributed along the boardwalk. As of this writing the ponds are significantly larger and deeper than they once were before the beavers made a concerted effort to dam the springs and in the process raised the water levels considerably. On the far side of the boardwalk the trail enters a shady stretch. Look for Blue Clematis, Western Canada Violet, Fairybells and Baneberry along this stretch, particularly if you are there in the early part of the season. After coming to one more viewpoint over the springs with a splendid view toward Yamnuska, the trail will gradually climb as it comes back to where it split earlier. Continue straight and you will soon arrive back at the parking lot for Many Springs.

Skirt the parking lot to the right and continue up the trail, moving primarily east through the woods. You will soon cross the park road again and arrive at the Elk Flats group camping area parking lot. Continue on the trail, moving through undulating country with several rocky meadows. The next T intersection is the Moraine Trail, so turn right and cross the park road to the north side of Middle Lake. At this point you can finish your hike or take one more diversion before you quit. Follow the Moraine

Trail around the east side of Middle Lake and you can start a gentle climb into the woods to the south of the lake. The trail extends as a loop above and around the lake, eventually bringing you back to the parking lot. As you move up the trail, look for a miscellany of wildflower species, the makeup of which will change with the seasons. In the early season you will find lots of Three-flowered Avens, Prairie Crocus, Shooting Star and Sweet-flowered Androsace (Rock Jasmine). As the season continues these are replaced by such things as Paintbrush, Western Wood Lily and White Camas – also known as Mountain Death Camas.

Middle Lake is a glacial relic. As the Bow Glacier receded thousands of years ago, it left behind a ridge of debris known as a terminal moraine. A large block of ice broke off the glacier in the area that would become the park, and as that ice melted it left a depression in the moraine known to geologists as a kettle. Over time the depression filled with clay, sand and small particulate matter that plugged up the bottom of the depression such that it would hold water. As the depression filled with seep water, Middle Lake was created as a kettle lake. Over time, the lake has been filling with decaying vegetative material, and is now only about 1 m deep. It will continue to get shallower as further deposits build up, eventually becoming a boggy marsh and then returning to forest cover.

As you are moving along the lake edge, keep an eye out for damselflies in the reeds and other vegetation at lakeside. They look like small dragonflies that fold their wings backward in a delta formation when they alight. The lake is home to millions of these creatures and they regularly emerge in the spring and early summer. During the emergence the damselfly nymphs swim to the lake edge, then crawl out onto lakeside vegetation to split their nymphal exoskeleton. From the nymphal shell the adult damselfly emerges, unfolds and dries its wings and then flies away. When the emergence occurs, it happens in such numbers that you can see thousands of the fluttering insects flying uphill from the lake. Their transparent wings catch the light as they move, giving the whole area a twinkling effect. On one occasion a few years ago I was hiking around Middle Lake with a friend when we stumbled into a damselfly emergence. As we made our way back to the car we discovered that there was a junior high school class at the lake for a science outing. In company with and at the direction of park staff, the students were collecting pails of water from the lake edge and carrying them up to tables above the lake. The damselfly nymphs were crawling from the pails and onto the students' outstretched fingers where they were hatching before the awestruck eyes of the students. I would submit that it is an experience that will stay with those students forever.

HOW TO GET THERE

Drive west from Calgary on the Trans-Canada Highway (Hwy 1) for approximately 61 km. Immediately after crossing the Kananaskis River bridge (a short distance past the exit to Hwy 40, the Kananaskis Trail) take Exit 114. After the exit, the road swings around to the north and goes to a junction with Hwy 1A, approximately 4 km away. You go only about 800 m and turn left into the signed entrance road for Bow Valley Provincial Park. Information about the park can be obtained at the Visitor Information Centre, which is on the right side of the road shortly after the entrance to the park. There are a number of paved roadways throughout the park. There is a seasonal closure on the roads beyond Middle Lake between mid-October and mid-May. Biffies are scattered around the park.

Gem Trek map "Canmore and Kananaskis Village." NTS map 82 O/03 (Canmore).

Above: Damselfly on fir
Below: Blue Columbine
Opposite: Yamnuska

Leather-leaved Saxifrage

Jumpingpound Summit and Ridge Trail

Jumpingpound Creek is crossed by the Trans-Canada Highway about 18 km west from the Calgary city-limit sign. The creek was so named because the Blackfoot used to gather bison by stampeding them over a high, steep bank of the creek near its mouth at the confluence with the Bow River. Jumpingpound Mountain takes its name from the creek because the creek rises on the mountain, gathers itself and percolates its way downhill to the Bow. As mountains go in this part of the world, Jumpingpound is not terribly imposing, topping out at 2225 m. However, it is unique in several respects. At or near its summit, Jumpingpound has alpine meadows and ridges that can be reached by a reasonably fit hiker in under two hours' time from the trailhead. That in itself is unusual because there are very few places in this area where one can get above treeline with such a modest expenditure of energy. With the trailhead only an hour's drive from Calgary, and some likelihood that this trail will be open by late May when other alpine areas are still buried in snow and weeks away from being accessible, Jumpingpound is singular as an early-season outing. It is also a place where the panoramas are breathtaking, in any direction you wish to face. At the top of Jumpingpound it is as if you are standing on the linchpin that secures the mountains to the foothills and the foothills to the prairies.

Once you reach the highland meadows on Jumpingpound Ridge you can meander for upward of 20 km in various directions. Lots of options are available, so you can tailor your hike to whatever will best satisfy you. For purposes of this text, the hike described is a one-way trip, with vehicles left at each of two trailheads – one to start and one to finish. The hike covers approximately 9.4 km and will involve an elevation gain of approximately 400 m. Bear in mind that this area is a popular destination for mountain bikers, so be alert to their approach and try to play nicely together. The hike described is certainly not the only route available, but it will introduce you to the area and other possibilities for a return visit.

205

Follow the directions below to get to the trailhead for Jumpingpound Summit. From the trailhead you enter a forest dominated by shady spruce and lodgepole pine and ascend in a northeasterly direction on a switchbacking trail. There are several bridge crossings along the way. On the ascent you might keep an eye out for such flowering plants as Wild Strawberry, Silky Scorpionweed, False Azalea, Bunchberry, Bracted Honeysuckle, Clasping-leaf Twisted-stalk, Heart-leaved Arnica, Jacob's Ladder and Grouseberry. Just over halfway up the hill, at coordinates 11U 0646078 5645771, there is a spur trail that leads southeast about 50 m to a bench that overlooks the Elbow River valley. After taking in the view, return to the main trail and continue to climb until you top out on a ridge at a signed junction at coordinates 11U 0646580 5645988. The sign is a map of the Sibbald/Jumpingpound Trails. Bear left and continue in a northeasterly direction through open forest cover. At the next signed fork, bear right and make for the summit of Jumpingpound Mountain, which you will see ahead. The tree cover will dwindle further as you move upward, and the open meadows below the summit are a riot of colour with thousands of wildflowers of various hues swaying in the breeze. The summit is a grassy knoll fringed with rocks. Take a rest, have a drink and enjoy the vistas. You should also pay some close attention to where you are stepping, because the alpine floral community is spread among the rocks at the summit – a natural rock garden. Look for Shooting Star, Spotted Saxifrage, Alpine Forget-me-not, White Mountain Avens, Roseroot, Rock Jasmine, Moss Campion, Globeflower, Western Anemone, Mountain Heather, Lyall's Ironplant, various Rock Cresses, Bearberry, Leather-leaved Saxifrage and many others.

From the summit, continue downhill in a northwesterly direction and intersect with the Jumpingpound Ridge Trail heading northward. The trail will follow the nearly level grassy ridgeline for a couple of kilometres, passing a lovely small tarn that reflects the snowy silhouettes of the Front Range mountains to the west. Keep your eyes open for more alpine flowers as you go. Any rock outcrops are worth investigating for flowers. In reasonably short order you will re-enter the trees as the trail slides off the ridge to the east. At about 5.9 km into the hike you will encounter a signed junction at coordinates 11u 0645623 5649042. The trail to the right connects to the ridgeline going to Cox Hill. The trail to the left heads northwest and descends 3.5 km in a series of switchbacks leading to your waiting vehicle in the parking lot at the Lusk Pass trailhead.

After completing the hike and retrieving the vehicle left at the Jumpingpound Summit trailhead, you can return home by reversing the routing that brought you to the trailhead. If you wish to experience a different return route, however, I would strongly recommend a return to Calgary by heading north on the Powderface Trail. That road runs for approximately 17 km before it intersects with Hwy 68, the Sibbald Creek Trail. If you turn right (north) at the intersection of the Powderface Trail and Hwy 68, it will deliver you to the Trans-Canada after 23 km. At the Trans-Canada turn east. The Calgary city limit is approximately 31 km east.

The spring of 2008 around Calgary was much wetter and cooler than "normal." At the conclusion of a hike to Jumpingpound Summit in the late spring/early summer of that year, we returned to Calgary along the Powderface Trail, connecting to the Sibbald Creek Trail as described above. By going slowly and "botanizing" from the vehicle, with frequent stops we recorded the following species in bloom along the roadway before we got to Sibbald Creek Trail:

Silky Scorpionweed (*Phacelia*), Yarrow, Yellow Columbine, Round-leaved Alumroot, Stonecrop, Smooth Blue Beardtongue, Red Paintbrush, Canada Anemone, Tall Lungwort (*Mertensia*), Cow Parsnip, Creamy Peavine, Shrubby Cinquefoil (*Potentilla*), Early Yellow Locoweed, Windflower (Cut-leaved Anemone), Saskatoon, Heart-leaved Alexanders, Brown-eyed Susan, White Geranium, Purple Avens, Western Canada Violet, Harebell, Showy Locoweed, Blue-eyed Grass, Tall Larkspur, various Goldenrods, Large-leaved Avens, Wild Rose, Northern Gooseberry and Northern Bedstraw. That list alone would constitute a successful wildflowering excursion, and it could have been had by walking the road and never stepping much past the ditches.

Clockwise from above: View to the west; viewpoint along trail; Spotted Saxifrage; Jumpingpound ridge meadow

HOW TO GET THERE

Note that the Powderface Trail and the portion of Elbow Falls Trail (Hwy 66) to the west of Elbow Falls are closed from December 1 to May 15. For the above-described hike you require two vehicles, spotting one at each end of the hike. The hike can be completed by going from south to north or from north to south. The commentary here assumes the hike will be done starting from the south and moving to the north. If you wish to reverse that direction, simply reverse the instructions accordingly. If you do not have two vehicles or do not wish to bring two vehicles, make the hike to the summit of Jumpingpound Mountain from the same trailhead as described, wander about on the ridge for as long as you wish, then retrace your steps to your vehicle.

If you are starting from Calgary, follow the most convenient of the following routes:

- If you are starting from the northern parts of Calgary, your best option is probably to get on the Trans-Canada Highway (Hwy 1) headed west. Follow Hwy 1 west from the city limit sign for approximately 14.2 km to the intersection with Hwy 22 (the Cochrane/Bragg Creek interchange, Exit 161A) and exit heading south on Hwy 22 to Bragg Creek. From the stop sign at Bragg Creek bear left on Hwy 22 and continue south to the intersection with Hwy 66 (Elbow Falls Trail), or
- If you are starting from southwest Calgary near Sarcee Trail, go to the intersection of Sarcee Trail and Hwy 8. Go west on Hwy 8 to the traffic circle where Hwy 8 joins Hwy 22. From the traffic circle, proceed south to Bragg Creek. From the stop sign at Bragg Creek bear left on Hwy 22 and continue south to the intersection with Hwy 66 (Elbow Falls Trail), or
- If you are starting from the south end of Calgary, travel west on Hwy 22x (the Marquis of Lorne Trail), past the turn to Turner Valley, past the Priddis turn and continuing westbound to the intersection of Hwy 22 and Hwy 66 (Elbow Falls Trail).

The coordinates for the intersection of Hwy 22 and Hwy 66 (Elbow Falls Trail) are 11u 0671395 5643925.

From the intersection of Hwy 22 and Hwy 66, proceed west on Hwy 66 for 27.6 km and look for the turn onto the Powderface Trail (just before the Little Elbow Campground). The coordinates for that intersection are 11u 0652011 5630372.

Turn north onto the Powderface Trail. The Powderface Trail is a winding gravel road that is basically going north and west. Continue on the Powderface Trail for 18 km to an unmarked trailhead just after crossing Canyon Creek. Parking is on the left (west) side of the road. The trailhead for Jumpingpound Summit is across the road. The coordinates for the trailhead are 11u 0645151 5645062.

If you are going to start the hike from here and go one way only, you should continue on the Powderface Trail with both vehicles for another 6.1 km to the trailhead for Lusk Pass. Drop one vehicle there for retrieval at the end of the hike. The coordinates for the parking lot at the Lusk Pass trailhead are 11u 0643591 5650594. After spotting a vehicle there, return to the trailhead for Jumpingpound Summit for the start of the hike.

If you want a longer hike, one option you may want to consider is to drop a vehicle at the parking lot for the Dawson Equestrian Campground, which is 10.7 km farther along the Powderface Trail from the Lusk Pass trailhead. The coordinates for the Dawson Equestrian Campground are 11u 0648543 5654592. You then proceed to the trailhead for Jumpingpound Summit and start the hike as above described. At the point during the hike where you arrive at the signed junction that takes you either right to Cox Hill or left to Lusk Pass trailhead, go right to Cox Hill and continue on Cox Hill Ridge to the Dawson Equestrian Campground. The total distance for that hike is approximately 17 km.

Gem Trek map "Bragg Creek & Sheep Valley – Kananaskis Country." NTS map 82J/15 (Bragg Creek).

Golden eagle

The Eagle Highway: Rocky Mountain Migration of Golden Eagles

March 20, 1992, is a singularly important day in the annals of birdwatching. On that day, Peter Sherrington and a colleague, Des Allen, were doing a bird survey in Kananaskis Country near Mount Lorette, a peak that stands just northeast of the Nakiska ski hill. During the watch Sherrington noticed an adult golden eagle soaring above the Kananaskis River valley east of Mount Lorette, and drew it to the attention of Allen. A short time later, the two men observed a pair of adult golden eagles soaring above the valley, and while they watched, the pair was joined by a third bird. The three birds disappeared toward the northwest. After another short hiatus, more eagles were seen moving from the southeast to the northwest, mimicking the pattern followed by the first four birds. With their attention piqued, Sherrington and Allen continued to watch, and by day's end they had seen and recorded 103 golden eagles following essentially the same route. The men suspected they had stumbled upon a hitherto unknown migration route for the large raptors, but further research would be required.

Sherrington returned two days later with a group of naturalists. The object of the excursion was, of course, to see if any more eagles might be seen. By that day's end the group had recorded 247 sightings, with all the birds moving along a route similar to that travelled by the birds seen on March 20. Sherrington posited that the birds were moving systematically along a determined route, and the second day's observations seemed to support the hypothesis that a new migratory route had been discovered.

At the time of the original discovery, the idea of a mass migration along the Front Ranges of the Rockies flew in the face (who could resist?) of all commonly accepted wisdom concerning the migratory habits of golden eagles in this area. Up to that time it was thought that golden eagles migrated mainly in the foothills of the Rockies; that there were relatively few migrants; that what migration did occur was in April and October; and that the migrants were mainly young birds. The new evidence suggested otherwise, and Sherrington set out to further test the hypothesis.

In the autumn of 1992, volunteer observers were enlisted for the project, and they spent 33 days watching the area around Mount Lorette for passing golden eagles. During that time the watchers recorded 2,672 raptor sightings, of which 2,043 were golden eagles. In the spring of 1993 the observers attended at the site and noted 4,140 eagles. In the autumn of that year, the count jumped to 4,499. There now seemed little doubt that the hypothesis was correct and a new migratory route for the large birds had been discovered. As time went by, the Rocky Mountain Eagle Research Foundation was established, and through that foundation a consistent study of the migration has been undertaken. After the first 14 years of observation, volunteers have counted more than 107,000 migrant raptors, of which 89,600 have been golden eagles and 7,500 have been bald eagles. The migration route has been fittingly dubbed "the Eagle Highway." The Mount Lorette site is unique in that it is manned daily during the migration time, and it monitors a significant portion of the total population of golden eagles in North America.

The overwhelming majority of the raptors counted in the migration are golden eagles. In the spring the birds are moving from their wintering ranges in the southern Great Plains of the United States and from the mountains as far south as Mexico. After they pass through southern Alberta, they continue to nesting grounds in Alaska and the Yukon. For most of the birds, the area where they are being observed in southern Alberta is about halfway along their migration route.

Golden eagles are considered by many to be emblematic of wilderness – particularly mountain wilderness. Their scientific name is *Aquila chrysaetos*. *Aquila* is classical Latin meaning "eagle," and *chrysaetos*, somewhat redundantly, is derived from the Greek *chrysos*, meaning "golden," and *aetos*, which means "eagle," a reference to the colouring on the crown, sides of the face, and cape (nape of the neck) of the bird. The common name arises from this coloration. Adult birds can weigh up to 6.5 kg, with a wingspan of up to 2.3 m, and a length of up to 90 cm. They can fly up to 130 km/h on occasion, though they move more slowly (30–50 km/h) most of the time. Top speeds of 320 km/h can be achieved during dives. Golden eagles have legs that are feathered all the way to the toes. The birds can vocalize, but seldom do so, even when defending a territory. A mature bird can carry over 3 kg in flight. Females are typically larger than males, weighing up to one third more than males of the same age. Maturity is not achieved until the animal is four to six years old, and breeding may be delayed until the animal is seven years old. Lifespan in the wild has been noted at up to 32 years, while it is not uncommon for birds in captivity to live to be 40 or more years old.

The golden eagle has exceptional eyesight, with a resolving power said to be more than eight times more powerful than humans. In mature birds the eyes are brown, and the talons and bill are black. The talons are used for killing and carrying prey. The hooked beak is used only for eating. The bird is considered to be an avian apex species – which is to say that a healthy adult bird is not preyed upon in its environment; it is at the top of its food web. Poaching and collisions with powerlines are the most frequent causes of injury or death. The golden eagle is known to often hunt in pairs, with one bird driving prey toward its partner. Its diet usually consists of rabbits, hares, hoary marmots and other small mammals, as well as birds from time to time. In times of food shortage, it may feed on carrion.

Nesting sites are usually on a ledge or cavity high on a rock face. Nests are sometimes built in trees, but that is more an exception than the rule. The nest is build with stout twigs and lined with soft materials. A nest might be used for many successive seasons, with enlargements added each year. Small birds and mammals that are too small to be of much interest to the eagles as food often shelter in the aeries. The normal predators on these creatures generally stay away because they are fearful of the "landlord."

A female golden eagle will usually lay two eggs, which are incubated for about 45 days before hatching. Newborn chicks are completely white and they are fed for about 50 days before their first flight attempts. In most cases only the first hatchling survives. The later hatchling usually does not leave the nest alive. The common wisdom is that this is a survival strategy adopted by the species. The parent birds are only called upon to care for one hatchling, thus reducing the work involved in raising the young, and also thereby allowing for more attention to be paid to that one offspring. In the event that the first hatchling fails to survive for some reason, the second hatchling is a reserve chick to take its place.

It takes several years for young golden eagles to attain the plumage colours of an adult bird – chocolate brown body, dark tail and dark golden cape and crown. Immature birds may be darker than mature birds, but one-half or more of the tail is white above a terminal dark bar. They also exhibit white on the wing tips and may show white patches on the ventral surface of the wings. golden eagles and bald eagles are similar in size, but they have some distinguishing features. A mature bald eagle has a white head and tail, yellow eyes and bill, and only has feathers that reach about halfway down the leg. A mature golden eagle has a golden head and nape, brown eyes, a black bill, no white feathering, and its legs are feathered all the way to the toes. An immature bald eagle may be conflated with a golden eagle, but it will not have the golden colour and will not have feathering extending all the way to the toes.

Should you wish to see what is happening at the Rocky Mountain Eagle Research Foundation's observation site, the public is invited to visit to learn more about the migration and about the foundation and its projects. Memberships in the foundation are available and donations are welcome. The foundation is a registered charity and can issue tax receipts for all cash donations. To learn more about the foundation and its work, check out its website at www.eaglewatch.ca. Email correspondence can be forwarded to rmerf.eagle@gmail.com. Peter Sherrington is the research director for the foundation. Volunteer opportunities include an array of jobs – fundraising, fieldwork, newsletter preparation, data recording and compilation, and more. Volunteers can also expect to learn a tremendous amount about the project and its subjects from others. The sites are consistently staffed by very knowledgeable and committed people who are happy to share their information with those who are interested.

As of this writing, the observation site adjacent to the Kananaskis River near Mount Lorette (often referred to as the "Hay Meadow site") is staffed by volunteers daily from the middle of February until late May to record the spring migration, then resumes in late August and continues monitoring until the middle of December to record the southward movement of the raptors. In addition to the Hay Meadow site, other organized observation posts have been set up at other points along the migration route, including Barrier Lake, Plateau Mountain and the South Livingstone Raptor Watch in the Crowsnest Pass area.

During the peak of the migration, it would not be unusual to see 200 or more birds during the day. The peak of the spring migration occurs from March 10 to the first week of April. The peak of the autumn migration occurs from the end of September to the end of October. Weather on any given day can alter the migration for that day. All things being equal, the afternoon is usually the better time during the day for seeing the greatest numbers of migrants.

If you wish to observe the goings-on or take part in the count, bring along food, water, binoculars or tripod-mounted spotting scope and a lawn chair. Bear in mind that spotting is an activity that involves little moving around, so dress warmly, depending on the weather and the time of the year. Warm footwear, hat, gloves, sweater or fleece, raingear and sunscreen should be on hand if required. It is probably always best to assume the weather will be worse than you think it will, so you go prepared for anything. If you have a bag of cookies, candies, a thermos of coffee or tea and other goodies to share with others on arrival, you will be most welcome.

In October of each year the Town of Canmore holds a "Festival of Eagles," and the public is invited to attend events like guided hikes, bird walks, interpretative displays, theatrical performances and various programs by guest speakers. Check with the Chamber of Commerce in Canmore for more information.

Mount Lorette Hay Meadow

HOW TO GET THERE

The Hay Meadow site can be accessed as follows: go west on the Trans-Canada Highway (Hwy 1) from Calgary for 57 km. Turn south at Exit 118 onto Hwy 40 (the Kananaskis Trail) and go 23.2 km to the sign for Kananaskis Village and Nakiska. Turn right and go west for 1 km. Pass the turn on the left to Kananaskis Village and immediately turn right onto a gravel road signed as "Stoney Trailhead." Park in the lot a short distance down the road near a gate. From the north side of the parking lot turn right onto the ski/hiking trail and follow it to the site. The walk to the site takes about 15 minutes. There are two small wooden huts there. The site is adjacent to the Kananaskis River at coordinates 11u 0630831 5645242.

The South Livingstone Raptor Watch site can be accessed as follows: from Hwy 3, go north on the Frank Slide Interpretation Centre access road. At the hairpin bend, continue straight ahead and cross the cattle guard ("Texas gate") and go 3 km east. As a landmark, there is a road to the left at 1.7 km. The road is gravel and steep in places. At the end of the 3 km, park in the open grassy area at coordinates 11u 0690636 5497945. From the parking area walk northeast on a trail to a wooded gully, then follow the red tape up the gully to an old hoist house. From there take the road north to the site. The site is on an open knoll with a fibreglass tower at coordinates 11u 0691258 5498619.

Great horned owl

Alberta Birds of Prey Centre

In 1982 Wendy Slaytor and Colin Weir approached the Alberta Fish & Wildlife Division with their proposal to start and operate a privately funded, volunteer-staffed wildlife rescue facility catering exclusively to birds of prey – hawks, falcons, eagles and owls. At that time there was no such facility anywhere in the province or indeed in the whole of western Canada. Furthermore, it was then illegal for private individuals to possess wildlife for any purpose. After discussing the proposal with the powers that be, Slaytor and Weir were given a special dispensation from the wildlife regulations by the provincial minister in charge, and they moved forward with the establishment of their rescue facility. The facility today remains a privately licensed not-for-profit raptor rescue and rehabilitation centre. It is operated by a foundation that is a registered charity under the income tax laws of Canada. Their mission statement includes caring for and rehabilitating injured raptors with a view to returning them to the wild as soon as possible; operating captive breeding programs and releases into the wild of threatened or endangered species; studying and monitoring wild populations of birds of prey; and advancing and encouraging public education on conservation issues concerning raptors specifically and habitat and environmental awareness generally. The centre neither seeks nor receives any operating subsidies from government, choosing instead to rely exclusively on donations from the public by way of funds, gifts in kind and volunteer assistance. No administrative wages are paid by the foundation, and they do not hire professional fundraisers. Admissions are charged to tour the facility, but the proceeds from the admissions are used for operating costs. Though the centre is not precisely a "natural phenomenon" in the same way as the other subjects in this book are, it is, as grandma used to say, "close enough for the girls you go with," and therefore deserves to be touted as a place you should visit and support.

The Alberta Birds of Prey Centre today consists of various buildings, aviaries, ponds, islands and wetland habitat, all contained within a 28-ha site. Historically the land was a wetland marsh, but prior to 1982 it had been dredged, drained and dewatered in order to make it into marginally productive agricultural land. Because the land was low-lying and subject to periodic flooding, the property was then designated as a regional storm water retention area. When work commenced on the centre, the volunteers, working in conjunction with provincial and municipal representatives, brought an enormous amount of foresight and ingenuity to the task and reclaimed the land by recreating it as a wetland habitat. The innovative thinking and enlightened land use policy applied to the restoration ensured that the property would fit precisely with the work done by the centre.

As its primary focus, the centre accepts injured birds of prey and, as much as possible, rehabilitates them with a view to releasing them back into the wild. When birds cannot be returned to the wild, for various reasons, they are housed and taken care of permanently at the centre. Those birds may become part of the educational program operated by the centre or they may become "foster parents" to orphaned juvenile birds brought to the facility. The centre is also engaged in a captive breeding program for endangered burrowing owls. School children and other groups are regular visitors to the centre to take advantage of the educational opportunities presented there. In addition, from time to time, centre personnel conduct programs in other facilities such as parks. It is possible that visitors to the facility may see all manner of birds of prey on display, including burrowing owl, snowy owl, American kestrel, prairie falcon, peregrine falcon, golden eagle, great grey owl, great horned owl, bald eagle, ferruginous hawk, red-tailed hawk and many others.

HOW TO GET THERE

The Alberta Birds of Prey Centre is located in Coaldale, Alberta, a short drive east from Lethbridge. The centre is located north of Hwy 3 and just west of Secondary Hwy 845. The facility is open from 9:30 a.m. to 5 p.m. seven days a week from May 10 to September 10. Admission fees are charged. For more information, please consult the centre's website at www.burrowingowl.com or call (403) 345-4262.

222

Above: Red-tailed hawk
Below: Burrowing owl

Flame-coloured Lousewort

Plateau Mountain

Plateau Mountain is in the Livingstone Range at the southern end of Kananaskis Country. It is accessed by hiking up a service road that is gated and locked and used for maintenance of a couple of gas wells at the top of the mountain. From this rather inauspicious beginning, the prospects for an interesting and enjoyable outing are not particularly promising, but the flowers abounding along the road instantly tell you that you are in a rather special place. Once you reach the road's end you will soon realize you have arrived in a place that is quite unlike any other in the province. From the top of Plateau Mountain at 2438 m the vistas in all directions are breathtaking, the flora and fauna are diverse and in keeping with Arctic tundra, and the landforms are curious and intriguing.

Plateau Mountain was named in 1915, and the name is an accurate reflection of the appearance of the summit – a virtually flat area that runs for 8 km north to south and covers some 14 km^2. Indeed, other names often applied to the mountain are Flattop and Table Mountain. The mountain was a nunatak – an island above the ice – during the most recent glacial advance, which ended some 10,000–12,000 years ago. It was a refugium – an area that remains today much as it was prior to that latest advance of the glaciers. There is plenty of evidence that the glaciers were nearby, as witnessed by cirques on the flanks of the mountain, but the summit itself was not ground down by the ice. Cirques – from the Latin *circus*, meaning "arena" or "stadium," by way of the French for the same idea – are amphitheatre-like valleys formed by erosion at the head of a glacier.

Though not glaciated, the summit was battered by what are known as periglacial conditions. Periglacial is an adjective that refers to locations on the edges of glacial areas that were subjected to severe freezing conditions like those associated with permafrost. That intense freezing and freeze/thaw cycles were responsible for creating many of the surface features on the mountain that are called "patterned ground." These peculiar rock formations (patterns) appear in several configurations: as circles, polygons, steps, stripes or lines, some symmetrical and others not, some with relatively uniform sizes of stones and others not. The best scientific explanation for these phenomena is that repeated freezing and thawing of subsurface groundwater forced the stones upward from depth and piled them on each other, in the process forming the patterns. The numbers and range of these features on Plateau Mountain are unmatched anywhere else in the province. In addition, there are places on the summit that exhibit stone features referred to as felsenmeer – fields of large, angular, often jagged stones. These features are the result of a process known as ice wedging. As water freezes it expands by as much as 10 per cent in volume. If the water is in interstitial cracks in stone, the pressures associated with the expansion of the ice can be significant and certainly sufficient to cause the rocks to split.

In addition to these features, there is an ice cave located on the north end of the plateau, but it is not accessible to the public. It once was, but the publication of its existence and location led to visitations that caused so much damage that a quick determination was made that human activities in the cave were detrimental to the fragile ice structures located there. Indeed, smashed ceiling pendants were confirmed, and it was discovered that the visitations were raising the cave temperature, causing many of its ice plates to melt. In 1971 the provincial government recognized that the ice cave was a fragile and unique feature requiring protection, and designated the area around the cave as the Plateau Mountain Natural Area. The cave was gated and permanently blocked off in 1972. In her book *Kananaskis Country Trail Guide, Volume 2*, Gillean Daffern describes the ice cave as follows:

> Inside it's a glittering fairyland of hexagonal, plate-like ice crystals, extruded fingers of ice, rare and delicate ice flowers and corkscrew stalactites. Apparently, the entrance leads to a larger room partially floored with ice. Two decorated passages leave the room, one with a floor of ice and walls and roof covered by ice crystals. The ceiling gradually lowers until it's necessary to crawl under pendent ice crystals into a small ice-filled grotto.

In 1991, recognizing the unique and diverse landscape features on the mountain and wishing to extend further protection to them, the government repealed the Plateau Mountain Natural Area and in its place created the Plateau Mountain Ecological Reserve. The reserve includes the whole of the mountaintop, as well as its flanks on the north and south. The gas wells on top of Plateau Mountain were drilled in the early 1950s by Husky Oil (as it then was), and are now being operated by Petro-Canada. When commercial production from the wells ceases, the wells will be abandoned and there will be no further oil and gas exploration or development in the reserve. In the usual course, the mountain experiences cool summers and cold winters. Most of the annual precipitation falls as snow. It can (and often does) snow during any month of the year. Winds are reasonably constant and can be quite strong. They often move snow to the lee sides of small ridges, leaving travel corridors for animals on the top of the mountain.

Plateau Mountain supports a wide diversity of plants, mostly of the alpine tundra type. A total of about 500 species occur here, including wildflowers, lichens, shrubs, trees, grasses, sedges etc. Some of the plants are considered rare in the province, such as the Pygmy Bitterroot (*Lewisia pygmaea*), Moss Gentian (*Gentiana prostrata*) and Flame-coloured Lousewort (*Pedicularis flammea*). Plants commonly found on the mountain include Sulphur Hedysarum, Purple Fleabane, Spotted Saxifrage, Sandwort, Sitka Valerian, Stonecrop, Yarrow, Heart-leaved Arnica, Jacob's Ladder, Alpine Chickweed, False Dandelion, Silky Phacelia, Alpine Forget-me-not, Showy Locoweed, Yellow Columbine, Wild Chives, Mountain Groundsel, Leather-leaved Saxifrage, Bracted Lousewort, Mountain Fireweed (River Beauty), Moss Campion, Alpine Spring Beauty, White Mountain Avens, Inflated Oxytropis (Stalked Pod Crazyweed), Ground Plum, Tufted Fleabane, Paintbrush, Sweet-flowered Androsace (Rock Jasmine), Alpine Bistort, Mountain Goldenrod, Alpine Speedwell, Mountain Death Camas, Yellow Heather, Elephant Head, Roseroot, Northern Gentian, Four-parted Gentian, Silver Rock Cress and many others. The mountain also provides habitat for bighorn sheep, hoary marmots, white-tailed ptarmigan, and the highest elevation known in the province for pocket gophers.

HOW TO GET THERE

Note that there is an annual winter road closure on Hwy 40 between the Kananaskis Lakes Trail turnoff and Highwood Junction from December 1 to June 14 inclusive, and Hwy 940 is closed between Cataract Creek Recreation Area and Wilkinson Summit from December 1 to April 30 inclusive.

From Calgary, go south on Hwy 22, to Longview, and either:

- turn west on Hwy 541 and go to Highwood Junction (where Hwys 40, 940 and 541 meet). Turn south on Hwy 940 and continue for 25.4 km to the unsigned Plateau Mountain Access Road at coordinates 11u 0674561 5563103. Turn left onto the access road and proceed uphill for 3.7 km. Park just below the locked gate, or
- continue 28 km south to the junction with Hwy 532 (just north of Chain Lakes). Go west on Hwys 532 and 940 for 31.6 km and then take the unsigned right turn (north) onto the Plateau Mountain Access Road just before the winter gate at the coordinates shown above. Continue up that road for 3.7 km to the locked gate and park downhill from the gate.

If you desire a different look to the scenery going in and coming out, go to the trailhead by one of the above-described routes and return by the other.

After passing through a pedestrian passageway on the right side of the locked gate, proceed uphill on the road until you reach the top of the mountain beside some gas production facilities. At the top, the road runs south to a gas well near the south end of the mountain, at 11u 0676838 5563610. If you turn north when you reach the top, the trail goes for approximately 4 km, ending at 11u 0676786 5569865. The total distance from parking to the top of the mountain is approximately 4.3 km.

Bicycles are allowed on the road, so be mindful of their approach.

Gem Trek map "Highwood & Cataract Creek." NTS map 82J/02 (Fording River).

Above: Moss Gentian
Right: Little Elephant Heads
Below: View from the top plateau

229

View of Dinosaur Provincial Park

Dinosaur Provincial Park

Dinosaur Provincial Park is in the valley of the Red Deer River approximately 100 km downstream from Drumheller, Alberta. Like the Drumheller area, and indeed the country at Writing-on-Stone Provincial Park discussed elsewhere herein, the park is in badlands, a starkly beautiful landscape of strange landforms and colours that is fascinating in itself. But quite apart from the stunning scenery, this park is the final resting place of a large number and variety of dinosaurs, the great beasts that roamed and ruled the earth millions of years ago and still excite intense amazement in children of whatever age. The bonebeds here are some of the most prolific in the world, and from here have been taken specimens of almost 40 species of dinosaurs, representing every known group of dinosaurs of the Cretaceous Period. Indeed, over the years, some 300 museum-quality specimens have been taken from this place and now reside in museums all over the globe. Since its opening in 1985, the Royal Tyrrell Museum of Paleontology in Drumheller has been the recipient of most of those specimens. In addition to the dinosaur remains, the bonebeds here also contain fossil remains of such diverse creatures as flying reptiles, marsupials, turtles and lizards. Here is another magical place that you really ought to see.

PREHISTORY

Seventy-five million years ago, present-day southeastern Alberta was a low-lying, often marshy area adjacent to an enormous, shallow inland sea. The climate at that time was subtropical, similar to that enjoyed by present-day Florida or Cuba. The landscape was populated by a diverse flora including huge ferns, mosses and trees; and a fauna comprised of primitive mammals like shrews and other rodents, crocodiles, turtles, lizards, primitive birds, fish and a wide array of dinosaurs. Many rivers emptied into the sea, bringing with them sand, mud, clay and other sediments entrained in the waters' flow. When some of the local animals died their bodies lay in the channels and mud flats of the rivers' deltas and were eventually buried under layers of arriving sedimentary material. The dinosaurs in the area died off about 65 million years ago, for reasons that are still not altogether clear, though there are some cogent theories about what happened. Over millions of years a combination of pressures, anaerobic conditions and the deposition of various minerals caused the animal remains to become fossilized, i.e., portions of the remains hardened into rock and were thereby preserved, buried under layers of sediments.

As discussed earlier, commencing about 110,000 years ago the landmass known today as western Canada experienced a period of glacial advance known as the Wisconsinian glacial episode, which saw most of the area covered with an ice sheet hundreds of metres thick. This ice sheet did much to scrape off the top layers of the sedimentary rocks formed earlier in the inland sea. When the ice began to melt approximately 12,000–13,000 years ago it generated enormous volumes of meltwater that made their way generally eastward, further altering the landscape by virtue of significant erosion of some of the remaining softer sedimentary rock formations. The waters gouged the landscape to produce the Red Deer River valley, with some rents in the sedimentary rock extending 100 m deep from prairie level to valley bottom. When the deluge was over, the valley was festooned with mesas, coulees, ravines, pinnacles, gullies, sculpted landmasses and strangely shaped hoodoos. It was now country that the Sioux called *makhosica*, or "bad land," the French trappers called *des mauvaises terres à traverser*, or "bad lands to cross," and the Spanish called *tierra baldía*, or "waste land." Indeed, this had become the largest area of badlands in the whole of what would become Canada. In the process, the water also exposed fossil-bearing sediments that have proven to be the largest concentration of late Cretaceous dinosaur fossils on the planet – the 27-km stretch of the Red Deer River that is now within Dinosaur Provincial Park. Erosion by wind and water persists in the area, and the landscape is still altering inexorably. As time goes by, more fossil remains will surely be revealed.

THE DINOSAUR HUNT

In 1874 George Mercer Dawson, a Canadian scientist and surveyor, while working as a representative of the International Boundary Commission in what would become southern Alberta, discovered fragments and large bones of a duckbill dinosaur. This is generally accepted as the first discovery of dinosaur remains in southern Alberta. Dawson later made a number of other significant contributions to science in Canada – including discovering Mount Assiniboine – and he is memorialized by having the communities of Dawson City, Yukon, and Dawson Creek, British Columbia, named after him.

In 1881 the Canadian Pacific Railway, in a surprise move, altered the routing for its railway to almost 300 km south of its originally announced course, putting the rail corridor into southern Saskatchewan and Alberta on a latitude with Regina and Calgary. At that time the Geological Survey of Canada (GSC) knew little about the geology of that part of the country, so it dispatched Dawson back to Alberta in company with several other staff members of the GSC. During the ensuing several years Dawson and his colleagues learned a great deal about the geology of southern Saskatchewan and Alberta, including the locations of coal resources that would be needed by the fledgling railway. One of Dawson's underlings was a young geologist named Joseph Burr Tyrrell, and in April 1884 Dawson ordered Tyrrell to do some geological investigations in territory north of the Bow River. While completing those instructions, Tyrrell and several assistants canoed portions of the Red Deer River near present-day Drumheller. The story goes that Tyrrell went to a nearby creek to wash off his lunchtime dish and stumbled across a piece of what appeared to be bone protruding from the streambank. The bone was excavated and it turned out to be a relatively intact skull of an unknown large dinosaur. It would later be christened *Albertosaurus sarcophagus* and it would forever be connected to its discoverer, Joseph Burr Tyrrell. Indeed, the Royal Tyrrell Museum of Paleontology in Drumheller is named for him. Interestingly, the discovery of albertosaurus was the only foray Tyrrell ever made into the world of dinosaurs, and that one was completely serendipitous. He was a geologist by training and interest, and when he quit the GSC in 1899 following a salary dispute with the agency's director, George Dawson, he went on to become a gold-mining consultant in the Klondike. Later he made a fortune in the management of gold mines in Ontario and eventually retired there as a wealthy orchardist, developing a variety of apple called – what else? – the Golden Delicious. The Toronto Zoo now sits on the orchard once owned by Tyrrell.

Following Tyrrell's find, the interest in dinosaur remains in southern Alberta was piqued, and over the ensuing years several staff from the GSC were sent to the area to collect specimens of dinosaur remains. Unfortunately, these delegations were too feebly supported financially and in manpower to ever do justice to the task at hand. There were simply too many bones for the limited personnel to deal with. Though the GSC was strapped, other parties interested in fossil collecting were not so constrained.

In the fall of 1909 a man named Barnum Brown was in Montana wrapping up his summer's field work and preparing to return to New York City, where he worked for the American Museum of Natural History (AMNH). Barnum Brown was born in Carbondale, Kansas, in 1873. He was named after P.T. Barnum, the famous circus impresario, although it is unclear from the historical record just exactly why his parents felt compelled to so honour Mr. Barnum, or, as some might say, burden the child with such an appellation. Brown became a paleontologist

Above: Barnum Brown
Right: Joseph Burr Tyrrell

and worked for the AMNH for virtually his whole adult life, travelling worldwide searching for and collecting fossils by discovery, bargaining, trading and outright purchase. Over the years Brown obtained thousands of specimens, and they arrived at the museum in great volume with great regularity. In 1902 he was working at a dig in Montana where he discovered and excavated the first documented remains of a dinosaur to be called *Tyrannosaurus rex*. With that discovery and his successful collection efforts on behalf of AMNH, Brown was soon acknowledged as one of the most famous fossil hunters of the early 20th century. He was an eccentric character by all reports, always appearing impeccably dressed, and was said to sometimes conduct digs in a fur coat, tie and top hat. Some say he was the prototype for the Indiana Jones character, but that is far from certain.

Before Brown departed Montana, he received a communiqué from Henry Fairfield Osborn, his immediate superior and the curator of paleontology at the AMNH. Osborn directed Brown to make a side trip north to Alberta before returning to New York. Once there, Brown was instructed to seek out a rancher named John L. Wagner and accept his invitation, extended to Osborn, to view some ancient bones on Mr. Wagner's property.

In this regard, there is a story, almost certainly apocryphal, that Mr. Wagner had made a trip to New York City in the summer of 1909 and visited the AMNH. While there, he viewed the dinosaur exhibit and was said to have exited the hall laughing. Fairfield Osborn, hearing Wagner's outburst, confronted him to find out what had so amused Wagner in the exhibit. Wagner responded that he found it amazing and amusing that people thought so much of the "old bones," because he had so many of them on his ranch in Alberta that the "cattle tripped over them all the time." According to the story, it was then Osborn's turn to be amazed, and he solicited an invitation from Wagner to visit, then communicated with his assistant Brown.

While the story might not be absolutely accurate, there appears to be little doubt that Wagner did visit the AMNH and did speak with Osborn about some bones on his place in Alberta. As it turns out, Osborn already knew about the existence of fossils in Alberta as a result of correspondence with one of his former paleontology students, Lawrence Morris Lambe. Lambe worked for the GSC and had made many trips to Alberta, starting in 1897. For over a decade he had discovered, collected and identified fossils of dinosaurs, and his published works helped immensely in making the public aware of the existence of dinosaurs in Alberta. Lambe was honoured in 1923 when a genus of duck-billed dinosaurs, *Lambeosaurus*, was named for him.

It is also noteworthy that it was the same Henry Fairfield Osborn who, in 1905, finally settled on the name albertosaurus for the creature so inadvertently discovered by Joseph Burr Tyrrell 20 years earlier. The genus name honours Alberta as the place the species was first found, together with the Greek *sauros*, which means "lizard" and is a common suffix in dinosaur names. For that alone, it can hardly be said that Osborn was unfamiliar with the existence of dinosaurs in Alberta.

In any event, Osborn realized that the time was propitious to investigate Alberta and he sent his ace fossil collector instructions to make the detour to Alberta before returning to New York. During that short sojourn in Alberta Brown realized that a full-blown expedition should be planned for the summer of 1910 and he reported accordingly to his superiors at AMNH.

In the early summer of 1910 Barnum Brown arrived in Red Deer, Alberta, and, without really intending to, quietly started the Great Canadian Dinosaur Rush, a somewhat frenetic exploration that would carry on for years. After his arrival in Red Deer, Brown contracted to have a large, flat-bottomed, steerable barge constructed, which was going to be his mobile laboratory on his bone hunt. The craft had a tent amidships which acted as a shelter and included a wood-burning stove, and considerable deck space both fore and aft for carrying artifacts. After completion, the vessel was launched in the Red Deer River and it set off downstream, reminiscent of Huckleberry Finn and Jim on the Mississippi. A few anxious moments occurred in the early going, but soon the barge reached sections of the river that were sedate enough that navigation was not problematic. The process worked splendidly, allowing Brown and his assistants to watch for likely-looking collection sites along the banks and adjacent cliffs while drifting, stopping often to closely examine prospective areas. By the end of the trip, Brown had collected a very impressive quantity of fossils of various descriptions, all of which he then shipped off to New York for further study. In the following year Brown and his crew returned to Alberta and, starting near Drumheller, repeated the procedure, once again recovering large quantities of paleontological artifacts that were crated up and sent off to New York.

During those two years Brown had been working with the knowledge, and presumably the approval, of the GSC, but as the volume of materials leaving western Canada grew, so did the objections from those who saw the process as a ransacking of Canadian historical treasures by foreign fossil hunters. Indeed, exhibits at the AMNH were now showing up made up entirely of Alberta artifacts, and Brown's successes were becoming only too painfully obvious to many in Canada. As the voices of protest became louder, the GSC realized that something had to be done, and quickly. The agency first considered barring Brown from further expeditions in Canada, but that course was fraught with problems, given that it could create enormous ill will toward Canada within the scientific community. Instead, the government of Canada insisted that the GSC take action to compete directly with Brown and move to collect the artifacts themselves. That sounded logical, but the practical difficulty was that the GSC did not have any qualified staff who could attend to the identification and collection of the dinosaur remains. As a result, the GSC resorted to hiring private fossil hunters to work on its behalf in the bonebeds of Alberta.

And thus was Charles Hazelius Sternberg engaged as a fossil hunter for the GSC. Sternberg was born in 1850 in Cooperstown, New York, and as a young man had moved to his brother's ranch in Kansas. His brother, Dr. George M. Sternberg, was a US Army surgeon who was an early and avid fossil collector in Kansas, and that interest captivated young Charles. Shortly after graduating from Kansas State Agricultural College (now Kansas State University), Sternberg took a job collecting fossils for Edward Drinker Cope, an eminent paleontologist of the time. When hired by the GSC, Sternberg was, like Brown, quite well known in the paleontology community as a fossil hunter, though he was not formally trained as a scientist and did not have any advanced degree in paleontology. He did, however, have a wealth of field experience, and he also had three imminently qualified sons – George, Charles Jr. and Levi – to assist him. The Sternbergs arrived in Alberta in 1912 and the Great Canadian Dinosaur Rush heated up. When Brown arrived for the new season's activities, he was surprised to find competition on hand. The Sternbergs equipped themselves in a fashion similar to Brown, and the two parties of bone hunters set off floating down the Red Deer River on their explorations. The collecting seasons for 1912 and 1913 were spectacularly successful for both groups, with most of the work being done in or near present-day Dinosaur Provincial Park. The hunters worked in close proximity to each other much of the time, and a certain rivalry soon arose. Fortunately that rivalry was, for the most part, civil – quite unlike the so-called "Bone Wars" that had been experienced in the United States for 15 years starting in 1877.

The Bone Wars was a period of intense and acrimonious rivalry between Edward Drinker Cope, of the Academy of Natural Sciences in Philadelphia, and Othniel Charles Marsh, curator of the Peabody Museum of Natural History at Yale – unquestionably the two most influential American paleontologists of the age. The two men hated each other intensely, and during the Bone Wars each of them employed the most underhanded and unethical methods to out-compete the other in the quest for fossil collection, often resorting to bribery, theft, prevarication, even property destruction,, to get ahead. During the 15-year period the two men squandered their personal fortunes and besmirched their professional reputations in pursuit of what they considered paleontological supremacy. No bounds were recognized, including personal attacks in scientific publications and attempts to see that project funding from third parties was withdrawn by the donors. In the end both men were ruined and neither could be said to have been the victor. However, the collections they amassed were astonishing, eventually yielding to science over 140 new species from the fossil evidence. The very public war also stimulated the public interest in the subject of dinosaurs, which probably led to further explorations. Both combatants in the war were known by Brown and the Sternbergs, and the Bone Wars might well have been an object lesson to keep the Canadian Dinosaur Rush within the bounds of peaceful coexistence.

The nearest Brown and the Sternbergs came to a "war" of their own was during the collection season of 1914. At that time Brown's assistant, Peter Kaisen, established a camp in the heart of present-day Dinosaur Provincial Park and let it be known to the Sternbergs that the American party had "laid claim" to all of the badlands within proximity of the camp – essentially telling the Sternbergs that they were trespassing should they come nearby in search of dinosaur remains. After consulting Lambe at the GSC in Ottawa, Sternberg decided to ignore the "claim," and he entered and dug wherever he wanted for the balance of the season. That action may have annoyed the Americans, but they kept their own counsel on the matter, at least for a while. Late in that year George Sternberg found and excavated a dinosaur skeleton that apparently had been missed by the Americans and the dispute blossomed into full flower. The Americans confronted the Sternbergs, but cooler heads prevailed when it was pointed out that there were plenty of remains to go around, and indeed neither party could even hope to excavate all it found in a season. The tension broken, civility was reclaimed.

In 1915 the GSC split its party of hunters, leaving Charles Sr. where the work had been done in the previous year, sending George upstream to a site near Drumheller, and sending the other Sternbergs to the Milk River country to the south. All of the parties continued to make some discoveries, but nothing like the numbers seen at the main bonebeds around Dinosaur Provincial Park. That year was also the last for Brown, who left the digs at the end of the season with tons of bones, never to return to Alberta.

With the outbreak of the First World War, the Canadian Dinosaur Rush stumbled falteringly to an end. By 1916 most government budgets were dealing primarily with the war effort and dinosaurs were off the front page. One exception was the British Museum of Natural History, which commissioned Charles Sternberg Jr. to collect and send specimens. The first shipment arrived safely, but the second was lost at sea when the freighter it was riding in was attacked by a German warship and sunk. That was the epitaph of the Dinosaur Rush.

In 1955, as part of Alberta's 50th Jubilee Year celebrations, the Steveville Dinosaur Provincial Park was dedicated in an effort to preserve and protect the bonebeds. The name Steveville attached to the original name of the park was in recognition of a hamlet that once existed adjacent to the park. Steveville was started in the early 1900s by a homesteader named Steve Hall. The place never attracted many settlers, but the Hall family were an enterprising lot and they operated a number of businesses there, including a ferry across the Red Deer River, a boarding house, a general store and a post office. Unfortunately for the Halls, the town soon failed and only the name remained in 1955. That name, however, proved to be problematic because after the dedication of the park, lots of would-be visitors got lost trying to find a place called Steveville, which of course had long since ceased to exist. In 1962 the name of the park was shortened to Dinosaur Provincial Park, which pretty well says what it means.

The park was declared a UNESCO World Heritage Site in 1979.

CLIMATE

The climate at the park is warm and sunny in the summer, with temperatures often reaching 35°c. The spring and fall tend to have unpredictable weather, but it is usually sunny and temperatures moderate quickly in the evenings. The winter months commonly bring snowfall and temperatures that can easily fall into the range of -30°c. Chinook winds may moderate winter temperatures from time to time, and the area is generally subject to windy conditions. Precipitation is light, usually in the range of 400 mm per year, with most of it falling as rain in the late spring and early summer.

ACTIVITIES IN THE PARK

Dinosaur Provincial Park is comprised of approximately 7330 ha, but about 70 per cent of that total lies within a natural preserve and the public is restricted from entering that area except on guided tours and hikes. According to the regulations, only credentialed scientists may freely roam in the preserve. This restriction is to ensure protection of the resources in the park, and to allow scientists to work without interruption from the public. A field team from the Royal Tyrrell Museum works in the park every summer, actively searching for and recovering dinosaur remains in the preserve. In fact, on average the teams find six complete dinosaur skeletons per season, so it is fair to say that the park is an active hive of paleontological activity. The closure in the park also has a great deal to do with promoting public safety. Without a guide or familiarity with the terrain it is quite easy to get lost in the badlands. Landmarks are difficult to differentiate and many things look much the same, so getting "turned around" is quite common. Apart from the problems of navigation, there are other perils to deal with such as getting stabbed with cactus spines, falling off rock ledges, sunstroke (hyperthermia, or heat prostration) and encounters with venomous snakes and "wee beasties" like black widow spiders and scorpions. In addition, the bentonite clay that makes up part of the badland features can be a problem. Bentonite contains a high concentration of minerals known as smectites. When it rains, smectites absorb a large volume of water and can swell up to ten times their dry volume. Microscopically, smectites are a series of plates that slide against one another, and when wet they do so with a great deal more facility, thus making the bentonite slimy and slippery. Indeed, the clay can get so slick when wet that it can make footing perilous. When it rains or threatens to, the best advice from park staff is to return to your vehicle straightaway.

All users are asked to stay on the established trails to avoid increased erosion, destruction of rare plant species and damage to paleontological resources. The trails are for pedestrians only; no bicycles are allowed. It should be noted by all visitors that since 1978 fossils have been protected in Alberta under the Historical Resources Act, and all fossils found in the province are the property of Alberta. It is illegal to sell, trade or alter any fossil in the province, and it is likewise illegal to remove any fossil from the province without proper certification and documentation by government officials. Excavation of any fossil embedded in the ground requires a permit before the excavation is commenced, and such permits are only

Signs and views from inside the park

available, on application, to professional paleontologists with postgraduate degrees in the discipline. Surface collecting of non-embedded fossils may be permissible on private property with the consent of the property owner, but all collecting of fossils is prohibited in national and provincial parks. If you see what you believe to be a fossil, do not attempt to pick it up. Leave it *in situ* because that is how the scientists would wish to see it.

Dinosaur Provincial Park is classified as being in the dry, mixed-grass subregion of the grassland natural region, the warmest and driest subregion in the province. Generally there is flora and fauna in three distinct communities – prairie grasslands, badlands and riverside, or riparian, habitat. There is a broad diversity of species in the park, and they bear a decided similarity to those that exist in Writing-on-Stone Provincial Park – including the prairie rattlesnakes (see page 95).

There are several ways in which visitors can explore the park. A self-guided tour is available by walking several short interpretative loop trails on your own. These trails are reached from the main road in the park or the Visitor Information Centre. All of them have educational signage along the way, and as a whole they will give visitors an overview of the park. All of these trails are rated as easy and each of them can be completed within about an hour. In addition, there are interpretative programs and educational exhibits at the Visitor Information Centre and you should attend there to obtain schedules for the programs.

For those visitors who wish to have a more in-depth look at the park there are regularly scheduled guided bus tours and guided hikes that take you into the natural preserve with park staff. The bus tours and hikes usually take about two to three hours. All of these guided activities are on a ticketed basis, and tickets are sold for moderate prices. Each activity also has a maximum number of allowed participants. Information concerning ticketing can be found at the park's website or by calling or dropping in to the Visitor Information Centre. The guided activities are extremely popular and all spaces for ticketed events can be reserved in advance. Indeed, reservations are highly recommended, particularly during the busy summer months. There is an enforced limit of one ticketed event per person per day.

As examples, you may wish to book on the Fossil Safari Hike. It is rated as easy to moderate, takes about three hours and visits a fossil site in the natural preserve. The Centrosaurus Bonebed Hike is rated as moderately strenuous, takes about three hours and visits an excavation site that was active for over a decade starting in 1979. The Great Badlands Hike is rated as strenuous, takes about four hours, is available only at limited times, and covers an extended route through rugged badlands terrain.

On all hikes in the park you should take plenty of water. Daytime summer temperatures can top 35°c, and there are no facilities to obtain more water after you start the hike. Water should be in resealable containers, and all containers should return with you to your vehicle after the hike. Canned beverages are not recommended. There are no waste receptacles along the way, so plan to carry out everything you carry in. A hat, sunscreen and insect repellent are also musts. You should confirm your start time and place when you pick up your ticket for the event. On guided hikes only sturdy footwear with "closed toe and heel" is allowed – no sandals or flip-flops are permitted.

HOW TO GET THERE

Dinosaur Provincial Park sits 48 km northeast of Brooks, Alberta; 200 km east of Calgary; and 100 km southeast of Drumheller. Go east on the Trans-Canada (Hwy 1) to the western edge of Brooks and then follow the signs to the park. The Visitor Information Centre is open to the public seven days a week during high season (May through August), and operates on more limited hours during the balance of the year. The field station for the Royal Tyrrell Museum is also open for visitors, but you should check the hours of operation before arrival. The website for the park is at www.tpr.alberta.ca/parks/dinosaur. Reservations for hikes can be made through the website or by phoning toll free in Alberta 310-0000 and requesting extension (403) 378-4344.

Limestone pavement

Leaf Peepers and *Larix*

When the autumn frosts arrive in New England and many parts of eastern Canada, the deciduous trees start to change their leaf colours from the greens of summer to the vibrant reds, oranges and yellows of fall. The changing colours also herald the arrival of the "leaf peepers," a colloquial name in New England for tourists who drive very slowly along the roads, staring wide-eyed through the windows of their rental automobiles at the annual foliage colour change, stopping at frequent but irregular intervals to leap from the car, camera in hand, to snap photographs. If you have never seen the display, try to take it in sometime. It is quite amazing. Just be careful of the traffic dangers.

In southern Alberta we are not blessed with the variety of deciduous trees that exist in the east, but our cottonwoods, aspens and shrubs give a good account of themselves in the colour change department. The star attractions for most of our local leaf peepers, however, are the *Larix* – the larches – whether they be the Western Larch (*Larix occidentalis*) or the closely related Alpine Larch (*Larix lyallii*). Both of these members of the Pine Family act in a very anomalous way for conifer trees by turning their leaves (needles) bright yellow and dropping them in the autumn. When this happens in the shortening days and gathering frosts of the fall season, it seems to create a stir in the local hiking community, which suddenly comes out in renewed numbers to witness the event. And why not? It is one of the most beautiful times of the year in the mountains – crisp temperatures, blue skies, fluffy white clouds and twinkling yellow foliage.

There are a number of places to take in the brilliantly coloured larches, but undeniably two of the preferred venues are on the Kananaskis Trail (Hwy 40) near Highwood Pass, and on the Smith-Dorrien/Spray Trail (Hwy 742) near Spray Lakes. At the former venue there are two short hikes to Ptarmigan Cirque and Pocaterra Tarn, while at the latter there are longer hikes to Rummel Lake and Chester Lake.

For hikes to Ptarmigan Cirque and Pocaterra Tarn the pertinent maps are the Gem Trek map "Kananaskis Lakes" or NTS maps 82J/10 (Mount

Rae) and 82J/11 (Kananaskis Lakes). Both hikes start at the parking lot at Highwood Pass, said to be the highest-elevation public road in Canada, at coordinates 11u 0642541 5606833. Because you start so high, the move into the alpine happens quite quickly here. The trail to Ptarmigan Cirque is a designated and maintained parks trail, while the trail to Pocaterra Tarn is not. Route-finding should not present any problem. Indeed, if you require help, there will almost undoubtedly be some other hikers to consult on these popular trails. If you require any other information, contact the Visitor Information Centre in Peter Lougheed Provincial Park at (403) 591-6322 or at Barrier Lake at (403) 673-3985.

The hike to Ptarmigan Cirque is only 3.6 km return, with an elevation gain of 230 m. Leave the parking lot going north, cross a wooden footbridge, and continue north into a willow-strewn meadow. After going a few hundred metres you will encounter a signed junction directing hikers bound for Ptarmigan Cirque to turn right and (carefully) cross Hwy 40. On the east side of the highway the trail resumes and starts climbing in a zigzag fashion up through the trees. Before long you will encounter a spur trail to the right. If you move onto the spur a few metres, you will have a wonderful view looking south. Depending on the time of year, the vista looking uphill from the spur trail could find the whole slope covered in a myriad of colourful wildflowers. Back on the main trail, at about 1.3 km from the trailhead, you will reach a T junction with a trail coming in from the right. It is signed as "one way–do not enter," so keep straight and continue to climb. The trail up to and around the cirque is a loop, hiked in a clockwise direction. The "one way" trail is the return heading down from the cirque, so you will see it later. Keep moving upward and you will soon break out of the trees and into alpine meadows. Once there, you can wander up the cirque as you wish. Depending on the time of year, the wildflower array in the meadows can be wonderful.

The cirque sits between Mount Rae and Mount Arethusa. Mount Rae was named by John Palliser in 1859 to honour Dr. John Rae, who conducted several expeditions to the Canadian Arctic for the Hudson's Bay Company. Mount Arethusa is named for HMS *Arethusa*, a Royal Navy cruiser that was sunk by a mine during the First World War. The ship

Ptarmigan flowers

Large waterfall from Ptarmigan

in turn was named for a mythological water nymph. The views from the cirque are quite panoramic, and the yellow of the larches stretched out before you will be impressive in the autumn. If you look west, you are looking at the valley wherein lies the Pocaterra Tarn.

Ptarmigan Cirque takes its name from one of its permanent residents, the white-tailed ptarmigan (*Lagopus leucura*), the smallest member of the grouse family. The birds live in the alpine environment in the mountains of western Canada and the US. They are well camouflaged in both winter and summer, looking like snow in winter and rocks in summer, but you could well see one or more on this hike.

You should also keep an eye out for the never shy hoary marmots (*Marmota caligata*) that live here among the rocks. They are the largest North American ground squirrel. "Hoary" is a reference to the silver-grey fur on their shoulders and upper back. The animals are often referred to as "whistlers" or "whistle pigs," on account of the alarm noise they utter. As a matter of interest, Whistler, British Columbia, the 2010 Winter Olympics venue, takes its name from this animal's nickname, hoary marmots being indigenous to that area as well.

There is a small creek percolating down the cirque, and it forms a small waterfall. The return trail is on the south side of the creek and is accessed by a rock-hopping crossing just above the waterfall. As you make your way down, you will soon re-enter the trees. Keep an eye over your left shoulder every now and then and you will probably see a much grander waterfall where the creek from the cirque falls off the escarpment. Before long you will encounter the T junction with the "one way" sign. Turn left and continue down to the highway and the parking lot.

The hike to Pocaterra Tarn is slightly longer than that to Ptarmigan Cirque, being 4.2 km return from the parking lot. There are moderate elevation gains to the tarn, but most of the steeper uphills will be met on the return journey. From the parking lot, cross the footbridge and enter the meadow, but stay left on the narrow trail instead of crossing the highway as you would for Ptarmigan. Approximately 700 m north in the meadow there is a large rock on the right side of the trail, and at that point the trail bends left, heading uphill into the trees. Climb up along a

Above: Hoary marmot
Below: Mount Galatea and Rummel Lake

small spring into a damp spruce forest. This area can get quite muddy and is extremely fragile owing to the short growing season at this elevation. Straying off the trail exacerbates the problem, so stick to the main trail as much as possible. You will soon reach a high point, and the trail starts a steep, twisting descent onto a lush avalanche slope. Pocaterra Creek can be seen ahead, gurgling its way down the mountainside. As you climb up the creek toward the tarn, the creek will disappear underground beneath rubble. You will soon come to the tarn, at coordinates 11u 0641230 5606460, sandwiched between scree slopes on one side and larch-strewn meadows on the other. Return to the parking lot by reversing your outbound route.

Pocaterra Tarn takes its name from George Pocaterra, an Italian by birth who came to Canada as a young man and eventually established the historic Buffalo Head Ranch in the Highwood Valley. Pocaterra was an early explorer of what is now Kananaskis Country, and his name is attached to Pocaterra Ridge, Mount Pocaterra, Pocaterra Creek and Elpoca Mountain. For more information on Pocaterra, I highly recommend *The Diva & The Rancher: The Story of Norma Piper and George Pocaterra*, by Jennifer Hamblin and David Finch, published by Rocky Mountain Books. Parenthetically, Pocaterra sold the ranch to Raymond Patterson, who wrote a celebrated book *The Buffalo Head*, which details many of Patterson's adventures in frontier Alberta in the 1930s and 1940s. The book was republished in 2005 by TouchWood Editions, and continues to be an excellent read.

If you want a longer outing than those provided by Ptarmigan Cirque or Pocaterra Tarn, follow the directions below to the trailheads for hikes to Rummel Lake and Chester Lake. The pertinent NTS map is 82J/14 (Spray Lakes Reservoir). Both hikes are also shown on the Gem Trek map "Kananaskis Lakes," though going past Rummel Lake to Rummel Pass will run off the top side of the map and technically you will also require Gem Trek's "Canmore – Kananaskis Village."

Of the destinations off the Smith-Dorrien/Spray Trail, it is probably fair to say that Rummel Lake, despite its beautiful setting and splendid scenery, particularly when the larches are in colour, seems to receive little attention when compared to some of its neighbours. For those who have been to Rummel, this seems somehow mysterious, but those familiar with uncrowded Rummel would probably be quite happy to have it remain somewhat a secret.

Rummel Lake and Rummel Pass take their name from Baroness Elizabeth "Lizzie" Rummel, who was born in 1897 in Munich, a member of the German aristocracy. As a young girl she travelled to Canada with her family for vacations, but her Canadian residency became permanent with the outbreak of hostilities in the First World War. The dislocations of the war stripped the family of their wealth, so they took up residence on a family-owned ranch in southern Alberta. Lizzie's dream was to operate a guest lodge in the Rockies, and her dream came true as a result of her hard work and determination. Indeed, during her lifetime she operated two different backcountry lodges – one at Sunburst Lake in the Mount Assiniboine area of eastern British Columbia, and the other at Skoki Lodge in Banff National Park. In those capacities she became famous, particularly with the hiking and mountaineering crowd. In 1980 she was awarded the Order of Canada. The citation reads: "Mountaineer par excellence, protector of the environment, authority on local flora and fauna, and friend to countless hikers in the mountains near Banff. She has enriched her country by sharing her deep love of the Rocky Mountains with all who met her." Lizzie Rummel's life is chronicled in Ruth Oltmann's book, *Lizzie Rummel: Baroness of the Canadian Rockies*, published by Rocky Mountain Books of Calgary.

The hike to Rummel Lake has a return distance of 8.6 km with an elevation gain of 355 m. If you wish to continue to Rummel Pass, add another 5 km and 185 m to the totals. The trailhead for Rummel Lake is on Hwy 742, just across the highway from the entrance to Mount Engadine Lodge. The coordinates for the trailhead are 11U 0616768 5633244. There is no parking lot; just a pull-off beside the road. The trail starts on the east side of the road, where it gently climbs, going southeast, more or less parallel to the highway, into an old forestry cut block. After about 1 km the trail meanders to the east, then turns north and east and continues to climb gently for another kilometre. At that point the trail turns decidedly east and begins to climb in earnest toward higher ground. Near the top the views of Spray Lakes from this leg of the trail are spectacular. Continue on the well-worn trail to a junction at coordinates 11u 0618628 5632333. The fainter of the two trails continues straight (south), eventually connecting to the Chester Lake trail. For Rummel Lake turn left (east), as indicated by an arrow nailed to a tree beside the trail. Shortly after you take the left turn, the trail meets Rummel Creek and arrives at a bridge over the creek at 11u 0619086 5632323. Cross the bridge and continue climbing. Above the bridge the trail becomes somewhat fainter and some trail-finding is required before you get to the lake. The trail is marked with yellow diamonds nailed on the trees, but you need to keep your head up to see them. There is a split in the trail at coordinates 11u 0619688 5632662, but either fork will lead to the lake. The southwest end of Rummel Lake, near its outflow, is at 11u 0619945 5632805.

Mount Galatea, standing 3185 m tall, dominates the view to the east from this end of the lake. Like Mount Arethusa, this peak too was named after a warship and a nymph. HMS *Galatea* was a Royal Navy light cruiser that was the first ship to open fire during the Battle of Jutland in the First World War. The ship in turn was named for a mythological sea nymph.

The trail to Rummel Pass follows along the west side of the lake, then turns north and continues to angle upward into the trees to the north and east. You will soon get above the trees into the scree slopes approaching the pass. The trail becomes somewhat faint through the rocks, but the way is marked with several cairns as it continues alongside several small tarns, eventually arriving at Rummel Pass, elevation 2393 m at 11u 0621259 5634469. From the pass you are looking down into the valley of Galatea Creek and Lost Lake.

If you favour wildflowers, Rummel Lake is a worthy hike even when the larches are not in colour. In early July 2008 we hiked the Rummel trail after a spring that had been decidedly wet and cool, with snow packs lingering in the high country several weeks later than usual. As a consequence, the wildflowers bloomed late that year, and we were seeing what are usually early-blooming species still appearing at a time one would normally expect them to be gone. At the conclusion of the hike I sent a report to a friend in the Visitor Information Centre at Kananaskis Country as follows:

> We went on a hike to Rummel Lake and Rummel Pass today with a group from High River. For a trail report we found the hike to the lake snow free, with some snowbanks at the pass but no problem negotiating the whole distance. The weather was good, with lots of wind at the pass but no rain or thunderstorms. On the trail we found the following plants in bloom, in no particular order: Hooker's Thistle, Red-stemmed Saxifrage, Wild Strawberry, Mountain Sorrel, Globeflower, Alpine Buttercup, Purple Saxifrage, Silver Rock Cress, Yellow Draba, Western Anemone, Glacier Lily, False Azalea (Fool's Huckleberry), Alpine Speedwell (in bud), Bracted Lousewort (in bud), Bog Laurel, Yellow Heather, White Heather, Purple Heather, Elderberry ssp, Sitka Valerian, Alpine Spring Beauty, Paintbrush in yellow, red and pink, Meadow Rue (male and female), Blue Clematis – a surprise this late – Bracted Honeysuckle (Black Twinberry), Heart-leaved Arnica, Roseroot, Bladder Locoweed, several Potentillas, Round-leaved Violet, several Pussytoes, Black Gooseberry, White Camas (in bud), Hedysarum, Fireweed (in bud), Grouseberry, Labrador Tea, Bunchberry, Sweet-flowered Androsace (Rock Jasmine), Moss Campion, various Milk-vetches, White Mountain Avens and others that I omitted to record, no doubt. A great hike altogether.

The hike to Chester Lake is hugely popular. The route is 9 km return, with an elevation gain of 315 m. If you wish to extend the hike, there is a very popular option that adds Three Lakes Valley to the Chester Lake trip, lengthening the whole hike to 13.5 km with a 550 m elevation gain.

The trail to Chester Lake starts from the northeast corner of the parking lot, above the biffies. The hike begins on an old logging road that has been converted into a hiking, skiing and biking track. In short order you will pass through a gate to a junction. Turn left and cross a bridge over Chester Creek at coordinates 11u 0619901 5628143. Continue on the main road, taking every uphill option, until you arrive at a signed five-way junction, where you turn right. The road continues straight, then soon turns uphill and to the right into a long traverse. At the end of the traverse, there are bicycle racks that mark the boundary for bikes and the end of the logging road. The coordinates at the junction are 11u 0619764 5629391. Head left up the narrow trail into the trees and climb a grade. When it levels out, you will alternate between forests and meadows as you move along. Some of the meadows are "bumpy" owing to frost heaves during the winter.

At the second meadow the ski trail will come in from the left. The trail then climbs a little more, then levels again as you enter a large meadow that has Chester Creek babbling away on the right side. The lake is straight ahead at the foot of the cliffs of Mount Chester. In the fall this meadow is ringed with golden-needled Larch trees. In the early season, it is equally popular with hikers when covered, as it then is, with bright yellow Glacier Lilies (*Erythromium grandiflorum*), a flower that is virtually emblematic of the high country.

The trail splits when you get to the lake, with one branch bridging the outflow from the lake and the other following the western shoreline. If you walk the western shoreline the trail splits again at coordinates 11u 0621514 5630424. Go left to cross the ridge into Three Lakes Valley. The less-used trail to the right continues to climb into the valley below The Fortress.

If you climb along the trail to Three Lakes Valley you will soon come to an area filled with enormous boulders, all scattered around as if they were toys abandoned by a giant. These are known as the Elephant Rocks. The floral community in and around the rocks is quite impressive, making a careful examination worthwhile. Moving farther up Three Lakes Valley will bring you, successively, to the lakes. They are more appropriately termed tarns, but the vistas and the vegetation are worth the added extension to the hike. The third tarn is often dry by the fall. Return to the trailhead by retracing your steps.

Chester Lake and the looming Mount Chester also take their name from a warship – HMS *Chester* – another cruiser that engaged in the Battle of Jutland, the largest naval engagement of the First World War. HMS *Chester* was heavily damaged during the battle, and many of its

Above: Elephant rocks
Below: Mount Chester

crew were casualties. One of those was John ("Jack") Travers Cornwell, a seaman who was posthumously awarded the Victoria Cross, the youngest person ever to receive the decoration. He became a wartime combatant casualty at the ripe old age of 16. The gun on which Cornwell served is preserved in the Imperial War Museum in London. Mount Cornwell, a mountain on the Continental Divide in the Highwood Valley is named for him.

If you are looking for a more challenging hike, the trail to Headwall Lakes starts at the parking lot for Chester Lake. This hike is just under 14 km long return and has an elevation gain of approximately 450 m to the upper lake. Start at the southeast corner of the parking lot by getting onto the road marked with a blue cross-country ski trail sign (coordinates 11U 0619779 5627973). The trail meanders through the forest, generally heading southeast. At 1.0 km you will cross a former clear-cut and reach a junction with a map sign at 11U 0620583 5627289. The right trail is marked as a yellow ski trail. Go straight on the blue/yellow ski trail. At 1.9 km you will intersect a road marked with a yellow ski trail sign at coordinates 11U 0621406 5627040. Go left and continue ascending. At 2.6 km there is another junction in a second regrowing clear-cut at coordinates 11U 0621852 5626764. At this junction the road marked with an orange ski trail sign goes up to the left (north). You want to go to the right on the road marked with the yellow ski trail sign. At 3.2 km you will drop to a bridge over Headwall Creek. Cross the bridge and follow the road. The road curves south and ascends steeply. Where the road levels at 3.7 km, look left for a cairn at coordinates 11U 0622203 5627227 that indicates where to leave the road and turn east onto a single-track trail. Once on the trail, you will ascend in the forest in a north-northeasterly direction. Soon you will come back to Headwall Creek. At that point you will have a view up the valley, with Mount Chester on the left and Mount James Walker on the right. Mount James Walker is named for the man selected from thousands of nominees as Calgary's "Citizen of the Century" during the city's centennial year in 1975. Walker's career included being a member of the North-West Mounted Police on the trek west, a stint as manager of the Cochrane Ranche, a mill owner/operator in the Kananaskis valley and a military officer during the First World War.

The trail continues along the bank of Headwall Creek, first through willows, then through forest, and eventually below a scree-covered slope. Follow the cairns along the bottom of the scree slope. At the end of the scree the trail suddenly begins a very steep, twisting climb to the treeline. At the top, the trail turns left and follows two traverses upward to arrive below the first headwall, a white rock face. Climb up the right side of the scree to the top and Lower Headwall Lake at coordinates 11u 0623547 5629216.

At this point you will be standing on what is known as "limestone pavement," a type of natural karst landform. Karst landforms are made by the dissolving action of water on carbonate bedrock. Keeping the explanation short and simple, what happens is that an advancing glacier scrapes away non-soluble overburden to expose horizontally bedded carbonate rock. That rock is somewhat water soluble, and over huge spans of time, rainwater falls on the rock, dissolving it slowly and leaving the peculiar landscape seen here.

Continue to move around the right side of Lower Headwall Lake and you will see the second headwall ahead. The second headwall has a tumbling stream spouting out of it about three-quarters of the way up. The trail climbs up the headwall on the right side of the stream. Upper Headwall Lake sits almost exactly 7 km from the trailhead, at an elevation of 2340 m. The Fortress, standing at 3000 m, looms behind Upper Headwall Lake. The Fortress is considered by many to be the most spectacular peak in the Kananaskis Valley, what with its vertical cliffs rising in symmetry to the flat summit. It is quite unique and the official name testifies to that character. After enjoying the views around the Headwall Lakes, return to the trailhead by retracing your route up.

HOW TO GET THERE

Note: Hwy 40 from Kananaskis Lakes Trail to Highwood Junction is closed December 1 to June 15.

The trailhead for the hikes to Ptarmigan Cirque and Pocaterra Tarn are both at the parking lot at Highwood Pass. To get there from Calgary, go west on the Trans-Canada (Hwy 1) for 57 km to the intersection with Hwy 40 (Kananaskis Trail, Exit 118). Turn south on Hwy 40 and continue for 67.4 km to the parking lot. If coming from the south, go to Highwood Junction (where Hwys 40, 541 and 940 intersect) and then go north on Hwy 40 for 37.7 km to the parking lot. There are biffies at the parking lot.

The hikes to Chester Lake and the Headwall Lakes both start at the parking lot for the trailhead to Chester Lake. To get there from Calgary, go west on the Trans-Canada (Hwy 1) to Canmore, exit into the town centre and follow the signs going uphill to the Canmore Nordic Centre. Pass the turn for the Nordic Centre and continue on the Smith-Dorrien/Spray Trail (Hwy 742) for 41.5 km to the parking lot for the trailhead for Chester Lake. The parking lot is on the east side of the highway, across from the Burstall day-use area. The parking lot is at coordinates 11u 0619759 5627948. If travelling from the south on Hwy 40, go 17 km north of Highwood Pass and turn southwest onto Kananaskis Lakes Trail. Proceed for 2.2 km and turn right (northwest) onto the Smith-Dorrien/Spray Trail (Hwy 742) and follow it for 22.2 km to the parking lot.

To get to the trailhead for Rummel Lake, follow the above directions for the Chester Lake parking lot, but if you are approaching from Canmore on Hwy 742 (Smith-Dorrien/Spray Trail) look for the sign for Mount Engadine Lodge and park just off the highway near the access road to the lodge. If coming from the south, pass the Chester Lake parking lot and proceed an additional 6.3 km north to the access road to the Mount Engadine Lodge. The coordinates for the trailhead for Rummel Lake are 11u 0616768 5633244.

Lower Headwall Lake

Photographic Credits

Glacier Lilies near Chester Lake

Index of Principal People & Places, Flora & Fauna

More Titles from Rocky Mountain Books

Prairie Beauty

Wildflowers of the Canadian Prairies

by Neil L. Jennings

Prairie Beauty explores the wildflowers and flowering shrubs commonly found in the prairie environment of western Canada. Written for the enjoyment of all who venture outside and wish to identify the wild flowering plants they encounter, the book is directed at readers with little or no background in things botanical.

ISBN: 978-1-894765-84-8 | $24.95

Alpine Beauty

Alpine and Subalpine Wildflowers of the Canadian Rockies and the Columbia Mountains

by Neil L. Jennings

Alpine Beauty explores the wildflowers and flowering shrubs commonly found in the subalpine and alpine environments in the Rocky Mountains of western Canada. Due to harsh weather conditions, the plants that exist at higher elevations are generally different than those at lower elevations. In this environment, low shrub and herb communities become the rule.

ISBN: 978-1-894765-83-1 | $22.95

Uncommon Beauty

Wildflowers and Flowering Shrubs of Southern Alberta and Southeastern British Columbia

by Neil L. Jennings

Uncommon Beauty explores the wildflowers and flowering shrubs of a large area from Jasper down to Creston, over to Glacier National Park in Montana, and up through Lethbridge and Edmonton. Extensively researched by author and outdoors enthusiast Neil L. Jennings, this guide will inform and intrigue the reader, while also assisting with plant recognition and identification.

ISBN: 1-894765-75-3 | $22.95

Coastal Beauty

Wildflowers and Flowering Shrubs Of Coastal British Columbia and Vancouver Island

by Neil L. Jennings

Coastal Beauty and Central Beauty are follow-ups to three previous volumes on wildflowers written by Neil Jennings and published by Rocky Mountain Books. All five books include exceptional photographs and interesting information about each plant. For ease of reference, the books are arranged by flower colour and by plant family. A complete index is included, using both the common and the scientific names for all plants.

Coastal Beauty explores the wildflowers and flowering shrubs commonly found in the coastal regions of British Columbia, including Vancouver Island, and also Coastal Washington and Oregon.

ISBN-13: 978-1897522028 | $26.95

Central Beauty

Wildflowers and Flowering Shrubs of the Southern Interior of British Columbia

by Neil L. Jennings

Central Beauty explores the wildflowers and flowering shrubs commonly found in the portions of British Columbia typically known as the southern interior - very roughly an east/west line drawn through Williams Lake, BC. The southern limit of the area extends well into the states of Washington, Idaho and Montana.

ISBN-13: 978-1897522035 | $26.95

Behind The Counter

Flyfishing Tips, Techniques and Shortcuts

by Neil L. Jennings

Neil Jennings started getting serious about flyfishing in 1973 and has fished that way exclusively ever since. From 1982 through 2003 he was a partner/owner in a retail flyfishing shop in Calgary, Alberta. During that time Neil was behind the counter, answering questions and giving advice to thousands of flyfishers, from "wannabes" to seriously talented anglers. Over the years, Neil learned a lot about flyfishing, some of it by good example and some of it by bad. This book is a distillation of the best of that experience.

ISBN-13: 978-1894765923 | $24.95

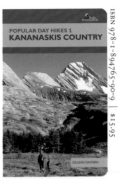

ISBN 978-1-894765-90-9 | $15.95

Popular Day Hikes 1
Kananaskis Country

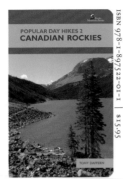

ISBN 978-1-897522-01-1 | $15.95

Popular Day Hikes 2
Canadian Rockies

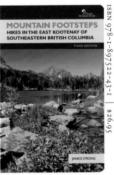

ISBN 978-1-897522-43-1 | $26.95

Mountain Footsteps
Hikes in the East Kootenay of
Southeastern British Columbia

ISBN 978-1-897522-48-6 | $19.95

The David Thompson Highway
A Hiking Guide

ISBN 978-1-897522042 | $26.95

Exploring the Castle
Discovering the Backbone of
the World in Southern Alberta

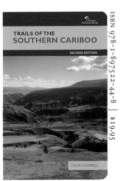

ISBN 978-1-897522-44-8 | $19.95

Trails Of The Southern Cariboo